Pakistan

The Taliban, Al Qaeda, and the Rise of Terrorism

WILLIAM J. TOPICH

Praeger Security International

 PRAEGER™

An Imprint of ABC-CLIO, LLC
Santa Barbara, California • Denver, Colorado

Library of Congress Cataloging-in-Publication Data

Names: Topich, William J., author.
Title: Pakistan : the Taliban, al Qaeda, and the rise of terrorism / William J. Topich.
Description: Santa Barbara : Praeger Security International, 2018. | Includes bibliographical references and index.
Identifiers: LCCN 2018013297 (print) | LCCN 2018017027 (ebook) | ISBN 9781440837616 (ebook) | ISBN 9781440837609 (alkaline paper)
Subjects: LCSH: Terrorism—Pakistan. | Radicalism—Pakistan. | Islam and politics—Pakistan. | Taliban. | Qaeda in the Indian Subcontinent. | Pakistan—Politics and government. | Pakistan—History.
Classification: LCC HV6433.P18 (ebook) | LCC HV6433.P18 T67 2018 (print) | DDC 954.9105/3—dc23
LC record available at https://lccn.loc.gov/2018013297

ISBN: 978-1-4408-3760-9 (print)
        978-1-4408-3761-6 (ebook)

22 21 20 19 18 1 2 3 4 5

This book is also available as an eBook.

Praeger
An Imprint of ABC-CLIO, LLC

ABC-CLIO, LLC
130 Cremona Drive, P.O. Box 1911
Santa Barbara, California 93116–1911
www.abc-clio.com

This book is printed on acid-free paper (∞)

Manufactured in the United States of America

Contents

A photo essay follows page 100.

Acknowledgments

I want to thank Pulaski Academy for their continued help and support and especially the first rate Social Science instructors I have had the privilege of working with: Angela King, Beth McCandless, Mary Muldrow, Jody Musgrove, Adam Penman, Rachel Primm, and Anthony Simmons. The Pulaski Academy administrative team: Alecia Castleberry, Greg Griffeth, Diane Lafferty, Leesa Renshaw, Matt Walsh, and Cheryl Watts, all provided needed encouragement during the turbulent times of working on this manuscript.

The inspiration for this book came from my travels to the region in 2010, which would not have been possible without the assistance of the Lone family: Binish, Fasal, Sarish, and, most importantly, Mohammad Ashraf Lone. Their friendship and hospitality during our stay in the country was beyond generous. Traveling with my former students and comrades, Kensey Berry, Jessica Berry Conway, Ian McMath, and Kristin Topich as well as Binish, Fasal, and Sarish Lone made this an unforgettable experience.

The editorial assistance from Nicole Topich was unbelievably helpful, and the book could not have been completed without her insightful editing skills. The project also benefitted from the timely formatting assistance from my former student Akhil Maddukuri. My daughter Kristin Topich provided breathtaking photography of the region for the book during our trip in 2010. The assistance from the staff at the Youngstown Public Library was very valuable during the two long summers of writing the manuscript.

The encouragement from the team at Praeger Press, including Steve Catalano and Padraic (Pat) Carlin, was extremely helpful as political changes in Pakistan led to numerous alterations in the manuscript along the way.

Finally, I thank my wife, LaDonna, and my daughters, Nicole and Kristin who were very supportive and encouraged me to pursue this timely and important project.

Introduction

The never-ending problem of terrorism in Pakistan continues to disrupt the political situation in South Asia and complicates attempts at peace and reconciliation within the region. As a volatile nuclear state, Pakistan is of concern for policy makers in the United States and globally. From the inception of Pakistan, troubling trends emerged pertaining to national identity and the role of religion in the newly formed country. Pakistani paranoia centered on the obsession with the perceived threat from India and the realization that Pakistan could not match their power. Further complicating the Pakistan situation was the artificial nature of the country. Especially troubling was the inhospitable and ungovernable tribal areas bordering Afghanistan. This region became a center stage regarding terrorism, and all parties involved in anti-terrorism efforts entered the area with caution and forewarning of the difficulty in attempting to pacify the area.

The regional upheaval that eventually led to Pakistan becoming the epicenter of global terrorism would not have taken place without the damaging role of General Zia-ul-Haq. In his decade-long tenure, General Zia promoted a radical Islamization program and planted the seeds of extremism that grew into a full-fledged terrorism problem. Zia's zealotry coupled with the proxy war against the Soviet Union in neighboring Afghanistan created the perfect storm for regional chaos and the strengthening of extremism. The subsequent period of state failure led to the birth of the Taliban movement in Afghanistan. This radical Wahhabis-influenced movement was in essence a creation of the Pakistan security apparatus, most notably the ISI. As the Taliban went from an insurgency movement to the governing body of Afghanistan, Pakistan had the ideal situation to strengthen their position regionally.

This changed forever with the events of September 11, 2001. Pakistan became a lynchpin of the U.S. efforts in the global war on terror. Pakistani president Musharraf became a vital link in the American efforts to dismantle the Al Qaeda terrorist network and to remove the Taliban regime in Afghanistan. As U.S. efforts proved initially successful, the militants fleeing Afghanistan ultimately sought sanctuary in neighboring Pakistan.

By 2002, Al Qaeda was dislodged from Afghanistan and firmly planted in Pakistan. Some terrorists sought the anonymity of the densely populated urban centers but most opted for the inhospitable tribal regions and sought sanctuary in areas such as Waziristan. The Taliban were ousted but had set up a governing structure in the Pakistan city of Quetta. Efforts to prosecute the war on terror in Pakistan were a troubling prospect for numerous reasons. The Pakistan military and intelligence service had nurtured and helped to create the same militants that the United States was now asking them to hunt down and kill. The vast majority of Pakistani officials did not feel this would be in the national security interest of the country and never seriously entertained this idea. Furthermore, an aggressive campaign against terrorist elements, many with ethnic or tribal ties to Pashtun insurgents in the country, could ultimately destabilize the fragile regime of Musharraf. The survival of elements from the former Taliban regime was considered a high priority to the ISI and factions of the Pakistani military. A pro-Pakistani government in Afghanistan was essential to combat the existential threat from India.

For the next decade, Pakistan would play a dangerous double game regarding relations with the United States and combatting terrorism. At times, the regime would orchestrate operations to flush out militants in the tribal areas. Other times, the government seemed quick to cut deals with insurgents to mitigate potential losses. It was common knowledge that Pakistan was a torn country regarding anti-terrorism efforts.

By 2007, the unrest in Pakistan was reaching a new level of intensity. The civil society efforts of the Lawyer's Movement, the horrific siege of the Red Mosque, and the triumphant return and tragic assassination of Benazir Bhutto were obvious examples of the peril Pakistan was engulfed in during this year. Finally, in December, the insurgents forged a lethal alliance that would become known as the Pakistan Taliban or TTP.

It was becoming evident that the Musharraf era was quickly coming to a close. As the government transitioned to Asif Zardari, the situation on the ground did not improve. The decision by the United States to implement the drone policy to target and assassinate militants further exacerbated tensions within the country. The countermeasures from terrorist groups included the increased use of suicide bombers, which heightened tensions along sectarian lines. At times, Pakistan seemed on the brink of civil war.

This chaos within the country was most evident in the Swat region, where extremists and government forces engaged in fierce battles.

By 2011, the situation reached a new low as Osama bin Laden was killed in Abbottabad and U.S. bombers accidently killed Pakistani troops close to the Afghan border. American officials openly called into question the Pakistani authorities' complicity with regional terrorist elements.

The struggle does indeed seem to be never-ending as the Pakistan Taliban and now ISIS are engaged in trying to ferment chaos within the country. As a nuclear state in one of the world's most vital and volatile regions, Pakistan is and will remain a centerpiece of U.S. efforts to combat global terrorism. No easy fix is within reach and success in promoting stability within the country remains distant.

PAKISTAN

Administrative Divisions

UZBEKISTAN

★ DUSHANBE

TAJIKISTAN

CHINA

TURKMENISTAN

GILGIT-
BALTISTAN

Gilgit ◉

KHYBER
PAKHTUNKHWA

1972 Line of Control

KABUL ★

Muzaffarābād ◉

AFGHANISTAN

Peshāwar ◉

AZAD
KASHMIR

★ ISLAMABAD

FEDERALLY
ADMINISTERED
TRIBAL
AREAS*

ISLAMABAD
CAPITAL
TERRITORY**

Lahore ◉

PUNJAB

Quetta ◉

NEW DELHI ★

BALOCHISTĀN

IRAN

INDIA

SINDH

International boundary

Province-level boundary

★ National capital

◉ Province-level capital

Pakistan has four provinces, one territory,
and one capital territory**.*

*The Pakistani-administered portion of the
disputed Jammu and Kashmir region
consists of two administrative entities:
Azad Kashmir and Gilgit-Baltistan.*

*Azad Kashmir and Gilgit-Baltistan are not
constitutionally part of Pakistan.*

Karachi ◉

| 0 | 100 | 200 Kilometers |

| 0 | 100 | 200 Miles |

Arabian Sea

Scale 1:10,000,000

Boundary representation is
not necessarily authoritative.

LAMBERT CONFORMAL CONIC PROJECTION; STANDARD PARALLELS 23°33' N 35°44' N

803473AI (G02807) 12-10

Central Intelligence Agency

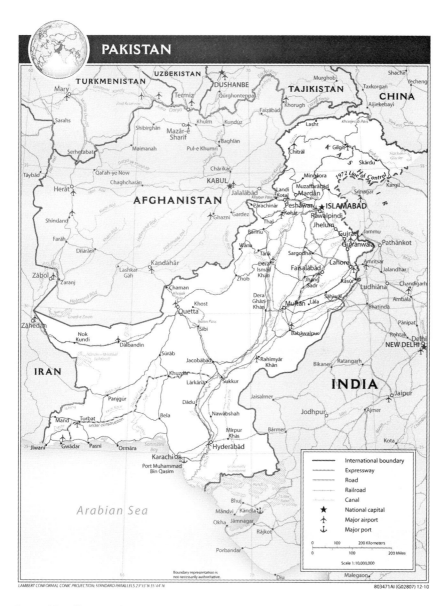

PAKISTAN

TURKMENISTAN
UZBEKISTAN
DUSHANBE
TAJIKISTAN
CHINA

Mary
Termiz
Qūrghonteppa
Khorugh
Taxkorgan
Shache
Yecheng
Aijiekebayi

Sarahs
Shibirghān
Khulm
Kundūz
Faizābād
Lasht
Khunjerab Pass

Serhetabat
Mazār-e Sharīf
Baghlān
Chitrāl
Gilgit
Skārdu

Tāybad
Maimanah
Pul-e Khumri
1972 Line of Control
Kargil

Qal'ah-ye Now
Chārīkār
Mingāora
Muzaffarābād
Srīnagar

Herāt
Chaghcharān
KABUL
Jalālābād
Landi Kotal
Mardān
ISLAMABAD

AFGHANISTAN
Ghazni
Gardez
Parachinār
Peshāwar
Kohāt
Rawalpindi
Jammu

Shindand
Thal
Jhelum
Gujrāt
Pathānkot

Farah
Bannu
Wana
Sargodha
Gujranwala

Dilārām
Tank
Dera Ismail Khān
Jhang Sadr
Lahore
Amritsar
Jalandhar

Zābol
Zaranj
Kandahār
Lashkar Gāh
Chaman
Zhob
Kāsūr
Ludhiāna
Chandigarh

Khost
Dera Ghāzi Khān
Lala
Sāhiwāl
Ambala

Zāhedan
Quetta
Sibi
Multān
Bhatinda

Nok Kundi
Dalbandin
Sūrāb
Bahāwalpur
Pānipat
Rohtak
Delhi
NEW DELHI

IRAN
Jacobābād
Rahimyār Khān
Bikaner
Ratangarh

Khuzdar
Lārkāna
Sukkur
Jaisalmer
INDIA
Jaipur

Panjgūr
Dādu
Nawābshah
Jodhpur
Ajmer

Mand
Turbat
Bela
Mīrpur Khās
Bārmer
Kota

Jīwani
Gwādar
Pasni
Ormāra
Hyderābād

Karachi
Port Muhammad Bin Qasim

Arabian Sea

Bhuj
Māndvi
Kāndla
Okha
Jāmnagar
Rājkot

Porbandar
Diu
Malegaon

———	International boundary
~~	Expressway
——	Road
·-·-·	Railroad
····	Canal
★	National capital
✈	Major airport
⚓	Major port

0   100   200 Kilometers
0   100   200 Miles
Scale 1:10,000,000

Boundary representation is
not necessarily authoritative.

LAMBERT CONFORMAL CONIC PROJECTION; STANDARD PARALLELS 23°33'N 35'44'N

803471AI (G02807) 12-10

Central Intelligence Agency

CHAPTER 1

The Evolution of Pakistan: Origins of the Terrorism Issue

Few states in modern history are more vital to the security of humans than the Islamic Republic of Pakistan. A nuclear state nestled in the fastest-growing region of the world, South Asia, the future of Pakistan hinders on the ability of the fragile government structure to control and ultimately eradiate the terrorist threat within its borders. The problems besetting Pakistan are multifaceted and, if left unchecked, this important regional power could become a security nightmare for the United States and the global community in general. In order to understand the current crisis engulfing Pakistan, it is important to analyze the difficult and troubling emergence of the world's fifth largest and populous country.

ETHNIC DYNAMIC OF PAKISTAN

One of the defining features of the ethnic and linguistic makeup of Pakistan is language. Over 20 languages are spoken in Pakistan with the most common being Punjabi, Sindhi, Urdu, Pashto, and Balochi. Most belong to the Indo-Aryan branch of the Indo-European language family. Language diversity has always been a challenge for South Asia in general and Pakistan in particular. Many communities are unable to communicate with neighbors in different regions, hampering economic development as well as national unity.

Close to half of all Pakistanis speak Punjabi with Sindhi being the second most common language spoken at 12 percent. Urdu and Punjabi are spoken by 8 percent with Balochi at 3 percent (Blood, *Pakistan: A Country Study*, 11). The educated class and businesspeople speak Urdu, which happens to be the official national language. This is partially due to the use of Urdu during the Mughal period of South Asian history. Because of Urdu's ties to Hindi, many Muslims look at the language as a unifying aspect for all of South Asia. During the colonial period, English became a second language to many elites within the subcontinent and eventually a de facto national language. English continued to be prominent and the language of instruction in schools until the 1980s. This was altered by General Zia-ul-Haq in an attempt to promote Pakistani nationalism.

The language issue was used by the independence leaders from the Muslim League as a way to promote Pakistani unification. This created a significant problem in East Pakistan, where the Bengali population speaks Bangla, and Urdu is not commonly spoken. Thus, the East Pakistanis did not want a single state language and in 1948 launched a movement to promote the Bengali language. This mobilization led to the outbreak of violence in the early 1950s, culminating in the recognition of Bengali as one of the state languages of Pakistan (Javaid, 101–102).

EVOLUTION OF PAKISTAN

Chaudhary Rahmat Ali, a student at Cambridge University in the 1930s, was the visionary for the future state of Pakistan. He published a manuscript in 1933 titled *Now or Never, Are We to Live or Perish Forever?* The name Pakistan is an acronym compiled from the names of the areas of Punjab, Afghanistan (including the North West Frontier Province), Kashmir, Sindh, and Baluchistan. In addition, Pakistan also means land of the pure in Persian and Urdu (Ziring, 13–15). A glaring omission from Ali's definition was that the eastern province of Bengal was not included. The cultural dissimilarities of the Bengali region and people were a point of contention for the early part of Pakistani history. In addition, the demographic momentum of the eastern region created anxiety within the groups that would later constitute western Pakistan. Many political leaders within the Muslim community at the time disregarded Ali's idea as unrealistic.

Mohammad Iqbal also promoted the concept of a Muslim state in the Indian subcontinent. A gifted philosopher and poet, Iqbal worked closely with the leadership of the organization, but he was the first to take the daring step of calling for a full-blown separation from India (Ziring, 14). During the 1930 meeting of the Muslim League, he spoke of the dire necessity for Muslims to secure a separate state apart from the Hindu-majority India. Iqbal felt that Hindus were the main beneficiaries of British educational policies as well as promotions in the civil service and bureaucracy. This favoritism was just one factor in the push for Muslims needing a separate political entity. Iqbal's proposal did not necessitate a total divorce from India, but, at the very least, a significant amount of autonomy.

Advocates of separatism believed that Muslims could not be tricked into any sort of Hindu-dominated federation.

The founding father of modern Pakistan was Muhammad Ali Jinnah, a middle-class lawyer from Bombay and the leader of the Muslim League. Jinnah was a leader in the anticolonial struggle and worked his entire life to secure independence from Great Britain. From the founding of the All-India Muslim League in 1916 until 1937, Jinnah was focused on independence for India as a whole and not necessarily a separate state of Pakistan. Initially, Jinnah had partnered with Indian leaders Jawaharlal Nehru and Mohandas Gandhi to obtain Indian independence. He became convinced that attempts to form any sort of confederation with the soon-to-be independent India would be problematic for the Muslim majority in the subcontinent (Lieven, 54–56). Eventually, Jinnah denounced the Indian National Congress and Hindu-dominated political movements that attempted to keep British India together under Hindu political control. The Congress Party had been insisting on a unitary state, something Jinnah and his associates in the Muslim League felt was totally unacceptable. Jinnah claimed that Muslims had to fight for safeguards without losing sight of the wider interest of the country as a whole. By the mid-1930s, Jinnah and the league emphasized that Muslims of all backgrounds and sects should come under the banner of a single all-India party. However, the election results of 1937 spelled a clear rejection of a unified Muslim political front. The league won less than 5 percent of the total Muslim vote cast. After the debacle, the league was excluded from the process in a meaningful way. If Jinnah was to be successful, he had to avoid having the Muslim population divided and disorganized. Above all, he needed to promote the idea of Muslim distinctiveness with the basis being political and not religious opposition to the Congress Party.

At the 1940 Muslim League meeting in Lahore, Jinnah explicitly called for a division along communal lines. He referenced self-determination and nationalism. The Lahore resolution called for the grouping of provinces in northwestern and northeastern India into independent states that would be autonomous and sovereign (Lieven, 55–57). Jinnah called for the Muslim regions to support him as he negotiated with the Congress Party as well as the British. The claim that a Hindu-controlled democratic solution was the answer was rejected. The majority would impose its will on the Muslim minority population, which was politically unacceptable. The fear of Muslims being treated as second-class citizens loomed large in the discourse. The language of the resolution passed was vague and left many questions unanswered. Furthermore, no mention of either the partition or Pakistan was stated in any of the documents from the meeting. Evidence points to the belief that Jinnah saw Pakistan remaining part of an all-India whole. He claimed that his movement was not an enemy of Congress and that a working relationship between the two states was essential. The key, which always remained problematic, was that any future arrangement had to be based on parity. Jinnah was also plagued by the fact that he was not the unanimous voice speaking for all Muslims regionally. The factionalism within the Muslim communities was more significant than with the Hindu cause being championed by the Congress Party. The conflicting rhetoric and language used by Jinnah meant that his intent and goals were changing over time.

By the end of World War II, the Muslim League was able to rebound and score electoral gains in 1946. Over 75 percent of the provincial assembly voting was in favor of the league. These results gave Jinnah's claim of parity with the Hindus newfound legitimacy. Interestingly, many of the Muslim voters in Punjab and Bengal (the two most contentious areas) did not realize that their votes could lead to an eventual partition based on religious self-determination (Jalal, 50–52). Jinnah saw the vote as a referendum on the league's demand for Pakistan. This desire for what is known as the "two-nation" formula was an integral part of the Pakistani mind-set.

Jinnah's view of Pakistan was not about religion as much as political rights and standing. Jinnah was a member of the Shia sect of Islam that constitutes only 10 percent of all Muslims worldwide and subsequently 15-25 percent of all Muslims in what would be Pakistan. As with many of the leaders in the anticolonial struggle, Jinnah was not particularly religious; he rarely attended the mosque and was not considered devout by most of his associates. Pakistan was to be a Muslim homeland rather than an Islamic state. According to a statement issued by Jinnah several days prior to independence, "You may belong to any religion or caste or creed . . . that has nothing to do with the business of the state. . . . We are starting with this fundamental principle that we are all citizens and citizens of one state" (Riedel, 5).

Muslim conservatives have a long history of activism dating back to the 19th century. The Sepoy Rebellion of 1857 (sometimes referred to as the Indian Mutiny) was a religiously inspired uprising against British colonial policies. Subsequently, the jihadist Deobandi movement emerged from the post-rebellion period in the 19th century. Devout conservative Muslims, who had goals that included reestablishing Muslim control in South Asia, constructed a madrassa near Deobandi to advocate a fundamentalist ideology.

This religious conservatism momentum carried over in the debate that ensued concerning the postcolonial structure of South Asian Muslims. Numerous religious political movements emerged in opposition to Jinnah's Muslim League. Several of the parties favored an Islamic state in Pakistan, with most following the lead of journalist and scholar Abul Ala Mawdudi. In 1941, Mawdudi formed the right-wing Jamaat-i-Islami. In theory, the movement was linked to the Muslim Brotherhood in Egypt, which was founded in 1928 in response to the fears of growing secular and Western influence encroaching into Muslim society. The party advocated peaceful change and the imposition of sharia throughout Pakistan. Mawdudi's rigid definition of Islam ultimately excluded the majority of Muslims in South Asia. The conservative religious parties formed an alliance together in opposition to the Muslim League whom they felt was too centrist. The coalition also felt that the ruling elites were corrupted by the immoral lifestyles of the Western elites.

The Jamaat-i-Islami drew membership from all three major branches of Sunni Islam but was highly selective with official membership. However, the party rallied millions in times of collective action. One major point of disagreement between Jamaat and the Muslim League was whether to stay in a unified India. Surprisingly, early on, Mawdudi favored remaining part of India, hoping to convert Hindus to Islam and also out of the fear of dividing Muslims in South Asia. Mawdudi eventually turned the Jamaat-i-Islami into a nationalistic party and focused much of his attention on anti-Hindu rhetoric (Jaffrelot, 442–443). The party drew support from the educated and middle class.

The second major religious party, but far less significant, was the Pashtun majority Jammiat Ulema-e-Islam or JUI. The party was centered in the Northwest Frontier Provinces (NWFP) and part of Baluchistan. The Deobandi influence was significant in the JUI. The party tended to draw more from the poor and uneducated segments of Pakistani society.

The Pakistani Nationalist Movement was obsessed with the state being put on equal terms with India. Indian leaders felt that with a majority Hindu population they were justified in controlling the political situation in any sort of political arrangement. Numerous popular writings were reluctant to grant this sort of equal status to Pakistan; references to Muslim autonomy in India or the "improbable country" of Pakistan were commonplace. This lack of legitimacy for status to Pakistan probably helped to fuel the paranoia already in place at the time of partition.

THE PARTITION

A Muslim homeland in South Asia was to be born out of bloodshed and chaos, and the military was to have a disproportional role in subsequent events. The regional rivalry with India put the military, and the army in particular, in a position of strength in numerous levels of government affairs. In addition, the ensuing politics of the Cold War also emboldened the military establishment (Aqil Shah, 13–14). The institutional structures of Pakistan were established in a way in which power was disproportionally placed in the center that lent itself to an easy drift away from democracy to authoritarianism. The building of democratic institutions was not a high priority for the new state. The focus of Pakistan was a centralized bureaucracy with a strongly supported military establishment. The sense of an immediate threat from India consumed all decision making for the new state. The critical issue of the security threat in Kashmir made the role of the military of paramount importance.

The victory of the Labor Party in 1945 helped to push Great Britain toward a quick resolution to the decolonization of India. The announcement by Prime Minister Clement Attlee that Britain would transfer power by June 1948 was considered to be a fairly quick departure. Ultimately, the timetable was accelerated and the date of August 15, 1947, was decided (Jalal, 37–38).

The British military advisors were wary about the strategic defense of Pakistan because the two main land frontiers of the subcontinent in the northwest and the northeast could not effectively be partitioned from the main body of what was to be an independent India. The British were concerned that Pakistan had neither the military nor industrial base for an effective defense. Fundamentally, from its inception, Pakistan was put in a precarious situation as it had approximately 17 percent of the financial assets and 30 percent of the defense forces of the undivided subcontinent. In addition, revenues of the Indian provinces were over 40 percent higher than in the Pakistan area. A final factor creating severe anxiety was the massive refugee influx in South Asia. These glaring discrepancies and serious problems kept a dark cloud over the potential development of the state (Jaffrelot, 97–99).

THE INTRACTABLE DISPUTE: KASHMIR

Following the partition of India in August 1947, Kashmir technically was "independent" with an understanding that it would decide to either become part of India or Pakistan in the very near future. Once Sheikh Abdullah and the National Conference colleagues were released from prison in late September, they immediately decided on standstill agreements with both India and Pakistan in order to give the people of Kashmir time to decide.

As long as Great Britain remained in control over South Asia, the conflict between the competing nationalistic movements in the subcontinent remained dormant. Politically opportunistic movements strived to turn the partition of India into a religious conflict. Intense rhetoric and fear led to one of the most significant migrations in modern world history (Ziring, 40–41). Nearly 7 million Hindus in Pakistan fled for their lives to India, and approximately the same amount of terror-stricken Muslims departed from India into Pakistan. This mass exodus of refugees did not even count the internally displaced populations in both countries. The chasm between these two faiths was significant and, with the intense politicization of religion from both faiths, tragedy seemed inevitable. This successful fulfillment of nationalist desires was marred by the bloodshed of the partition.

The partition also impacted the economic status of the subcontinent as the region was split into three parts (India, West Pakistan, and East Pakistan). The complicated situation of merging the two sectors of Pakistan together that were separated by 1,000 miles of Indian territory would prove challenging as the areas had nothing in common except for religion. The three distinct regions did not cooperate economically and ultimately had severe disagreements that harmed the future developments of the societies. As the hostilities boiled over, the economy was devastated.

When the British decided to withdraw from the region, the princely states were given three options: accession to India, accession to Pakistan, or independence. All but three opted to join India or Pakistan. Out of the three clamoring for independence, only the state of Kashmir proved to be problematic (Schofield, 32–33). The sheer size of Kashmir and the fact that it was highly coveted by both countries created a major problem. Kashmir proved to be the breaking point in the India-Pakistan dispute. The area historically known for its scenic beauty was also of enormous strategic value to both countries. The core of the dispute over Kashmir was centered on the disagreement between the ruler of the princely state and the subjects governed. The maharajah of Kashmir, Hari Singh, was Hindu, but approximately 75 percent of the population was Muslim. Singh tried to buy time by proposing a "standstill agreement" with both countries to obtain as much freedom as possible for their region.

The increasing violence engulfing the subcontinent was bound to drag Kashmir into the fray. Incursions from Muslim tribesmen from the northwest region of Pakistan frightened Singh, who pledged accession to India in exchange for military help against the insurgents, who were within a few miles of the Kashmiri capital of Srinagar. Lord Mountbatten accepted the accession with the condition that as soon as the violence had quelled a plebiscite was to be held in order to give the population of Kashmir the final say about the future status of the area. India troops arrived in time to turn the tide against the Pakistani tribesmen. The fighting in Kashmir continued without a clear-cut victory for either side. India assumed that the international community would declare Pakistan as the aggressor in the conflict, which was a factor in deciding to send the matter to the United Nations for resolution. A United Nations-mediated cease-fire was worked out that led to an uneasy peace. The Pakistani tribesmen put up strong resistance and ultimately secured one-third of the state, which they proclaimed as "Azad" or free Kashmir. In the months following the cease-fire, India was confronted with the difficulty of sealing off the border between the warring factions. This was reminiscent of the situation the British had to deal with in this Frontier Region. By the summer of 1948, the Pakistani army moved into the Jammu and Kashmir regions claiming that the accession from the previous fall was fraudulent. The military tension accelerated as India sent in reinforcements and used airpower to bomb Gilgit. It was clear to outside observers that the people and majority of leaders in the region wanted to be a part of Pakistan. The international community was able to quell the violence and solidify a more formal cease-fire in January 1949 (Bose, 40–41).

Even though the standard view of this conflict has been one of a modern religious war erupting in the postcolonial era, the reality of the situation was much more complicated. Pakistani insecurities pertaining to water access to the Indus basin helped to fuel the Kashmir conflict. According to Ayesha Jalal, "Whatever the emotive claims of religious affinity with Kashmiri Muslims, it was effectively water insecurity that drove a barely armed Pakistan to make the incorporation of Kashmir one of its main strategic goals" (Jalal, 67). The religious motivations behind the conflict became more pronounced when Pakistan encouraged the Mehsud and Mohmand tribes of the Northwest to raid Kashmir in late October 1947. The tribesmen were encouraged to wage jihad against the Hindu aggressors, who were involved in serious violations of Muslim rights following the partition. Chaos ensued as property was damaged and widespread looting took place. This policy decision by Pakistan was a significant gamble with potential risks for the internal and external security of a state that had been in existence for a mere two months.

The heightened tensions in Kashmir played into the hands of elements in Pakistan that wanted to see a more assertive role for the military in politics. Ultimately, Pakistan president Muhammad Ali Jinnah bore some of the responsibility for the Kashmir crisis. As the father of Pakistan, Jinnah was guaranteed nearly unlimited power and unquestioned authority. This situation lent itself into an overly strong executive with no real checks on institution power. Jinnah's proclamation in favor of democratic norms did not match his somewhat authoritarian actions in dealing with Bengalis, the tension in Balochistan, and of course Kashmir. Jinnah felt he was guiding Pakistan toward state sovereignty and the preservation of national unity (Iffat Malik, 209–210). Unfortunately, Jinnah's death on September 11, 1948, dealt a blow to Pakistan at a time when a strong leader was an absolute necessity. Jinnah was fearful of what might happen as his health was rapidly failing, but he did not know what actions might mitigate the potential threat to the fledgling democracy.

The Muslim League that Jinnah had championed for so many years had become excessively corrupt with wealthy landlords-turned-politicians reaping the benefits of power. Many of the novice civil servants, bureaucrats, and legislators ultimately directed a disproportional amount of resources to the military rather than economic development policies. This was done in large measure because of the Kashmir crisis but also the West Pakistani fear of the growing Bengali political power. The decision to fund the military at a disproportional level angered local and regional political actors, who felt the central government was out of touch with the needs of the Pakistani people. With a lack of accountability in the newly formed state, the level of mismanagement grew at an alarming rate. Making matters worse, the state was dealing with an influx of refugees following the partition. Finally, the new regime of Liaquat Ali Khan was actively plotting to rig the first ever elections in the history of Pakistan.

Western powers, including the British, were encouraging Khan to agree to a resolution to the Kashmir problem by splitting the region at the Chenab River. This would have given Pakistan control over about one-third of the territory. Most of the Pakistani military leaders agreed with this assessment and believed this was the most realistic resolution at the time. Khan felt that this sort of compromise would weaken his position nationally. In response, he arrested several senior officers who had fought in the initial Kashmir campaign, including the popular chief of the general staff, Major General Akbar Khan. Liaquat believed the generals were conspiring to launch a coup d'état. What became known as the "Rawalpindi Conspiracy" included key generals who were conspiring with the USSR. Many active on the left in Pakistan were rounded up under suspicion of being in collusion with the plotters. This led to a further crackdown against civil liberties in Pakistan as unwarranted arrests and the suppression of the press became commonplace (Jahal, 80).

Pakistan was in need of financial and military assistance in order to effectively deal with the Kashmir issue. India had a noticeably growing military buildup, and the Americans were showing a strong interest in strengthening ties with the regime. The need for American military bases in the Indian Ocean and the vital interest the Americans had in the oil rich region of the Middle East made the partnership possible. Liaquat's productive visit to the United States in 1950 pushed the process along even further (Haqqani, 48–49). The shocking assassination of Khan in October 1951 left the United States concerned about a possible power vacuum in the region. Over the next few years, the Americans were able to secure a deal with Ayub Khan to place an American base in Pakistan in exchange for military aid. The decision to make a strong pro-American push was finalized.

The situation played into the hands of the military. As the Cold War heated up, the generals in Pakistan became compelled to take on a more assertive role. General Ayub told the political leaders that they must go wholeheartedly with the West. The political elites were warned not to interfere with the developing relationship. Pakistan signed two important security agreements with the United States: the Southeast Asian Treaty Organization (SEATO) in 1954 and the Baghdad Pact in 1955. A shift in the balance of power from elected to nonelected institutions was clearly in place by the mid-1950s. In 1958, the army was ready to act, and the first military intervention took place. What was emerging in Pakistan had long-term, detrimental implications for democratic development. A patronage system was

established that solidified the military power brokers along with a lucra-
tive political economy of defense. Ultimately, the military developed utter
contempt for the civilian leadership. It was the military that alone could
retake Kashmir and keep the Bengali situation under control. This trend of
the military being the savior of Pakistan has been endemic throughout the
history of the country and continues to the present.

By 1958, the fundamentals of civil society were eroding, and the fragile democratic system in Pakistan was vulnerable. The judiciary refused
to challenge the power structure in place and did not want to create anything resembling the checks and balances so important in the Western-
style democracies. In addition, the concept of rule of law was weak with
far too much power vested in the military. Ayub demanded blind obedi-
ence and total compliance by subordinates. The final move was to actually
declare martial law on October 7, 1958. In what was known as "Operation
Fair Play," President Iskander Mirza put an abrupt end to the less than
three-year experiment in parliamentary democracy. The state was facing
both economic and political difficulties at the time, which made the move
seem more credible. It was apparent that the military officials involved
had the blessing of both the United States and Great Britain as the powers
were assured that the new regime would be more pro-Western. As part
of the change, "Mirza suspended the constitution, dismissed the central
and provincial governments, dissolved assemblies, banned political parties, postponed elections indefinitely, and placed the prime minister and
his cabinet under house arrest" (Jalal, 98). The claim was made that the
coup was in the interest of the country. The crackdown and implementation of martial law was seen as a positive change by many of the citizens,
who believed that only the military could restore a semblance of order and
normalcy to Pakistan.

The idea of General Ayub sharing power with his coconspirator President Mirza was ill-fated and short-lived. Within a few weeks, the president was sent into permanent exile as Ayub solidified his dictatorship.
Direct martial law rule was brief as Ayub instead relied on two military
spy agencies, the Inter-Services Intelligence (ISI) and Military Intelligence
(MI), in order to control the watch over the civil bureaucracy. The initial
popularity of Ayub's rule attracted numerous young politicians, including
the future prime minister of Pakistan and young Sindhi lawyer Zulfikar
Ali Bhutto.

A new constitution was put into place on March 1, 1962. The system
shifted away from the British Westminster Model. The legislative branch
included a single chamber and a presidential form of government. In a
somewhat surprising move, the state's designation of the country shifted
from "Islamic Republic of Pakistan" to the "Republic of Pakistan" (Shah,
98–99). In addition, all references to the Quran and Sunnah from the 1956
document were deleted. Ayub detested religious leaders who tried to

make political advances in Pakistan through shamelessly peddling Islamic virtues. Ayub felt that the growth of Islamic parties was one of the most potentially threatening advances that could take place in Pakistan. He took steps to change Muslim family laws and strengthen women's rights. Ultimately, this drew the ire of Mawdudi's Jamaat-i-Islam, which accused the government of undermining the religious foundations of Pakistan. Politically, he did lack patience and wanted a system that would quickly rubber stamp policies so that Pakistan could industrialize and militarize in the shortest possible time. Many of these economic plans were more beneficial to West Pakistan, while the eastern area continued to suffer in abject poverty with the perception of little or no representation at the national level (Jalal, 129–131). This lack of concern for the situation in the eastern region continued to fester, as the central government did not respond well to natural disasters, such as flooding, and fed the general feeling that the Bengalis were treated as second-class citizens.

The growing disillusionment sparked opposition parties to form a coalition against Ayub. The parties lacked any clear direction, and the only point of unity was the desire to remove the current administration. The standard bearer of the movement was Fatima Jinnah, the sister of the founder of Pakistan. The electoral process was in all likelihood rigged, and Ayub won a landslide victory.

Ali Bhutto continually warned Ayub that Pakistan was gravitating too close to America in foreign policy matters. Bhutto wanted a more non-aligned position and possibly closer relations with China. Many within the military establishment felt that the close relationship with America made it more problematic to aggressively pursue Pakistani interests in Kashmir. The relationship with America became more complicated with the election of John F. Kennedy. The American goal of forging closer ties with India was apparent, as the United States saw India as a more important ally in both the realm of security and economic interests. This shift toward India seemed more logical with the outbreak of hostilities in the Sino-India War of 1962. The desire to counter Chinese power in the region made sense to the foreign policy team in the Kennedy White House. In an attempt to maintain some sense of balance at this time, the American "Atoms for Peace" program enabled Pakistan to further advance programs in nuclear science and technology (Haqqani, 103–105).

Pakistan did secure several trade and military agreements as the influence of Ali Bhutto was apparent. Furthermore, the disputed boundary between Pakistan and China was resolved. By compromising with the Chinese, Pakistan was able to procure more economic assistance that was needed because American aid was being curtailed. The successful deal with the Chinese allowed Bhutto to become the main point man in Pakistani foreign affairs. His recklessness and risk taking endangered the Pakistani state.

The population in Kashmir was growing increasingly disillusioned with Indian rule. Harsh treatment toward the population and constant human rights violations kept the resistance movement alive. A spark for the resistance was the April 1964 rearrest of Kashmiri leader Sheikh Abdullah. A brief but successful Pakistani military incursion into Rann of Kutch gave the regime confidence that a move against India in Kashmir might be successful. The plan was for the Kashmiri population to stage an uprising without necessarily having direct or explicit help from the Pakistani military. The Pakistani military and political establishment felt that this was the best opportunity they would have to retake some of the lost Kashmiri territory. Pakistan believed that India was vulnerable following the loss to China in the 1962 border war; a defeat that showed the Indian military weakness. Second, Pakistan felt that India would be strengthened in the near future because of the increased aid from the United States. Bhutto claimed that in two years India would have the ability to launch a war of annihilation on Pakistan and, if they did not act very soon, a major opportunity would be lost. Bhutto had unrealistic expectations for the Pakistani military, which he believed was vastly superior to the Indian fighters. In July 1965, the decision was made to launch an attack. Ayub was encouraged to take a tough stance in dealing with the United States—it needed Pakistan as a strong ally in Asia. If quick gains could be made in Kashmir, a cease-fire would be implemented, and the Pakistani gains could be secured. Bhutto assured Ayub that both the ISI and MI believed that Kashmir was ripe for an uprising against the oppressive Indian rule. In the subsequent military plans known as Operation Grand Slam and Operation Gibraltar, the Pakistani military saw disappointing results (Shah, 103). The eagerly anticipated uprising never materialized, and the forces that entered the Indian-occupied part of Kashmir were quickly defeated and captured. The Indian counterattack in September turned this into a full-fledged conflict. The United States opted to implement an arms embargo and remain neutral. The Americans were engulfed in the growing quagmire of Vietnam and could ill afford to get involved simultaneously in multiple Asian conflicts. Interestingly, it would be the Soviet Union that would take the lead in negotiating an end to the hostilities.

What was glaringly noticeable was the lack of support for the India war from East Pakistan. The Bengalis saw the conflict as a barrier to improved relations with the growing economic powerhouse that was India. The ultimate end of the war was a military and political stalemate for Pakistan, but a financial disaster. The UN cease-fire was accepted in late September with India's position in Kashmir as strong as ever. The Pakistani military command was perceived as inept, while relations with America continued to be strained. Pakistan felt betrayed by America, which they perceived as a "fair weather friend," a label that would dominate relations between the two countries up to the present times. The United States tried to mend the relationship by inviting Ayub to the White House for an official visit with President Johnson. The Pakistani delegation assured Johnson that they were a reliable ally and that a stronger relationship between China and Pakistan was not going to transpire. The United States convinced Pakistan that India would not be allowed to threaten the survival of the country (Riedel, 14–15). After the meeting with the Americans, Ali Bhutto was forced to resign, as he was seen as the most pro-Chinese member of the Pakistani government.

By the late 1960s, the impact of the "Green Revolution" was altering the economic situation in Pakistan. Landlords benefitted and were able to squeeze smaller farmers out of business, which led to a massive migration to urban areas. Food shortages in East Pakistan became commonplace, and subsequent natural disasters created despair in the region. In addition, the aftermath of the 1965 war left many in the East feeling resentful and ready to take action. Student and labor activism was becoming more pronounced, and, politically, the Awami League led by Sheikh Mujibur Rahman became the main voice for East Pakistanis. The desire for greater autonomy for the region and increased representation in the military and civil bureaucracy were part of the demands of the league's Six Point Program. Ayub's inability to correctly read the political climate and act in an appropriate manner spelled his demise. He did not foresee the serious nature of the threat from the now united Bengali movement in the East. Eventually, the Bengalis consolidated with other pro-democratic movements to demand changes in the Pakistan government. The coalition known as the Pakistan Democratic Movement demanded "the restoration of parliamentary government based on direct elections and universal suffrage; a federal center restricted to defense, foreign affairs, currency, communications and trade; separate foreign exchange accounts for the two wings based on their export earnings; relocation of the naval headquarters from Karachi to East Pakistan; and the achievement of parity in the state services within ten years" (Jalal, 130).

Ayub's paranoia was significant, and his apprehension of a CIA-inspired plot against him as well as his growing fears over secessionist elements in the East sparked irrational responses. Bizarre criticism of the Bengalis included that a West Pakistani felt like a foreigner in Dhaka (the capital of the East) and Bengalis were Hinduizing their language and culture. The response from Ayub and the West was to extend the state of emergency that had been in place since the outbreak of the conflict in 1965. Attempts to arrest Mujibur Rahman on trumped-up charges failed, as the Awami League leader became a driving force of Bengali nationalism.

It became apparent that the momentum was shifting away from Ayub. In addition to the Bengali upheaval in the East, the never-ending unrest in Balochistan was festering again. Making matters worse, the deposed Ali Bhutto launched the Pakistan People's Party (PPP) in December 1967.

The motto of "Islam as its faith, democracy as its politics, and socialism as its economy" resonated with numerous factions within Pakistan. With an aggressive populist agenda that attracted liberals and leftists, the party promised food, clothing, and housing. The regime's unpopularity grew, and Ayub retaliated by arresting key opposition leaders, including Bhutto and Wali Khan. Lawyers, civil society groups, and student activists began massive protests. This was an era in which protests were mounting globally in places such as Mexico City and Paris. The Pakistani democracy movement clamored for fundamental rights, including secret ballots, freedom of the press, an independent judiciary, and a recognition of the importance of checks and balances. None of these attributes were apparent under Ayub's reign. Following a heart attack in January 1968, his trusted military commander General Yahya Khan replaced Ayub. The new administration was somewhat factionalized with different commanders supporting several political party leaders (Jalal, 133). Exacerbating tensions was the fact that key politicians had different objectives and opinions of what constituted real democracy for Pakistan.

By early 1969, tensions in the East were increasing dramatically. Student organizations attending a rally of over 100,000 people clamored for the lifting of the state of emergency, release of previously detained political opponents, and halt of all political cases against eastern activists. The student protesters were more radicalized than the political leaders who were attempting to negotiate with the Ayub government. Mujib's main objective was to decentralize power in Pakistan. However, it was clear from private conversations that the Bengali leadership wanted to keep Pakistan together as one state and that secession was not under consideration (Lieven, 59).

The demand for decentralization angered the ruling elites in West Pakistan. The landlords and industrialists, who wielded economic power, wanted the regime to crackdown on the militants in the East. The idea of an open, transparent democratic system for Pakistan did not appeal to these groups. Economically, the disparity was clear, as the West received the lion's share of revenue for infrastructure development, and per capita income was significantly higher. Furthermore, electricity costs were increasing at dramatically higher rates in the East, and industrial leaders were departing from the East, which exacerbated the already troubling economic trends.

In March, martial law was declared, as Ayub Khan abdicated calling on Commander in Chief Yahya Khan to defend Pakistan from external threats and to save it from internal chaos (Jaffrelot, 216–217). The military deployed a large contingent of troops and equipment into the eastern wing, where the troop numbers surpassed 40,000. The political decision to declare martial law was in all likelihood taken to prevent a Bengali from becoming the next leader of Pakistan. The public response to the imposition was meek in the West, but in the East, the decision created anxiety and heightened tensions dramatically.

Yahya Khan was an unlikely leader of Pakistan. He was a Shia, and his family was Persian. However, the general showed resolve as he acted decisively to consolidate power. He dissolved the national assembly, abrogated the constitution, and issued decries to eliminate basic civil liberties. Many in the East were concerned that these moves would lead to the total collapse of the country.

By the end of the year, the general announced a date for general elections, which were scheduled for October 5, 1970. The negotiations ultimately ended by conceding the Bengali request of representation according to population. However, Mujib's demand for provincial autonomy was not mentioned. The general was concerned that this would be an initial step toward eventual secession. In the early election campaign, Ayub took several steps to strengthen his hand and limit popular sovereignty. Any attempts to shift the balance of power via the election of 1970 would face considerable roadblocks (Shah, 106–107). Power was to be centered with the military and the entrenched bureaucracy.

The West Pakistani elite and military distrusted the Bengali political leadership. It was believed that Mujib was working with India in order to dismember Pakistan. The pro-Islamic parties were supported by the military in order to counter the leftist Bengali movements and most notably, the Awami League. The regime was overconfident in their belief that the numerous parties would split the vote and allow the West Pakistani establishment to control the future political path of Pakistan.

THE STORM THAT SPLIT PAKISTAN

A massive cyclone hit East Pakistan on November 12, 1970. This disaster coupled with an already dire food shortage led to the death of over 200,000 citizens. Millions were left homeless in what is known as one of the worst natural disasters in modern history. The scheduled elections were postponed for a month, as a seemingly indifferent and lackadaisical response from the Pakistan authorities fueled intense anger in the East. The reaction played out most notably at the ballot box, as the Awami League won a resounding victory in the elections. The turnout in the East was astoundingly over 50 percent with approximately 75 percent of the votes cast for the Awami League. This meant that virtually the entire eastern electorate in the national assembly were Awami supporters. The votes in the West were more splintered with the PPP winning two-thirds of the seats. As events unfolded, it was apparent that no formula for power sharing would be viable and that political turmoil leading to the implosion of Pakistan was inevitable (Stoessinger, 125–127).

The stage was set for the tragic partition of Pakistan long before the elections of 1970. Authoritarian and discriminatory policies promulgated by elites in the West helped to heighten the tensions. The economic inequality coupled with the neglect of regional disparities worsened the situation. Furthermore, the Bengalis were culturally and linguistically homogeneous, which made nationalist aspirations more realistic. Finally, the crisis was fueled by the refusal of the West to grant more autonomy to the East and the passion and intensity felt by the Bengalis to change the status quo.

Most observers believed that the partition was due to political miscalculations on both sides of the disagreement. The elites in West Pakistan culturally alienated the Bengalis, and the perception of what has been coined "internal colonization" took place. Furthermore, policies promoting nationalism increased within the Bengali community. Decades of economic discrimination and political marginalization brought the country to the breaking point.

The first call for independence came from radical Bengali nationalist Maulana Bhashani. He refused to participate in the elections of 1970 on the grounds that it was time for an independent state to be declared. His decision was also a result of the callous indifference of the West Pakistani leadership to the death and destruction from the cyclone tragedy. Initially, the Awami League and Mujib did not call for such extreme action, but a dramatic increase in autonomy for the eastern wing. Mujib wanted the implementation of his Six Point Plan. An early meeting between Mujib and Yahya Khan in January 1971 by all accounts went well. Cooperation between the two and, subsequently, PPP leader Bhutto was key if partition was to be averted. These attempts were in all likelihood too late, and on February 22, after deliberating with intelligence officers, governors, and key administrators, the decision was finalized to use force to restore order in East Pakistan. The Awami League leaders faced arrest and charges of sedition.

In early March at a rally in Dhaka, Mujib called for armed resistance against the inevitable invasion. The struggle was now cloaked in terms of independence as the slogan of "Jai Bangla" (Victory to Bengal) was proclaimed. Last minute efforts to find a compromise governing structure failed.

It was clear that the military operations to suppress the Awami League were in the works long before February. The initial plan to restore law and order was code named Operation Blitz. Fighting broke out on March 23, and the West Pakistani forces under General Tikka Khan launched the first stage of the invasion that was known as Operation Searchlight. The goal of the army was not to quickly disarm the combatants but to violently destroy the opposition. At no time did Yahya Khan act to quell the violence or attempt to negotiate with the Awami League. The bloody carnage included the indiscriminate murder of innocent students and protesters at locations such as Dhaka University, as well as key areas where protesters were congregating. The accounts quoted from Archer Blood, the American consul general in Dhaka, in the seminal work by Gary Baas *The Blood Telegrams* depicted the unbelievable horrors that occurred during what he and many claimed were genocidal activities on the part of the West Pakistani regime. The leadership did not have a long-term plan nor did they consider the reactions from regional power India or for that matter the international community.

The Bengali resistance forces known as the Mukti Bahini (Liberation Army) quickly emerged and funded, supplied, and trained by Pakistan's rival India. The extremely difficult and watery terrain of the Bengali delta made the fighting challenging for the Pakistan forces. Eventually, the India regime under Indira Gandhi was faced with the dilemma of 10 million refugees on the border, who were becoming a nearly impossible financial and humanitarian strain on the state. After tense diplomatic rhetoric between the regional powers, Gandhi made the calculated decision to launch an invasion of Pakistan to help liberate the Bengalis and subsequently create an independent Bangladesh. The India government had earlier secured a treaty of friendship with the Soviet Union in order to protect them from any possible countermeasures from the United States on behalf of Pakistan. The end result was an utter catastrophe for Khan and the Pakistan military. By December, 93,000 Pakistani troops were captured. According to Tufts political scientist Ayesha Jalal, "Strategic blundering and political ineptitude combined to create a horrific nightmare for a military high command that was ill equipped to handle the situation. Once orders had been given to put boots on the ground and enforce law and order, pent-up frustrations shredded the last remnants of humanity still adorning the hearts of the West Pakistani troops. The ethical dilemma of killing fellow Muslims was quickly overcome. Bengalis were not just black men; they were Muslims in name only and had to be purged of their infidelity. Whatever the reasoning of the perpetrators, nothing can justify the horrendous crimes committed in the name of a false sense of nationalism" (Jalal, 175).

CHAPTER 2

The Birth of Extremism: Internal and External Factors

The dismemberment of Pakistan that resulted from the tragic 1971 war set the country on an eventual drift toward extremism. The fear of Indian encroachment and the possibility of the outright loss of Pakistan provoked numerous political changes. Both internal and external factors played into the decision making of the leaders as well as overall direction of the political climate. Before addressing the phenomenal changes orchestrated during the tenure of General Zia-ul-Haq (1977–1988), it is important to understand the impact of Zulfikar Ali Bhutto and the populist Pakistan People's Party (PPP).

POSTWAR DEBACLE: THE RISE AND FALL OF THE PPP AND BHUTTO

Following the debacle of 1971 and the eventual independence of Bangladesh, Pakistani society yearned for a departure from the inept military rule that had dominated the country for nearly two decades. Even though Zulfikar Ali Bhutto was associated with the previous administration, he was skillfully able to distance himself from the regime at key junctures. Bhutto was considered to be a savior of the new Pakistan, and he was able to use the state-controlled media effectively to neutralize the opposition and secure state power. Bhutto's political opposition was Muslim League leader Khan Abdul Qayyum Khan. The challenge was not serious as Bhutto had been deputy prime minister and represented Pakistan at the UN Security Council, while the negotiations to the conflict were ironed out. Bhutto led the walkout during the UN session, and his oratory skills made him a natural leader. He claimed to stand by the people at the most critical hour in the nation's history. The country and all institutions of Pakistan were in chaos, and restoration of national morale was urgent. Furthermore, Bhutto wanted a return to rule of law and a constitution that could guide the country toward democracy (Bass, 329–333).

Bhutto was the first leader of Pakistan to emerge from the indigenous feudal landed aristocracy. He was a Sindhi landlord educated in the West with a somewhat liberal lifestyle that seemed contradictory to the role he would need to fulfill.

Bhutto took the reins from a demoralized and shaken military that was in total shambles after the loss in 1971. Not only had they suffered their worst defeat in the history of Pakistan, the military also had to secure the release of 93,000 prisoners of war taken during the fiasco. It would take time for the military to reestablish credibility and regain confidence (Fair, "Fighting to the End," 149–150).

Bhutto was a populist and champion of the Third World agenda, including many socialist programs and policies. The issue of social justice was a priority for the new regime. The PPP slogan of "Islam is our faith, democracy is our polity, socialism is our economy, all power to the people," summarized the focus in the postwar administration. High on Bhutto's agenda was the formulation of a new constitution for Pakistan that included a parliamentary system of government in which power was vested mostly with the prime minister rather than the president. (This was something that Bhutto initially opposed, but eventually compromised on for the final document.) In April 1972, the national assembly convened to pass an interim constitution. A year later, the final document passed with an overwhelming majority. Over 90 percent of the national assembly voted in favor of the draft document. The meeting was held in a time of crisis as the regime was dealing with separatism in Balochistan (Lieven, 73–75). Bhutto needed to work with smaller parties in order to promote his agenda. He also wanted to build up civilian institutions and parliament in order to prevent too much power heading toward the military.

One of the problems Pakistan encountered in the transition to democracy regarded federalism. The question of how much power the central authority should have versus the four provinces was contentious. The issue of Punjabi control of the bureaucracy and the military alarmed other regions and ethnic groups. The official language being Urdu was also divisive. This frustrated Sindhi speakers and later clashes based on linguistics would be encountered. Ultimately, the center of power remained in the national government and not the provinces. In order for the government to be removed, a 75 percent majority was required. Every significant change to the governing structure of Pakistan in the mid-1970s strengthened Bhutto's authority at the expense of other branches or, in some cases, the citizenry.

The dangerous path Bhutto followed was most apparent regarding the relations with the military. His June 1972 meeting with Indira Gandhi in Simla was a step toward reconciliation that did not sit well in the military. In addition, to gain concessions, including the return of prisoners of war and occupied territory, Bhutto signed an official cease-fire agreement, which renamed the border the Line of Control (LOC). Finally, a clause was added to the 1973 constitution that made it illegal for the military to intervene in politics. Another ominous issue that developed was the emergence of the intelligence network in Pakistan. Bhutto felt that his administration was kept in the dark about some of the workings and programs of the ISI and other agencies. To gage the power of the military at this time, one only needs to look at the fact that 90 percent of the federal budget was allocated to defense spending, which left a paltry sum for the social programs so highly touted by the PPP leadership (Jalal, 194–196).

Ultimately, Bhutto was a populist who did not hesitate to nationalize industries. One of his initial moves was to gain government control of a number of heavy industries and public utilities. These early directives accelerated tensions between the regime and big business. Bhutto's announcement of the Economic Reforms Order mandated the takeover of nearly a dozen categories of industry that were beneficial to the people. Using bureaucrats with no experience to run industries that had been privately controlled created numerous problems to the economic stability of Pakistan. In addition, the accelerated speed of the nationalization process created economic uncertainty. Bhutto's and the PPP's initial popularity can also be attributed to the wave of populism and anti-capitalist sentiments that were popular during this period in the developing world (Shah, 128–129).

In order to suppress opposition, industrialists were detained, and the press was censored. Bureaucratic opponents were also replaced and in some cases imprisoned. The top level of the bureaucracy known as the Civil Service of Pakistan (CSP) was abolished. An unforeseen problem was that many civil servants were not trained properly in how to run the newly nationalized industries. The need for outside assistance opened up opportunities for corruption and political misdeeds. Political challengers were intimidated as Bhutto created a culture of fear. In addition, Bhutto challenged key members of the military hierarchy, including General Gul Hassan. Bhutto called for investigations into the causes of the military catastrophe of 1971, triggering the formation of the Hamoodur Rahman Commission. The military leadership was in conflict with Bhutto over issues related to labor unrest and government restructuring. A showdown ensued, which led to several key leaders, including General Hassan, being forced to resign. Bhutto realized that the possibility of a military coup d'état lingered. The military was adamant that any internal or external crisis that threatened Pakistan could not be tolerated and that they would not hesitate to intervene if necessary. Bhutto believed that a strong civilian political authority in control of the three branches of government (executive, legislative, and judicial) could keep the military in check (Shah, 128–129). In order to gain loyalty, Bhutto increased salaries and perks to officers and bureaucrats alike. The building up of a strong patronage system was essential.

Bhutto's strong relationship with organized labor in the urban areas was also beneficial. Reforms implemented during the summer of 1972 helped boost the popularity of the Bhutto regime. The minimum wage was increased, and benefits, including collective bargaining, the right of free association, and employee representation were all included. Labor troubles in urban areas were endemic. The worst incidents in Karachi led to workers being fired upon. The business community did not trust Bhutto or the PPP because their socialist policies firmly stated that they would side with the workers in any labor disputes (Ziring, 140–142).

During March 1972, Bhutto accelerated the land reform program. This helped to strengthen Bhutto's ties to the peasantry. Many loopholes in the system allowed the elite landholding families to keep the majority of their holdings, but overall, the power of large landowning families was curbed. In addition, and mostly important, he promoted land reform by doling out holdings to the mass of Pakistani peasantry. Bhutto wanted to distribute wealth more evenly and needed a steady growth rate in order to do so. Bhutto turned to the IMF and World Bank to help boost the Pakistani economy (Jalal, 198). In addition, the regime solicited help from the Gulf States. Economic analysts at the time felt that Pakistan was in better condition than either India or Bangladesh.

Bhutto's most controversial policy was the decision to accelerate the development of nuclear technology and ultimately advance the nuclear weapons program for Pakistan. The PPP successfully negotiated the lifting of the 10-year American embargo on arms to Pakistan. Once India tested a nuclear device in 1974, the stakes were raised. In one of the most famous quotes uttered by Bhutto, he stated that Pakistan would push ahead with the nuclear program "even if the country had to eat grass." The initial plans were kept secret, but the regime realized it was necessary to counter the growing strength of India. Bhutto wanted a rapid expansion of the program. During the Khan administration, the government had formulated the Pakistan Atomic Energy Commission (PAEC). However, Ayub Khan was apprehensive about the program because of fear of economic retaliation from the West. After assuming power, Bhutto felt that Pakistan needed the nuclear program in order to regain the international status lost during the 1971 conflict. The majority of nuclear scientists in Pakistan were on board with Bhutto, who promised to spare no cost in order to develop nuclear weapons technology (Haqqani, 210–213). Many within the country later commented about a sense of pride in being the first Muslim country to develop a nuclear weapon. One side effect of this ambitious program was the impact it had on Bhutto's populist domestic agenda. The financial burden derailed many of the programs and ultimately led to a domestic crisis in Pakistan.

The role of Pakistan on the global stage was complicated during the tenure of Zulfikar Ali Bhutto. At times, he seemed to advocate a shift toward the nonaligned mentality that was en vogue during the late 1950s to 1960s. During the 1970s, Bhutto withdrew Pakistan from SEATO and the Commonwealth. The goal of the regime was stronger relations with China and the Muslim world (Jalal, 200–201). The oil crisis of 1973 pushed Bhutto to pursue closer ties with the Gulf States in particular. Bhutto hosted the Islamic Summit Conference in Lahore in 1974. During the meeting, diplomatic recognition was granted to Bangladesh and relations with the Saudis (especially King Faisal) were strained as Bhutto attempted to dominate the proceedings. The meeting showed the clear rift in the Muslim world, as the Shah of Iran did not attend and instead hosted a visiting delegation from India. It was a forgone conclusion that Pakistan needed close ties to the United States. This relationship was complicated by the nuclear ambitions of the regime.

THE POLITICIZATION OF RELIGION AND THE FALL OF BHUTTO

The international changes occurring had domestic implications for Bhutto. Religious parties saw the tide turning globally and used this as an opening to reemerge on the political front domestically. Bhutto also alienated leftist elements that had been loyal to him throughout his tenure. His populist programs were more important than true democracy building. The religious parties took advantage of the discord from the Balochistan uprising (which also concerned Iran because of the possible spillover effect) and growing disillusionment with the PPP government. The issue that caused the most significant amount of trouble was the standing of the Ahmadis. The conservative Jamaat-i-Islami under the leadership of Mawdudi forged close ties to the Wahhabists in Saudi Arabia, who were calling for the excommunication of the Ahmadis. The key point of contention was that the Ahmadis professed the belief in a prophet after Muhammad. The sect was refused entry into Saudi Arabia to perform the Haj. This was an essential problem for the rigid fundamentalist mind-set. There were bizarre conspiracy theories that the Ahmadis were British agents during colonial times and, more recently, Israeli sympathizers. Proof of this plot was that Ahmadis held key posts in the government and military and welded considerable power in Pakistan overall. Many experts believed that amending the constitution to proclaim the Ahmadis a religious minority set the stage for further discrimination against minority populations (Ispahani, 46–47). This went against the concept of equal rights that had been a cornerstone of Pakistan since the creation of the state. Bhutto's weakness in dealing with the religious conservatives played a part in his eventual demise.

This victory for the religious conservative parties only emboldened the movement. The next step was to implement sharia and eventually an Islamic system of government. The middle and lower classes in Pakistan were susceptible to the rhetoric of fundamentalists. Jamaat weaved together a message that the lack of religious fervor in Pakistan was a key component in the losses it had incurred over the years. Only a religiously devout regime could lead Pakistan to its potential greatness. Bhutto realized that no matter what concessions were given, the religious elements would not be satisfied (Shah, 135–136). What they desired was a regime change.

In the period leading up to the 1977 election and subsequent crisis, Pakistan seemed to gain momentum in several key areas. The underclass, sympathetic to the religious conservative message, also benefitted from the populist programs of the Bhutto regime. Economic optimism was boosted by the PPP advocating universal education and comprehensive health care. These measures should have guaranteed continued loyalty to the regime. The economic revival and positive investment numbers in Pakistan led Bhutto to make the critical decision to call for nationwide elections in 1977. This decision proved to be his undoing.

A Bhutto victory was a forgone conclusion. In order to further secure his mandate, the prime minister cut taxes for the business community and implemented additional land reforms. The government also increased pensions for civil and military employees. Finally, the parties and movements opposing Bhutto seemed hopelessly factionalized. There was no need to manipulate the process or fudge the results.

The opposition coalition collectively known as the PNA won 36 seats in the parliamentary elections to the PPPs 136. In particular areas, notably Punjab, the victory was even more lopsided. The PNA demanded new elections and the resignation of Bhutto. The regime's approach was to jail some of the leadership, while calling for a dialogue to resolve outstanding issues. The opposition actions accelerated as protests increased during the spring and early summer of 1977. The well-funded PNA wanted a truly Islamic state in Pakistan, and external supporters were more than willing to donate financial resources to promote this agenda (Jalal, 207–209). The PNA claimed that the regime was too pro-Western and lacked the moral standing to legitimately govern the state.

The response by the PPP was to give in to numerous demands. Sharia was imposed by the end of the year, and alcohol and gambling were to be banned. Anarchy spread, as the death toll from the protests mounted, and major urban areas were in peril. Widespread damage occurred as the role of the military increased. Bhutto also faced mounting pressure from the new U.S. administration under Jimmy Carter to curtail the Pakistani nuclear program. Statements from the new regime spread paranoia within the PPP government. Bhutto publicly proclaimed an international conspiracy against his regime, and he believed the Jamaat and the military were also in collusion to topple him (Jaffrelot, 324–327). By the first week of July, Bhutto finalized negotiations with the PNA to strike a deal to end the protests and return the country to normalcy. However, the coup was already in the last stage of planning with General Zia-ul-Haq ready to replace the faltering leadership.

The earlier decision by Bhutto to promote Zia-ul-Haq was a safe bet. ISI chief Ghulam Jilani recommended the choice of General Zia. Six higher-ranking generals were passed over in order to select Zia. The background of the soon-to-be leader of Pakistan was modest and nonthreatening. Zia came from a middle-class background in East Punjab. By all accounts, the general was highly devout and had no base of support within the military. Zia was educated at St. Stephen's College in Delhi and began his military service in 1944. He had ties to religious conservatives, including key individuals in the Jamaat-i-Islami (Hiro, 159–162).

No single leader in Pakistani history changed the political and religious landscape as much as General Zia-ul-Haq. The longevity of his rule (1977-1988) had as much to do with the volatile international situation than anything else. As the military quickly implemented "Operation Fairplay," the former leader was placed under house arrest, and martial law was once again imposed. The national and provincial assemblies were also dissolved. What made the situation in 1977 unique was the fusion of the military and religious zeal. Zia considered himself a true soldier of Islam and promised to hold nationwide elections within 90 days.

General Zia was heavily influenced by the Wahhabist ideology and thus wanted to move Pakistan in a fundamentalist direction, which included returning to the times of the Prophet Muhammad. This was part of a seismic shift globally regarding religious fundamentalism. A rejection of Western values was underway, which led to changes in Iran and numerous other Muslim states. The influence of Gulf money in these efforts cannot be overstated. In Pakistan, a major reshuffling of the Council of Islamic Ideology was undertaken, and the attire of government workers changed to garb more in line with traditional Pakistani values rather than Western dress. Prayers were introduced in offices, and religiously observant Muslims were shown favoritism in hiring and promotion. These policies were collectively known as the Islamization of Pakistan.

It was clear to General Zia that his promise of holding elections within 90 days could not occur. The popularity of the PPP coupled with threats to try Zia on treason made the situation precarious. The announcement that Bhutto was arrested under a martial law order meant that the military was in this for the long haul. Zia proclaimed that only the military could stabilize the country and keep it from falling into chaos (Lieven, 76–78). The key strategic move by Zia was to manipulate the judiciary to ensure that any PPP or Bhutto loyalists were quickly purged. Zia's cronies, including new justice Anwar ul-Haq, stated that the coup was necessary to protect the welfare of the nation. The judiciary also ruled that General Zia could alter the constitution of 1973.

The final step was to quickly try the former leader. Bhutto was charged with criminal conspiracy to commit murder and was sentenced to death. The closed-door trial was a farce and ultimately one of the darkest moments in Pakistani history. Even though Zia could have commuted the sentence to life in prison, he ultimately followed through and had Bhutto hung in April 1979. Appeals from leaders across the world fell on deaf ears (Kux, 237–238).

The aftermath of the execution was Zia's attempt to secure a lengthy and more aggressively Islamic period of rule for his military regime. The direction of the courts shifted to sharia, while numerous rulings proved discriminatory to non-Muslims. One of the especially harmful areas was the treatment of women. Policies on adultery and rape were harsh and vindictive toward women. These *hudoods* or restrictions especially harmed women from underclass backgrounds (Jalal, 224). The key to Zia maintaining power was his close alliance with religious parties, especially Jamaat. The PNA coalition became an integral part of the national government.

Even with the base of religious support, Zia was in a dubious situation. His legitimacy was nearly nonexistent as former PPP members and other factions rallied against the regime, who were appalled by the general's decision to execute Bhutto. Additionally, the international community, most notably the United States, was fed up with the direction Zia was taking the country. The Carter administration suspended all economic and military aid to Pakistan under the Symington Amendment (Kux, 238–239). The growing frustration with the nuclear weapons program and Zia's rule in general put the alliance in a precarious state. General Zia had neither the political acumen nor intellect to weather the brewing storm. The regime needed a diversion to quell the onslaught and they got just that from the Soviet invasion of neighboring Afghanistan.

PAKISTAN AS A COLD WAR PROXY: THE AFGHAN CAMPAIGN

The late 1970s saw seismic changes to the dynamic of the Islamic world in groundbreaking ways. Several events shifted the balance of power away from the pro-Western secular direction that had emerged after World War I to a revival of Islamic fundamentalism. This change was part of a growing politicization of religion that occurred globally. The decline of Arab nationalism and the Pan-Arab movement was apparent as Egypt broke unity by signing the Camp David Accords with the United States and Israel. Conservative Islam filled this political vacuum. Second, the Soviet invasion of Afghanistan on December 25, 1979, led to the rise of a transnational Islamic mujahideen force to fight jihad against the godless communist behemoth. The Iranian Revolution also altered the power balance regionally. The subsequent hostage crisis forever altered the U.S. role in the region. An Islamic Revolution led by cleric Ayatollah Khomeini ousted a solidly pro-American regime under Shah Raza Pahlavi. The hostage crisis started on November 4, 1979, showed how strong the anti-American sentiments ran in the region. It is worth noting that the fact that Iran is a Shia-dominated country somewhat limited the overall impact of the event. Additionally, on November 20, during the Haj, 500 Muslim insurgents loyal to Juhayman al-Otaibi attacked the Kaaba. Thousands of Muslims attending the Haj were taken hostage by the fighters. Anti-Americanism also spread into Pakistan as student supporters of the Jamaat-i-Islami attacked the U.S. embassy in Islamabad (Kux, 242–244). Further violence against American interests in Lahore and Rawalpindi followed.

Ultimately, it was the Soviet aggression in neighboring Afghanistan that changed the political and economic dynamics in Pakistan. The relationship between Afghanistan and Pakistan had always been strained. A border dispute dating back to the 19th century was still a point of contention. In 1893, the British had drawn the 2,600-mile border between the two countries in a way that separated the region's largest ethnic group, the Pashtuns. British foreign secretary of India Henry Mortimer Durand was the architect of the line that bore his name. No Afghan government had ever recognized the line as being legitimate (Riedel, 22–23). Ultimately, Afghanistan did not vote for Pakistan's admission into the United Nations because of the controversy surrounding the Durand Line. Separatists who wanted an independent nation of Pashtunistan occasionally fermented problems regionally. This issue continued to cause significant problems that impact the region today.

The United States saw the Soviet invasion of Afghanistan through the prism of the Cold War. This was the first time since the end of World War II that the USSR invaded a country that was not a member of the Warsaw Pact (Schmidt, 69). Some foreign policy experts believed this decision by the Soviets was a first step for further encroachments into Pakistan, Iran, and the Middle East in general. The United States quickly realized that helping the "holy warriors" or mujahideen in Afghanistan was imperative. For the United States, this meant working more closely with the ultraconservative Saudi regime that was exporting a very conservative branch of Sunni Islam throughout the region. This also led the United States to aggressively back General Zia in Pakistan. The general had a long history of cooperation and friendship with Riyadh. Initial aid from the Carter administration started in July 1979. The administration's level of concern had grown significantly in 1978 with the Marxist takeover of Afghanistan in what is now known as the Saur Revolution. Covert action from America coupled with an increase of spending from the Pakistani defense and intelligence communities ensued.

The resistance to the Soviet occupation of Afghanistan has centered in Pakistan. The organizing, training, and equipping were mostly staged from the border region close to Peshawar. In the 1980s, Peshawar was a hub for everything related to the Afghan campaign. The fortunes of the Zia regime increased as he realized the position of strength from which he was operating. The resistance was tribal in origin but quickly became an Afghan jihad as religious extremism became main core cause. As expected, Zia benefitted financially from the increasing assistance from the Gulf States as well as the Western bloc nations. Zia rejected the initial offer of $400 million in aid offer from the Carter administration as "peanuts." The later Reagan offer of $7.2 billion was more in line with the expectations of Pakistan (Schmidt, 70). (Interestingly, the Saudis offered to match the American aid dollar for dollar.) To further benefit Zia and his supporters, the deal ensured that all aid to the rebel groups went through the Pakistani military. The issue of Pakistan's nuclear program was tabled for the entirety of the Afghan-Soviet struggle.

The aid served several purposes for Pakistan. It enabled Zia to increase his patronage network and establish a more sophisticated intelligence apparatus. Furthermore, it allowed Zia to effectively combat Shia discontent, most notably in the always-volatile region of Balochistan. The state also encouraged the building of more madrassas in the tribal region as well as the recruitment of radical Deobandi clerics (International Crisis Group, "Pakistan: Madrasas," 10–11). Most of the future leaders of the Taliban movement (such as Mullah Omar) emerged from the radicalization of the 1980s. One of the most significant long-term consequences that impacted the war on terror in Pakistan years later was that the balance of power in the tribal regions shifted from the tribal elders to the radical clerics. The assistance funneled into the conflict also led to radical jihadists from all across the world entering Afghanistan to fight in the holy war. Most prominently, Abdullah Azzam and his main protégé Osama bin Laden, as well as future Al Qaeda leader Ayman al-Zawahiri, all arrived in Afghanistan at different junctures in the 1980s.

Several unattended problems surfaced as a result of the frontline status of Pakistan. The flow of between three to four million refugees from Afghanistan was problematic both politically and economically. Most ended up in the impoverished areas of the Northwest Frontier Province (NWFP) or the Federally Administered Tribal Areas (FATA). The inability to manage the refugee flow in any significant way changed the culture of Pakistan and caused an enormous economic strain (Gunaratna, 777–778). The refugee camps that opened were a toxic mix of disease and violence.

Refugees were perfect recruits for the jihad movement in the tribal regions. Some refugees relocated to the growing urban centers of the country.

Violence became more commonplace in everyday life. Pundits labeled Pakistan and Afghanistan as the "Kalashnikov Culture" because of the rapid arms proliferation that consumed Pakistan during this period. In addition, the increased trafficking of drugs became an essential way to fund the rebel movements. The expanding drug trade and abundance of regional opium production led to both addiction problems as well as the increase of the illicit economy (Rashid, *Descent into Chaos*, 317–322). The madrassa networks also saw exponential growth in the period of the USSR conflict in Afghanistan. Many of the refugees sent their children into the system, which radicalized a future generation of militants, especially in the FATA and NWFP. In addition, efforts at democratization were put on the back burner because of the Afghan-Soviet War. Zia dismissed the idea of elections because of what he perceived as a national crisis. To this end, the security and intelligence apparatuses were emboldened during this time. The expanded role of the ISI included increased leverage in both domestic and international affairs. The group trained 80,000 to 90,000 Afghans during the course of the conflict. Many future jihadists, including Mullah Omar, would be trained by the ISI. Over time, the ISI was turned into a multilayered bureaucracy with sophisticated state-of-the-art equipment. The legacy of the ISI growth continued to damage Pakistan politically and economically as they shifted the jihadist focus toward the Kashmir quagmire once the Afghan conflict subsided (Hussain, 56). The Soviet-Afghan War was profitable for every sector of the Pakistani intelligence community. The enormous expenditures in these areas made the ISI untouchable and feared by every leader of Pakistan for the next three decades.

The anti-Soviet jihad consisted of seven factions that had varying ideological and ethnic dimensions. Any group wanting to receive funding or weapons was required to join one of these organizations. The party names were similar, but the funding sources and operational areas varied. Most of the groups emerged in the volatile border region between Afghanistan and Pakistan. The Afghan National Front was formed in 1978 and led by Sibghatullah Mojaddedi. The organization was based in Peshawar. The second faction was the Quetta-based Islamic Revolutionary Movement of Afghanistan led by Mawlawi Muhammad Navi Muhammadi. This faction had most of its support in southern Afghanistan and benefitted from a strong relationship with the JUI. Two factions of the mujahideen were subgroups of the Hizb-i-Islami. Yunus Khalis and Gulbuddin Hekmatyar were the factional leaders. Hekmatyar became the main benefactor of the Zia regime because of his rabid anti-communist ideology. Khalis co-opted the infamous Haqqani network into his faction (Brown, 40). The Pashtun-dominated tribal region of the NWFP and FATA had significant autonomy from Pakistan. The largest faction was the Islamic Society of Afghanistan (also referred to as Jamiat-i-Islami). This group was Tajik based and led politically by future Afghan president Burhanuddin Rabbani and militarily by the legendary commander Ahmad Shah Massoud. In addition, notorious warlord Ismail Khan from the Herat Province was part of this faction that posed the stiffest resistance against the USSR and Afghan communist forces. Over time, the fact that this group was ethnically Central Asian with few ties to Pakistan damaged their opportunities for funding and the sharing of intelligence. The sixth faction was the Islamic Unity Party led by Abdul Rab Rasul Sayyaf. This Saudi-supported group was formed in 1979. Finally, the National Islamic Front of Afghanistan was based in Peshawar and led by Pir Sayed Ahmad Gailani.

It is worth noting the importance of Hekmatyar in the overall resistance. At Kabul University in the 1960s, Hekmatyar was an active anticommunist organizer in the Muslim Youth Organization. His fluency in several languages, including French and English, allowed him to work with Westerners whenever needed. A trained engineer with intense religious zealotry, Hekmatyar was well connected in the Pakistan military and intelligence communities. These connections and his charismatic personality made his faction the natural main benefactor of all mujahideen groups (Abbas, 56).

This complex and multifaceted factionalism formed because of the significant amount of assistance available via the West and the Wahhabi elements in Saudi Arabia. Interestingly, the lack of a central leadership or chain of command did not hurt the military success of the resistance. A core characteristic of Afghanistan and the tribal region of Pakistan has always been factionalism.

THE DEMISE OF THE DICTATORSHIP

Zia-al-Haq was able to keep the Pakistani economy strong due to considerable foreign aid and solid agricultural gains. The thriving drug trade also benefitted numerous sectors of the society. Revenues, both legitimate and illicit, helped the regime increase patronage.

As the proposed date for elections neared, Zia orchestrated a crackdown on civil society. Media restrictions were tightened, student unions were banned, and opposition activity was suppressed. The election turnout was enormous, and the results spelled defeat for many of Zia's close associates. Even though the process was problematic, the tide was turning against the general. The last years of the regime saw growing opposition from the Pakistani community abroad as well as dissent from numerous avenues on the home front, such as artists, writers, and women's organizations. Calls for stricter public morality laws inevitability targeted women. Zia declared himself president for life and then subsequently lifted martial law (Ziring, 198–200). He took further hits as the Soviet withdrawal was completed and peace negotiations were finalized in Geneva. Also, Benazir Bhutto returned to Lahore from her time in exile to exuberant crowds. During the final stages of the regime, Zia clashed with Prime Minister Junejo over his refusal to accelerate the Islamization program, which eventually led to his dismissal.

Zia's decision to fly to Bahawalpur for military exercises proved to be a fatal mistake. Following the proceedings, he boarded Pak One along with numerous Pakistani generals and the American ambassador to Pakistan Arnold Raphel and General Herbert Wassom. The cause of the fatal crash that killed all 50 people on board remains a mystery. In all likelihood, it was sabotage.

Nonparty elections were finally held in Pakistan during 1985. The PPP was still mired in factionalism, and Bhutto's widow Nusrat and his eldest daughter Benazir were kept under house arrest in Karachi. The opposition to military rule had coalesced during 1981 and formed the Movement for the Restoration of Democracy (MRD). The anti-Zia momentum was temporarily derailed by the violent highjacking of a Pakistani airline flight orchestrated by two of Bhutto's sons, Murtaza and Shahnawaz. The 13-day high-profile drama ended with a prisoner release and paid ransom. Overall, it damaged the opposition and created a media spectacle that Zia was able to capitalize on. However, pressure continued to mount as the damage of the Zia years took its toll. According to political scientist Ayesha Jalal, Zia "promoted Punjabi chauvinism and a virulent kind of Sunnism, accentuating the alienation of non-Punjabi provinces and destroying the internal sectarian balance" (238). The ensuing civil disobedience campaign of 1985 rallied around multiple issues, including the denial of an elected Parliament, the total disregard of civil liberties and rights, and the lack of a constitutional government.

Without outside pressure from the United States, the Pakistani nuclear program continued to move forward in the 1980s. A significant percentage of the Western aid for the Afghan campaign was funneled into nuclear research. The now notorious Abdul Qadeer Khan headed the nuclear project known as "Operation Butter Factory." European powers sold the critical components to Pakistan, which enriched uranium by 1978. The program was immensely popular with the country and considered the best way to counter the always-present threats from India.

A PROBLEMATIC DEMOCRACY: PAKISTAN IN THE POST-ZIA PERIOD

One of the essential legacies of the Zia years was the dominance of Islamic conservatism over the institutions, structures, and socialization process of the military (Shah, 162). The use of religious texts as the basis for strategies and historical truth was stressed. Zia advocated that the professional soldier in a Muslim army, pursuing the goals of a Muslim state, must always base his activities on the will of Allah. Islamic militancy became an instrument of the national security policy during his tenure. The justification for war being waged in the name of God has had a disturbing legacy in Pakistan.

The decision by the military hierarchy to allow the democratic transition to continue was based on multiple factors. International and domestic changes along with an institutional crisis solidified the directional change in Pakistan. The United States exerted pressure on the military to progress with the planned elections. The Cold War was winding down, and the Soviet withdrawal from Afghanistan was progressing rapidly. The global push for democracy was apparent in the People's Power Movement in the Philippines that deposed longtime dictator Ferdinand Marcos placing Corazon Aquino at the helm. Further evidence of the democratization push was seen from movements in Latin America, Eastern Europe, and Africa (Jaffrelot, 239). Domestically, the immense popularity of 35-year-old Benazir Bhutto and mobilization from the PPP also showed that change was needed. The institutional crisis centered on the total lack of public confidence in military rule. Chief of the Army Staff (COAS) General Mirza Aslam Beg met with the additional chiefs and decided to appoint the chairman of the Senate, Ghulam Ishaq Khan, as acting president until elections could be held. Pakistan found out that holding elections was the easy part, but establishing a true democratic system proved to be much more daunting.

The 35-year-old daughter of the former leader Zulfikar Ali Bhutto, Benazir Bhutto, emerged as the political leader of the PPP. The party's motto of "bread, clothing, and shelter" resonated with the masses. Educated at Radcliffe and Oxford, she was imprisoned by the Zia regime on several occasions and returned from exile. She was married to Sindhi landlord Asif Ali Zardari, who had a reputation as a heavy partier and little concern for politics.

As was the case for every leader in the history of Pakistan, Benazir knew that without the approval of the all-powerful military, the chances of gaining power were nearly impossible. Bhutto convinced General Beg and the Pakistani bureaucracy that her intent politically did not include any sort of revenge for the killing of her father. Her interest was to promote democracy and development for the country. The lack of trust between the military, bureaucracy, and the soon-to-be leader mired this period of Pakistani political history (Jaffrelot, 244–245).

In the lead up to the elections, Pakistan was engulfed in chaos as the political culture of arms and drugs, coupled with an out-of-control debt and increasing sectarian conflict, made the democratic transition problematic. Bhutto's strategy included making alliances with business interests and the large landowning class. In many ways, this was a reversal of some of the key stances championed by her late father.

The opposition was a patchwork of several parties, including the Pakistani Muslim League (PML) that unified under the banner of the Islamic Jumhoori Ittihad (IJI). The ISI played a significant role in forming the alliance, which eventually decided on Nawaz Sharif as the candidate to lead the party (Rashid, 39–40). A last minute decision to require voter identification cards hurt the overall victory margin of the PPP. The 8 percent margin of victory gave the PPP the momentum to form the new government. Bhutto struggled to gain the leadership helm. Behind-the-scene negotiations with the military included guarantees that the PPP would not disrupt the Afghanistan policy or the highly valued nuclear program. In addition, no retaliation against the Zia family or any of the bureaucrats that were involved in her father's demise was promised. The swearing in of the first female prime minister of a Muslim country on December 2, 1988, was indeed a monumental event.

Initial decisions regarding her advisory team hampered her ability to govern effectively and probably precipitated her eventual fall from power. Her chief of staff, defense adviser, defense minister, and three of the four provincial governors were all retired generals and army officers (many being Zia loyalists). To further complicate matters, the IJI and PPP were off to a contentious start, especially in the Punjab region. Numerous elements in Pakistani society that opposed her election worked tirelessly to ensure her failure. Eleven long years of Zia's authoritarianism, economic mismanagement, and rigid Islamization policies could not be altered overnight.

Bhutto took over a Pakistan that was in peril. Crony capitalism, which included huge unregulated loans that were never repaid and favored an inner circle of elites along with excessive borrowing practices, spelled economic catastrophe. By the time Bhutto assumed office, the debt reached 19 billion, and the middle and upper classes still found loopholes to evade paying taxes. Even more depressing were the key societal indicators. Growing mortality rates, the highest birth rate in South Asia, a literacy rate of 26 percent, and a population in which over one in four citizens was unemployed made the task of governing a challenge for even the most savvy politician (Jalal, 265).

However, many of the problems with the Bhutto administration were self-inflicted. She ended up with a bloated cabinet (the largest in Pakistani history), along with endemic corruption that continued to plague the country. Most notably, her husband Asif became notoriously known as "Mr. Ten Percent" due to the fact that he took a cut of all business transactions coming through the government. Later, it was discovered that he had stashed millions in Swiss bank accounts and did significant damage to her regime (Farwell, 88–90).

Benazir also took considerable criticism for inking a deal with archrival India by signing an accord with Prime Minister Rajiv Gandhi. The IJI coalition brutally targeted Bhutto for having the same publisher as reviled author Salman Rushdie as *The Satanic Verses* controversy boiled over. Most of the attacks against Benazir were blatantly misogynistic as the conservative religious elements of the opposition were totally opposed to a female leading Pakistan. In a fairly short period of time, PPP officials began to bicker with the novice leader. The final obstacle that made governing Pakistan nearly impossible was the steadfast opposition from the Pakistan president Ishaq Khan. He realized how vulnerable Bhutto had become and stalled policy recommendations and political appointments. The Americans, no longer concerned with the proxy war in Afghanistan, warned Bhutto to pull back the nuclear ambitions. Eventually, the ISI planned a failed coup with disgruntled members of the PPP. The regime sputtered along until the summer of 1990, when the president, in collusion with the army, finally deposed Benazir Bhutto and accused her administration of corruption and mismanagement.

The subsequent elections spelled a humiliating defeat for Bhutto and the PPP as the IJI swept into power with a broad coalition. Nawaz Sharif was the new prime minister and forged a strong relationship with President Khan. Soon after the election, the United States invoked the Presser Amendment and cut all military and civilian aid to Pakistan. This was in response to the refusal by Pakistan to certify that it was not trying to produce nuclear weapons. The strategic value of South Asia had diminished significantly as the Cold War ended. The Pakistani military leader General Beg went as far as to oppose the U.S. invasion of Kuwait (Haqqani, 280–282). The new Pakistani leadership blamed the recently ousted Bhutto for this misfortune.

As with the previous regime, Sharif was marred in scandal and mismanagement. In a trend too familiar to Pakistan, the prime minister faced accusations of ill-fated investments, fraud, and nepotism. Crisis within the banking sector also surfaced as the opposition PPP led by Bhutto seized the opportunity to pounce on the regime. By far the most significant financial problem facing Pakistan in the early 1990s was the political economy of defense (Jalal, 275–276). Nearly half a billion dollars was tied up in projects connected to the military. Sectors such as arms procurement, banking, automobiles, agriculture, and telecommunications were connected to the military apparatus. Some of the economic ties were direct connections to the government, while others were in the private sector. Beneficiaries included retired and current members of all branches of the military and intelligence services. With such economic mismanagement, Sharif faced a difficult road.

The event that led to Sharif's demise was a dispute with the president over the appointment of the next army chief after the death of Asif Nawaz.

Ironically, the prime minister turned to his political rival Benazir Bhutto and the PPP in an attempt to diminish the power of the President. Bhutto was given an appointment as the chair of the Parliamentary Foreign Relations Committee, and her scandal-ridden husband Asif was released from prison in exchange for help in the move against Khan. The plan backfired on Sharif as several ministers abandoned him, and Benazir struck a deal with Khan that led to the government failing. Sharif's last-ditch attempt to impeach Khan failed, and a popular tide of discontent doomed the Sharif regime. Sharif's dismissal was based on accusations of lowering the prestige of the armed forces, subversion of the constitution, persecution of political opponents, and the lack of transparency. In order to secure Sharif's departure, Ishaq Khan was also forced to resign in a compromise deal negotiated in mid-July.

The second tenure of Benazir Bhutto was framed through building a coalition with several smaller parties. PPP member Farooq Leghari was selected as president secured the party's dominance for the near future. Benazir attempted to use her international prestige more effectively in her second term. She also made a significant effort to court the key members of the military establishment. Unfortunately, the male-dominated, misogynist mind-set of the military was impossible to overcome. The mounting problems in Pakistan made governing difficult. The strained relations with the United States and India over the nuclear issue were costly financially and diplomatically. Furthermore, sectarian problems were more troubling across Pakistan. The increase of the illicit drug trade and gunrunning continued to plague Pakistan, which were direct result from the Afghan war of the 1980s (Kux, 332–334).

Family drama made the challenges even more difficult for Bhutto. Her overreliance on Asif for domestic affairs put a cloud over the PPP administration. In addition, Benazir's mother Nusrat wanted to see her eldest son Murtaza return from exile (her youngest son Shahnawaz was poisoned in France). An expected pardon did not materialize, which caused an open and very public rift within the family. Murtaza's return from Syria prior to abolishing previous charges of terrorism and sedition led to his imprisonment. In the ensuing power struggle, Benazir's mother sided with her recently returned son. The sensational nature of the quarrel included her mother calling Benazir a liar and dictator. Benazir relied on her husband, which further polarized the situation (Jalal, 281–282).

As had been the case for the better part of a decade, the opposition pressed for change. Nawaz Sharif staged a walkout to protest the lack of transparency and true democracy under PPP rule. He received backing from the business community. Benazir's response was to further subvert democracy as she tinkered with judicial appointments and had the Sharif family charged with fraud and embezzlement. The regime quickly lost credibility.

To secure power, Benazir tried to appease the religious conservatives by wearing a hijab and refusing to shake hands with men. She also went after the Ahmadis and proclaimed them to be non-Muslim. Blasphemy laws were implemented, which further harmed civil society (Ispahani, 138–139). This change also impacted the Christian minority within the country. For the religious conservatives, Bhutto's shift in policy and personal action was not enough. She was criticized for allowing the World Trade Center bomber Ramzi Ahmed Yousef to be extradited from Pakistan to the United States (this gesture secured Pakistan $368 million in assistance from America). The accusations of Benazir being a Western agent persisted (Haqqani, 279).

The intelligence community, most notably the ISI, began promoting the Taliban movement in neighboring Afghanistan. Members of the Taliban had attended Deobandi madrassas in Pakistan run by the JUI in the NWFP and FATA. Bhutto did not oppose the ISI policy and the group was called "Benazir's Taliban." Since the JUI was part of her governing coalition and members of her cabinet were active supporters of the movement, she was constrained from opposing the group. Extremists in the tribal region were clamoring for the imposition of sharia, and Bhutto appeared inept for not dealing with the situation in an effective manner.

In addition, politically motivated violence in arguably Pakistan's most vital city, Karachi, was spiraling out of control. The MQM in Karachi were supporters of Sharif and felt that the city could provide the perfect staging ground to bring down the PPP regime (International Crisis Group, "Pakistan: Stoking the Fire in Karachi," 5–6). The violent government suppression was weakening the PPP's ability to govern. The same story of corruption and mismanagement continued to plague the regime as Asif held the investment portfolio in the government and his misdealing's led to the media referring to him as "Mr. 20 percent!" Mounting evidence of misappropriation and the downgrading of the country's credit rating created panic.

The situation got worse and more tragic for the Bhutto family. Murtaza Bhutto was killed in a police ambush in September 1996. Conspiracy theories ranged from Zardari having a hand in the murder to the military, intelligence sectors, and senior police officers. The mystery of the death was never solved, but Benazir's legitimacy was severely damaged. Many officials hoped for a chance to remove the family from Pakistani politics.

President Leghari established a judicial commission to investigate corruption and, with the backing of the military, he fired Bhutto, dissolved the national assembly, and appointed a caretaker government. The justification for the dismissal included a failure to control the violence in Karachi, wide-scale corruption, tampering with the independence of the judiciary, and making unsubstantiated accusations about her brother's killing. Subsequent arrests of PPP officials included Benazir's husband

Zardari. Benazir was the 15th prime minister, and the 10th to be dismissed. The public was in favor of the decision as expectations for competent government increased. The desire for democracy was maintained even in the face of continual corruption and mismanagement from multiple leaders.

The stage was set for the Pakistani Muslim League coalition under Nawaz Sharif to once again gain control of the government. The 1997 elections saw the lowest turnout in recent years with less than one-third of the population participating. Sharif initially attempted to work with the opposition to bring about a functioning multiparty system. Sharif realized the mismanagement and corruption of the bureaucracy had to be dealt with, and he pursued an aggressive campaign to clean up the system. The honeymoon period did not last long, as Sharif ended up in a fight with President Leghari and other top bureaucratic officials.

Sharif was quickly beset by the continuing economic woes of Pakistan. The trade deficit skyrocketed to $4.5 billion, and the external debt reached an all-time high of $34 billion. Inflation and youth unemployment were also significant problems facing Sharif in his second stint as prime minister. Sharif tried to alter the constitution in order to give the prime minister powers closer to an elected dictator. The main faction that made Sharif's moves difficult was the independent judiciary. Multiple attempts to rein in civil society were met with judicial opposition (Jalal, 294).

On the international front, Pakistan suffered from its diminished role in the post-Cold War era. The steadfast support for the Taliban regime in Afghanistan strained relations with both India and the United States. Pakistan's refusal to sign the Nuclear Nonproliferation Treaty (NNT) and its announcement of the successful intermediate-range missile test in April 1998 only further heightened global anxiety. Sharif continued to accelerate the Pakistan nuclear program against the wishes of U.S. president Bill Clinton, who had promised numerous incentives (F-16 deliveries and repeal of the Presser Amendment) to the regime if it promised to curtail the program. Sharif relished in the idea of being the first Muslim state to develop a nuclear weapon, but the price of rebutting the United States was substantial: international sanctions were imposed and debt relief was suspended (Haqqani, 293–294). Without gaining consent, the United States also used Pakistani airspace to launch an attack against Al Qaeda facilities in Afghanistan.

Sharif's goal was to tighten the reins on his power and, to help in this endeavor, he appointed Pervez Musharraf as the new army chief. Musharraf's family was Urdu-speaking migrants from New Delhi. Key Sharif advisors in the military and ISI felt that Musharraf would be working from a position of weakness. This was a safe bet because the lieutenant general lacked the experience and did not have a base of support within the military.

Soon afterward, the Pakistani military launched an incursion across the LOC into the mountainous region of Kargil. The operation named Koh-i-Paima was secret in nature with the prime minister having little fore-warn knowledge of the action. An angry Indian prime minister Vajpayee and President Clinton condemned the action, and a full-blown war was a distinct possibility. With both powers now in possession of nuclear weap-ons, the stakes were high. The incident and the subsequent international response spelled trouble in the relationship between Sharif and Mush-arraf. On a July 4 meeting between President Clinton and Sharif, the prime minister agreed to an unconditional withdrawal and conceded the Kargil operation as a mistake. Sharif was attacked by the political opposition and the military for caving into the American president. It was apparent that Sharif would move against Musharraf, but the general acted first and was able to orchestrate a coup in a skillful manner, in October 1999.

CHAPTER 3

Pakistan during the Musharraf Years: 1999–2002

The transition to another military dictatorship in Pakistan seemed business as usual. No demonstrations or chaos ensued in the streets of the capital as the fourth military government in Pakistan's history was installed. Previous coups by Ayub Khan, Yahya Khan, and Zia-ul-Haq had led to the military ruling for 25 of the 52 years of Pakistani history. The international community looked at Pervez Musharraf with mixed views. Even with the flaws of the previous regime, an undemocratic takeover was not justified at this point in time as democracy was trending globally. China viewed the takeover as disturbing because fundamentalism seemed to be gaining more traction in their neighbor to the west. Russia feared elements of the Chechen resistance could find more sympathy under the new regime. The Indian government was of course the most alarmed because of the coup. With the recent misadventure by the Pakistani military under Musharraf's leadership in Kargil, the fear was reasonable. Internationally, Musharraf was treated as an unreliable parish and a dictator not worthy of trust (Hussain, 10–11). Making matters more anxious was the fact that Pakistan had just recently acquired nuclear weapons. U.S. State Department analysts called South Asia "the most dangerous place in the world." Furthermore, the coup was a setback for American efforts to get Pakistani help in capturing Al Qaeda leader Osama bin Laden because the perception was the military regime would be less inclined to pressure the Taliban regime in order to get intelligence (Burke, 324).

THE ROLE OF PAKISTAN LEADING TO 9/11 AND THE
WAR ON TERROR

The emergence of the Taliban movement in Afghanistan and the subsequent evolution of the organization in Pakistan could not have occurred without the support of the Pakistani military and most notably the Inter-Services Intelligence (ISI), which serves as Pakistan's espionage network.

Regional chaos ensued in the aftermath of the Cold War campaign waged by the mujahideen against the Soviet Union. The postwar settlement signed in Geneva did not create a lasting peace in Afghanistan. The rise of non-Pashtun power in Kabul after the ouster of Dr. Najibullah had increased tensions especially with the majority Pashtun groups. A bitter and bloody civil war would engulf Afghanistan and jihadist violence ensued in Kashmir, northwestern China, and the former Soviet Central Asian states. In addition, Al Qaeda proclaimed a global campaign of political violence against the United States. The Taliban takeover of Afghanistan in September 1996 did not quell the regional instability.

Attempts to mediate between the warring factions proved unsuccessful as virtually every city and town came under the control of a local warlord. The key regional powerbrokers, the Haqqani family led by family patriarch Jalaluddin Haqqani, tried to build a coalition of Afghan mujahideen commanders into a broad-based government that would allow significant regional autonomy. Several cease-fires between rival factions were implemented without lasting effect. Moderate religious elements that might have forged a consensus were never able to control the situation on the ground. The two most significant Cold War warlords Gulbuddin Hekmatyar and Ahmad Shah Massoud fought a series of brutal campaigns with shifting alliances between other factions (Fair, 125–126). Hekmatyar had the solid backing of the ISI in Pakistan. This period of civil war was one of the bloodiest in Afghan history as Kabul was totally destroyed. In the south, warlordism led to homes and farms being seized, travelers being taxed, and women being sexually assaulted. More refugees streamed out of Afghanistan for the Pakistani border.

A direct consequence of this countrywide anarchy was the emergence of the Taliban movement. The group was a mixture of fighters who had been involved in the anti-Soviet campaign as well as youngsters trained in the madrassas that had proliferated across the region. Talibs (literally seekers of knowledge) were religious students who sought to bring a more just society to Afghanistan. These young students were bringing law and order to villages around the Kandahar area with a high level of success and overwhelming sympathy from a war-weary public (Abbas, 61–66). Mullah Abdul Salam Zaeef, the future Taliban ambassador to Pakistan, stated that the decision to officially launch the movement was made by 33 leaders at a meeting in a mosque in 1994. At first, the expectations were modest and the objectives were limited. As the group grew in prominence and power, the goals became much more ambitious and included the implementation of sharia, the defense of Islam, the restoration of peace to the country, and the disarming of the population. The Taliban leadership had a limited knowledge of Islam based on the fact that few in the group had knowledge of the Arabic language that is vital to fully understanding the faith. The leader of the Taliban was a 39-year-old veteran of the Soviet conflict from Kandahar, Mullah Mohammed Omar. He was relatively unknown and was not well connected. An important factor was that Omar did not carry any political baggage from the earlier conflicts. Mullah Omar had been wounded several times during the conflict, including the loss of his right eye. He was considered to be the most pious individual in the group, which led to the decision to elevate him to the leadership position.

By the winter of 1994, the Taliban was consolidating their power in southern Afghanistan by taking over Spin Boldak, a critical trucking route on the road to Pakistan and, more important, an ammunition depot formerly controlled by Hekmatyar. By 1995, several key areas in the north, most notably Herat, were under Taliban control. At this juncture in the civil war, the Haqqanis were placed in a somewhat awkward situation. At one point, Taliban fighters surrounded one of the Haqqani compounds and demanded the occupants surrender. Eventually Jalaluddin negotiated terms with the young Taliban insurgents. The Haqqanis were savvy entrepreneurs and had thriving business interests throughout the region and did not wish to jeopardize the status quo. The scrap metal business and later drug exportation would be cash cows for the family. The final deal negotiated between the Haqqani family and the Taliban gave the family regional autonomy in return for recognition. The tribal structure in the areas under Haqqani control would be left alone and no enforcement of Taliban law would apply to the highland tribes under Haqqani domain. The final decision by the Haqqanis to make peace with the Taliban may have been brokered by the ISI once they had thrown their support behind the movement (Brown and Rassler, 101–106). This alliance would prove beneficial to the Taliban as they proceeded to make a final push to capture Kabul. It was fighters from the Haqqani clan that were vital in the success of the operation. After suffering several defeats at the hands of Ahmed Shah Masood, the Taliban turned for help from the Haqqani fighters from Khost who provided 2,000 soldiers that helped to secure the victory.

The final triumph was the capture of Kabul in September 1996. The Taliban regime was still unable to totally vanquish the resistance of Tajiks and Uzbeks collectively known as the Northern Alliance under the control of Ahmad Shah Massoud. Pashtun tribal leaders had jumped on the Taliban bandwagon, which eventually convinced the Pakistani military and ISI to shift loyalty to the movement. Two other factors played into the Pakistani shift to the Taliban. One was that Hekmatyar had always remained strongly tied to the regime in Iran and this meant that the ISI did not totally trust him. Second, it became apparent to the Pakistanis that the militants fighting in the civil war would not be unified by any of the current factions, which had depleted resources and lost the trust of the population. The Taliban with its close connection to the conservative South Asian-based Deobandi sect of Islam was a natural fit for Pakistan (Schmidt, 101–102). The Deobandis wanted to lead a spiritual awakening in the region. The movement also adopted parts of tribal Pashtun code of pashtunwali and was interested in the implementation of sharia.

Over a period of several years, the philosophy of Al Qaeda also influenced the Taliban leadership. The contemporary religious origins of Al Qaeda date back to the 1950s and 1960s. Osama bin Laden came of age during the religious revival known as the *sahwa* or Awakening. This movement was in part a reaction to the devastating defeat of Egypt during the Six Day War in 1967 and the subsequent demise of Arab nationalism. For the future leader of Al Qaeda, this period of decline could be blamed on the fact that the Muslim youth had lost their way spiritually and had become decadent, falling into the trapping of Western hedonism. For bin Laden, the Muslim world had suffered decades of humiliation that date back to the post-World War I period. The Sykes-Picot Agreement that established the modern boundaries of the Middle East in 1916, along with the demise of the Ottoman Turkish Empire and the subsequent decision by Kemal Ataturk to abolish the caliphate, were devastating changes for Islam globally. Bin Laden referred to this period several times as "the 80 years of degradation" (Bergen, 27).

Bin Laden's family was enormously wealthy and owned one of the leading construction companies in Saudi Arabia responsible for expanding the holy sites in Mecca and Medina. Instead of living the comfortable life of luxury, Osama chose to live a pious life and led by example. He had rejected all the comforts of modern society. For example, he slept on the floor, ate modestly, and refrained from listening to music or watching television. According to friends and associates, bin Laden was extremely modest in his dress and with any interactions with females. The ultimate goal for bin Laden was to emulate the lifestyle of the Prophet Mohammed (Bergen, 13).

The Egyptian writer Sayyid Qutb was the main inspiration and motivation spiritually for Osama bin Laden. Qutb was the most significant philosopher of radical Islam and without a doubt the main inspiration for the ideology of Al Qaeda (Malik, 130). According to Qutb, the Muslim world was living in a state of paganism or *jahiliyyah* and until society changed nothing but misery and suffering would befall the people. Qutb had lived in the United States for a brief period of time around 1950. He was appalled by the materialism and depravity he witnessed during his stay in Greeley, Colorado. He was especially obsessed with the sexual openness of American society. He returned to Egypt convinced that if Westernization permeated Muslim societies that culture was doomed. His fanaticism and zealotry led to Qutb spending several years in jail for attempting to incite revolution and violence against the regime. While in prison, he wrote his masterpiece *Milestones*. Qutb believed that Muslims were living in a time similar to the pre-Islamic period that he referred to as *jahiliyyah*. Individuals who claimed to be Muslim but chose to live incorrectly could be excommunicated from the community and declared to be apostates. This process or declaration was known as *takfir*. Qutb also insisted upon the use of offensive jihad against the enemies of Islam, which included Middle Eastern governments that refused to fully implement sharia. Upon his release from prison, he was once again arrested and eventually sentenced to death by the Egyptian government of Gamel Abu Nasser. Qutb could have had his sentence reversed by making peace with the government, but he refused and was executed in April 1966. In death, Qutb had the status of a martyr and his writing would influence the next generation of radicals (Bergen, 22–23).

The second major influence on the future leader of Al Qaeda was the Palestinian cleric Abdullah Azzam. Instrumental in organizing the jihadist camps against the Soviet Union, Azzam directly mentored the impressionable Saudi activist. Azzam and bin Laden founded the Services Office in Peshawar in the early 1980s. The purpose of the organization was to provide support and relief for the mujahideen fighters arriving in Pakistan from the Middle East. The work of this group was vital in keeping the logistical support for the growing network in place.

Azzam was a renowned religious scholar with a doctorate in Islamic jurisprudence from the prestigious Al-Azhar University in Cairo. His 1984 *fatwa* ordered all Muslims to expel foreigners from Muslim lands. This edict was to have long-lasting and significant implications for thousands of young impressionable Muslim youth who joined the jihad and headed to Pakistan and Afghanistan. Azzam internationalized the conflict in Afghanistan, and the networking that took place was significant for bin Laden's ability to build and sustain Al Qaeda. From this point on, it was a truly global jihad. Bin Laden's decision to take a more active role in the actual fighting caused a rift with his mentor, who felt his talents were best served in administering and financing the organization and fighters. Azzam also disagreed with bin Laden over the creation of a separate Arab fighting force in Afghanistan. Azzam believed that having Arab fighters integrated with soldiers from throughout the Muslim world would indoctrinate them into the true Islam.

Another relationship bin Laden forged while fighting in Afghanistan was with Dr. Ayman al-Zawahiri. It was Zawahiri who further radicalized the sheik (Weaver, 232–233). He promoted the idea of revolution against the pro-Western Arab regimes such as Anwar Sadat's in Egypt. This idea of defeating the "near enemy" and promoting regional change to remove the apostate regimes was vital according to Zawahiri. He strongly supported the ideas of Qutb, especially the doctrine of *takfir* that could validate the killing of Muslims. Later, Zawahiri and bin Laden developed an informal partnership while fighting in the anti-Soviet campaign. Sources confirm that the relationship was symbolic: bin Laden was able to provide the financial support for some of Zawahiri's operations, while the Egyptian doctor was able to supply fighters for the jihad. The alliance was strengthened following Zawahiri's three-year prison stint for his role in anti-Sadat activities.

Zawahiri admired Qutb and was also influenced by Sheikh Omar Abdel Rahman. Sometimes referred to as the "blind cleric," Rahman was the spiritual leader of the Egyptian Jihad group, and he gave religious creditability to the Al Qaeda leadership. He was a cleric and religious authority with a doctorate from Al-Azhar University in Cairo. Rahman was imprisoned in the United States in 1996 for his role in plotting the first attack on the World Trade Center in 1993 (Jones, 113).

For the core leadership of Al Qaeda, a seminal event that led to a rise in anti-Americanism was the decision by the United States to oust Saddam Hussein out of Kuwait in 1991 and subsequently station American troops on holy sites. Bin Laden had offered the Saudi government his mujahideen forces from the Afghan campaign to defeat Hussein, but the royal family declined his offer of assistance. Several hundred thousand U.S. troops ended up stationed on Arabian soil. Many Muslims viewed this occupation as something similar to the Crusades. To make matters more humiliating, female forces were included in the U.S. contingent (Bergen, 19). Several Saudi clerics including Salman al-Awdah issued fatwas condemning the occupation that was done to protect American oil interests in the region.

Bin Laden also forged a relationship with the patriarch of the powerful Haqqani family Jalaluddin. The Haqqani's stronghold was Khost in eastern Afghanistan, and bin Laden would seek advice and at times sanctuary from Jalaluddin. The Al Qaeda-Haqqani relationship would be complicated at times as different factors and factions entered into the region (Brown, 108–109).

Bin Laden's actions in the post-Afghanistan War period were creating a rift with his country of origin: Saudi Arabia. In addition to the disagreement regarding the U.S. troop presence in the region, the kingdom was concerned over the disruption bin Laden and his followers were causing in neighboring Yemen. The removal of the socialist regime in southern Yemen became a high priority for Al Qaeda. Once bin Laden caught wind of the growing frustration with the Saudi dynasty, he made the decision to first briefly flee to Pakistan, but eventually settled in Sudan.

During his stay in Sudan, bin Laden's anti-Western plans were more clearly formulated. His paranoia increased when the United States decided to enter the Horn of Africa to deal with the crisis in Somalia. The U.S. "Operation Restore Hope" was viewed by bin Laden as another attempt by the West to occupy Muslim lands. This was part of a grand strategy to recolonize the region. In Somalia, the U.S. mission changed from one of humanitarian relief to hunting down the notorious warlord Mohammed Aidid. This subsequently led to the disaster in Mogadishu that became known as Blackhawk Down, which led to the deaths of 18 American servicemen. It is unclear as to how much involvement Al Qaeda had in the training of Somalia militants, but bin Laden was quick to take credit for the success of the operation (Bergen, "Manhunt," 18). Soon afterward, the Clinton administration made a precipitous exit from Somalia as public opinion quickly turned against American involvement in the conflict.

The Saudi regime was growing more concerned about bin Laden's activities in the region that included construction of new training camps in Sudan. The Saudis ultimately persuaded the Sudanese government to force his expulsion from the country in May 1996. Bin Laden blamed Western governments for his expulsion as he turned to the failing state of Afghanistan for sanctuary. He blamed the United States specifically, and it was at this time that he made his first public declaration of war against the West (Schmidt, 105–106).

Mullah Omar eventually encouraged Al Qaeda leader Osama bin Laden to move closer to the Taliban spiritual center of Kandahar. As the relationship evolved, bin Laden provided infrastructural improvements, the building of mosques, money, Arab fighters, and ideological guidance to the Taliban leader. Jihadist training facilities were established in the south and eastern sections of Afghanistan. Bin Laden was able to train over 30,000 fighters with enormous support coming from extremist elements in Pakistan who had financial and logistical resources to help the cause (Jones, 88–89). The Arab fighters would be of assistance as the Taliban attempted to gain control of the remaining 10-15 percent of the country. The post-9/11 period would reveal just how strong the ties between Al Qaeda and the elements within Pakistan had become.

Once Al Qaeda had established itself in Afghanistan, the strategic goal of attacking the "far enemy" was implemented. This was a reference to the United States, which had become the target of the global jihadist following the occupation of Muslim lands during the Gulf War and its continued support of authoritarian regimes in the Arab world. (The "near enemy" was a reference to the goal of deposing the regimes in the Islamic world that continued on a path of Westernization and pro-American policies.) The fact that the United States was being targeted was not a secret. In August 1996 and again in February 1998, Al Qaeda publicly stated that war was being waged on the United States and that the "killing of

Americans and their allies—civilians and military—is an individual duty for every Muslim who can do it in any country in which it is possible to do it." In 1998, at a spectacle attended by international media in remote Afghanistan, bin Laden and Al Qaeda supporters announced the "International Islamic Front to do Jihad against the Jews and Crusaders." This was the most significant declaration of global jihad ever issued by Al Qaeda (Bergen, 29–30). Part of the declaration was written by Omar Abdel Rahman (who at the time was in jail in the United States), which gave the decree more religious credibility. Rahman's credentials and prestige within the Muslim community is something that neither bin Laden nor Zawahiri had since they were not trained religious scholars or authorities per se. High profile interviews occurred with journalists from Britain, the United States, Pakistan, and China. The media was escorted around Khost to view the training facilities. This self-promotion by Al Qaeda infuriated the Taliban leadership and strained the relationship between bin Laden and his hosts. According to author and regional expert Vahid Brown, bin Laden used his relationship and leverage with the Haqqani network to circumvent Taliban restrictions at several junctures (113–114).

On August 7, Al Qaeda terrorists who had been trained in Khost simultaneously bombed the American embassies in Kenya and Tanzania, which killed 224 and wounded almost 5,000. Two weeks later, the United States retaliated by launching 75 cruise missiles against jihadi training facilities in eastern Afghanistan around Zhawara. The attack was a failure as no significant combatants were killed nor were any key installations eliminated. The attack also made the United States look weak and vulnerable in the eyes of the terrorists. According to Abu al Walid, the embassy bombings and failed U.S. response resulted in Al Qaeda recruitment increasing with followers flocking to the tribal regions of Afghanistan. The news was not all good for Al Qaeda. The ambitious moves and aggressive behavior of the organization led to increasing factionalism between elements within the terrorist group. The major point of contention was whether to focus on the domestic front or to take on a more international agenda. Walid stated that many elements among the Arab fighters felt that the bin Laden move was ill-conceived and would do long-term harm to the network. This rift factionalized the Taliban into pro- and anti-bin Laden camps. Over the next three years, the relationship between the Taliban and Al Qaeda was strained. Eventually, the Taliban sought to exert greater control over the Arab fighters living in Afghanistan. Several jihadi camps run by the Arabs were closed, and it was feared that the Arab fighters would be forced out of Afghanistan. The Arab contingent opposing bin Laden felt that no further provocation against the United States should be undertaken. This group included fighters from Libya. The Taliban went so far as to put forth a 13-point decree limiting the actions of foreign jihadists entering and living in Afghanistan. A few of the key stimulations included the following: "all foreign guests should have identity papers issued, no communications with governments outside of Afghanistan were permitted, no contact with foreign journalists is allowed, no suspects wanted for serious charges in other states would be allowed entry, and when jihad is waged it should be to help Muslims who have been victimized" (Brown and Rassler, 119).

The pro-bin Laden faction of the Taliban had the backing of religious authorities and Pakistani officials. The Pakistani clerics and their ISI backers encouraged the Haqqani family to support the Al Qaeda efforts and to end sanctuary to bin Laden supporters whenever needed. In November 1998, the Pakistanis interceded on his behalf, negotiating a truce in which bin Laden would pledge baya (allegiance) to Mullah Omar. However, within a month, bin Laden was once again granting interviews, reiterating his stance and the jihad against America. Bin Laden's bodyguard stated that following the interviews he was called to the Taliban headquarters in Kandahar where the regime demanded he prepare to depart Afghanistan. Carlotta Gall's account stated that according to retired Pakistani general Ziauddin Butt, who served in the ISI, Mullah Omar spoke of bin Laden being a "bone in his throat" (51). In 1999, a failed assassination attempt against Mullah Omar provided bin Laden a way back into his good graces. Osama promised to help investigate the issue and also to fortify Omar's compound and provide an elite team of bodyguards for protection. Furthermore, the importance of the Pashtun code of ethics, pashtunwali, made the final decision to force bin Laden's removal virtually impossible. Omar would not turn on his guest (Hilton, 6).

The Taliban was also seeing increased tension with the Haqqani network. Jalaluddin Haqqani personally supported local initiatives such as schools for girls. The group opposed some of the more draconian decrees issued by the Taliban. The brand of Islam practices by the Haqqani network was conservative, but not as extreme as the Taliban. The tension led to attempts by the Taliban to exert more control over the highland tribes that constituted the base of Haqqani support. The Taliban wanted more say over local appointments that in turn led to anti-Taliban rebellions in select areas. The Haqqanis pushed for autonomy from Taliban rule. Fearing that the uprising could spread and knowing the power of the Haqqani family, the Taliban leadership wisely acquiesced. The fact that the Haqqani network had a strong base of support in both Afghanistan and Pakistan would prove to be extremely important in the post-9/11 period. The center of global terrorism from 2002 to 2011 would be the tribal regions (most notably North Waziristan) where the Haqqani network was based (Gopal, 4–6).

Following the embassy attacks, further pressure was put on the Taliban regime and its supporters within Pakistan to help in the apprehension of Al Qaeda leader Osama bin Laden. The United States lacked significant leverage, and all attempts ultimately failed. A criticism of the Clinton administration at this time was that no attempt to strengthen the anti-Taliban resistance was offered. Furthermore, the key sponsors of the Taliban, the Saudi and Pakistani governments, were never pressured in a meaningful way to persuade the Taliban to hand over bin Laden (Rashid, 15). On the contrary, the Pakistani special unit known as the Frontier Corps was providing fighters to assist in artillery and communications. The situation accelerated when the American destroyer the *USS Cole* was hit by a terrorist attack on October 12, 2000. It was suspected, but never totally verified, that this was the work of Al Qaeda.

International efforts to pressure the Taliban and subsequently hold Al Qaeda accountable were difficult. United Nations resolutions demanded the regime turn over bin Laden and halt support for terrorist activities. Later resolutions called for a weapons ban against the Taliban regime and closure of terrorist training camps within the country. The UN also called for the freezing of all Taliban assets until the regime was in compliance. Discussions of sending UN monitors to the border to ensure enforcement were tabled when the regime as well as its Pakistani supporters threatened to harm any UN personnel attempting to interfere on the border region. The Taliban's primitive and troubling policy directives continued. The prominent issue that drew the most significant coverage internationally was the March 2001 decision to blow up the two famous historic Buddha statues in the Bamiyan valley in the heart of the Shia Hazara region. In addition, multiple massacres of the Hazaras occurred in the late 1990s escalating tensions in the north. International objections to the cultural destruction and human rights abuses were ignored, as the regime seemed oblivious to any outside pressure. Second, the Taliban shut down all foreign aid operations and closed multiple Western-run hospitals. Most dire was the halting of the polio immunization program. Finally, the rights of females working in Afghanistan were severely curtailed. This was part of a larger push by the regime to eradicate any substantial role for women in society in general (Burke, 13–15).

Afghanistan was falling deeper into despair. A severe drought had hit the country and the nation was dealing with both internally displaced persons (IDPs) and a growing refugee population. Significant migration to the urban areas was occurring as well as mass starvation. Approximately 3.6 million Afghans were refugees with another 800,000 having internally displaced peoples (IDP) status. To make the economic situation more severe, Mullah Omar banned production of the Afghan poppy in the summer of 2000 (Rashid, 63–64). The livelihood of millions of farmers was threatened by this decision. These problems were complicated by the Taliban's isolation from the international community.

The anti-Taliban opposition seemed to gain some momentum during the period preceding the 9/11 attacks. Ahmad Shah Massoud had clearly emerged as the Northern Alliance leader. In addition, exiled leaders were returning home, including Ismael Khan, General Dostum, and most important, Hamid Karzai. Additionally, the former king Zahir Shah was supporting the opposition more vocally (Jones, 70–72).

It cannot be said with any certainty whether the Taliban regime knew of the pending attacks that would take place on 9/11. The Pakistani government and most notably the ISI had invested years and millions of dollars into establishing a friendly state to its west. Whether the Pakistan intelligence establishment actually wanting Al Qaeda dismantled and bin Laden turned in is open for debate.

HOLY TUESDAY

The overall justification given by bin Laden for the 9/11 attacks is specifically centered on the evils of American foreign policy related to the Muslim world. This critique of American policy was centered on the U.S. support of Israel and subjugation of the Palestinians, the promotion of authoritarian regimes in the Middle East, and the increasing direct American presence in the region in the post-Cold War period. The Al Qaeda leadership had sent vague messages out about the impending attack against the United States. During an interview with the Middle East Broadcasting Corporation, Osama bin Laden and his top lieutenant Mohammed Atef mentioned that a major attack against the United States and Israel was imminent (Burke, 23). A few Western media outlets picked up the story, but it did not receive much attention. In addition, select members of the U.S. intelligence community had growing alarm about an impending attack. Further evidence that a major attack was pending was provided by the fact that bin Laden urged his followers to evacuate from the Taliban stronghold of Kandahar in early September because of possible bombings that might take place. At Al Qaeda training camps and guesthouses, talk of suicide missions against the West was buzzing during the summer of 2001. Al Qaeda was obsessed with secrecy on the specific details of the operations. Even Al Qaeda's second in command Ayman al-Zawahiri was not informed of the operational details until June 2001. Many leaders of Al Qaeda who held prominent roles would only find out about the attacks from the media after they had taken place.

Bin Laden termed the attack as the "Holy Tuesday" operation. Differing views have emerged about the anticipated damage the 9/11 attacks would inflict. Bin Laden stated in subsequent interviews that the impact of the planes hitting the targets would take out several floors of the World Trade Center towers and the intense fires caused by the jet fuel (and the fact that the planes were loaded down since the final destinations were the West Coast) would mean that the floors above the point of impact would subsequently be destroyed. Other accounts stated that several hundred casualties was the best-case scenario for the 9/11 attacks. The final death toll of 2,984 exceeded the expectations of Al Qaeda.

Around 50 Al Qaeda members gathered with bin Laden to listen to the radio broadcast as the attack unfolded. For the core followers of the sheik, this was joyous news as the success of the attack unfolded. Others, including factions of the Taliban leadership and some members of Al Qaeda, were horrified as they realized they would soon face the wrath of the U.S. military power. As news of the attack reached the Taliban, Foreign Minister Vahid Mojdeh realized that the regime's days were numbered. Within the Al Qaeda ranks, several leaders worried that the attack would cost the organization the support of the Taliban regime and would also mean the loss of key training facilities that were located in the remote tribal regions of the country. In addition, the killing of civilians was not justifiable to many within the Al Qaeda organization. However, by 2001, bin Laden's control over the policy and direction of Al Qaeda was absolute.

In the years leading up to the 9/11 attacks, bin Laden's views of the United States had become warped. His views were centered on the American defeat in the Vietnam War in the 1970s, as well as the failure of the marines to respond to the deaths of 241 servicemen during the barracks bombing in Beirut in 1983. Finally, the 1993 Black Hawk Down fiasco in Somalia that led to the deaths of 18 Americans was further evidence of the eminent U.S. decline. In one of bin Laden's earlier interviews, he referred to the United States as a "paper tiger" (Bergen, 6–7). He firmly believed America was on the same path of the Soviet Union. This hubris on the part of bin Laden would have dire consequences for the viability of "the base."

The attack provided a clear choice for the Muslims living within the region. In many ways, this was an ideological war within Islam as the followers of Al Qaeda and the Taliban wanted a rigid theocratic brand of Islam that was a return to the practices of the religion in the seventh century. The opposition on the ground, including most of the Northern Alliance factions, advocated a more moderate brand of Islam.

PAKISTAN IN A BIND

It is ironic that on the morning of September 11, the head of the ISI General Mehmood Ahmad was visiting Washington, D.C., to testify about Pakistani efforts to convince the Taliban to assist in apprehending Osama bin Laden. During the visit, the general was meeting with members of the State and Defense Departments as well as the CIA. Ahmad was summoned to D.C. because it was a forgone conclusion that any attempts to apprehend the Al Qaeda leader would need Pakistani assistance and an overall change in the mind-set of the military and intelligence sectors. Mehmood's view was that the United States needed to be conciliatory to the Musharraf regime, starting with the good faith effort of lifting sanctions. The Pakistani delegation said that the relationship was beset by misunderstandings. Mehmood felt the end of the Clinton tenure was toxic and counterproductive. The visit was important because this was an opportunity for a fresh start with a new regime in Washington, D.C., that had shown promise of being more encouraging of Pakistani demands (Schmidt, 122–123). By all accounts, Ahmad was one of a handful of policy makers in Pakistan who dictated the decision-making process in the government. Unfortunately, he was also part of the security apparatus that most aggressively supported Mullah Omar and the Taliban regime. Whether the general and other policy makers in Pakistan realized the Taliban regime was shifting in a more extreme direction is uncertain. Scholars disagree about the influence Al Qaeda and bin Laden had on this further radicalization. For Pakistan, the support of the Taliban was a high national security priority as securing the western border was vital in combatting Indian aggression regionally and providing the essential strategic depth necessary in any future confrontations. Additionally, support for the Pashtun-dominated regime made logical sense due to the significant Pashtun minority population in Pakistan. The non-Pashtun factions in Afghanistan had solicited support from regional rivals including India, Russia, and Iran (Schmidt, 130).

All of the negotiations and dialogue that preceded the 9/11 attacks became moot as the tone and language of the Bush administration changed quickly. It was now a basic question: Are you with the United States or are you with the terrorists? The United States was in no mood to negotiate. It became clear that it would be a take it or leave it proposition to the Pakistanis (Haqqani, 310).

Further complicating the situation was the Pakistani request to America to delay the pending attack until they had an opportunity to convince Mullah Omar to hand over bin Laden. Several days of talks between the Taliban leadership and an ISI delegation led by General Ahmad did not produce significant results. According to the Pakistani leadership, the delegation even attempted to use radical Deobandi clerics from Karachi, including bin Laden mentor Maulana Nizamuddin Shamzai, to convince Mullah Omar to turn over the Al Qaeda leaders.

U.S. intelligence sources discovered that just the opposite was occurring. It was becoming obvious that this was a ploy to stall the bombing campaign. It is believed that the Pakistani military leadership and the ISI actually encouraged Mullah Omar to hold tough against the impending U.S. campaign and to refuse all requests to hand over the Al Qaeda leader. Ultimately, Mullah Omar was probably never going to betray bin Laden. Indications both publicly such as his interview with the Voice of America and privately within the inner circle of the Taliban leadership state that giving up the Al Qaeda leader was never seriously considered (Gall, 52–54). Whether Musharraf knew about the backdoor negotiations is uncertain. The Americans found an outlet to the Taliban that was not through the Pakistanis. In the context of the brief talks, the United States tried to persuade Taliban military commander Mullah Akhtar Mohammed Usmani to convince Omar to hand over bin Laden to no avail.

Regional experts, including the Pakistani military establishment, underestimated the resolve that would be shown by the United States following the 9/11 attacks. Pakistan believed the conflict with the West would follow a similar pattern to what occurred during the Soviet campaign of the 1980s. It was also anticipated that the U.S. reluctance to utilize ground forces was a sign of weakness and uncertainty and would lead to the conflict dragging out into 2002. As the conflict progressed, the Taliban fighters were assisted by militant volunteers from Pakistani madrassas and the Central Asian regions, making the guerilla fighters more difficult to defeat (Rashid, 268–269). In clear violation of international law, the ISI continued to supply weapons, fuel, and supplies to the Taliban regime.

The attacks of 9/11 shook America to its core. The option of launching a cruise missile attack similar to the response by the Clinton administration in 1998 was quickly ruled out. The Al Qaeda camps were quickly deserted and such a reaction would be perceived as weak. A full-blown invasion was considered, but CENTCOM had no plan of action for such an invasion of Afghanistan. Military leaders realized it would take weeks of planning to put together a coherent plan. The logistics of the invasion were nightmarish, as the landlocked country did not provide easy access. The ghost of past invasions also merited consideration. The "graveyard of empires" might be a cliché, but the British and Russians historically and the Soviets more recently were humiliated in trying to subdue the country. Further complicating matters was the fact that the U.S. relations with the countries bordering Afghanistan were strained. Iran was outright hostile; Pakistan was nearly put on the list of terrorist sponsors; and the Central Asian Republics were authoritarian dictatorships that had limited contact with the United States (Haqqani, 312–313).

The finger pointing quickly ensued as the intelligence failures were targeted as the main problem. Nineteen suicide attackers entered the country undetected and were able to pull off the most devastating terrorist attack in American history (Bergen, 39–42). The CIA director George Tenet stepped in with a plan to use Northern Alliance fighters with CIA and Special Operations Forces for the initial incursion. The use of air power and sophisticated technology would lead to minimal boots on the ground. By all accounts, this was a high-risk proposal. President George Bush signed on to the plan on September 17 after meeting with key advisors at Camp David. This decision gave the CIA enormous decision-making power during the early stages of the war on terror in order to capture or kill key Al Qaeda members. Covert operations were essential and the total budget allocated may have exceeded $1 billion. The first American contingent into Afghanistan was a small CIA team led by Gary Schroen.

No one including the CIA had prepared for any involvement in Afghanistan. The shift away from using human intelligence meant that few operatives had knowledge of the language and culture. With rare exceptions, no U.S. official had been in Afghanistan for nearly a decade. In addition, our ties to the key players and factions had greatly diminished in the post-Cold War period. The main leader the United States had dealt with in our limited involvement in the region had been the ethnic Tajik leader, Ahmad Shah Massoud. Unfortunately, the "Lion of Panjshir" who had so dramatically defeated the Soviet forces was no longer able to assist the American war effort. Two days prior to 9/11, Masood had set up an interview with two Tunisian reporters at his base in northern Afghanistan. The reporters were actually suicide bombers working for Al Qaeda. The camera was rigged with explosives and Masood was killed. The most celebrated warlord and resistance fighter in modern Afghan history was dead. The timing of the attack was to ensure that the impending U.S. invasion following 9/11 would have no leader to turn to rally in the forces in the country. Bin Laden knew that by killing the charismatic leader of the Northern Alliance, he would fatally damage the movement. Everyone was in agreement that Masood was the heart and soul of the Northern Alliance (Rashid, 20–22). Abdullah Abdullah, a close associate of Massoud's in the movement, believed the Northern Alliance was finished with the assassination of his friend. The organization tried to keep his death secret, but reports quickly surfaced that the assassination was successful. Al Qaeda felt that the resistance in Afghanistan would not be sustainable with the loss of Massoud.

The U.S. plan for the war in Afghanistan was Operation Enduring Freedom. The plan had four phases but was limited to simply military action and did not address the aftermath of the Taliban reign. The Bush administration made it clear that the operation was about justice and not nation building. Four aircraft carriers and 32 naval vessels would be deployed with limited ground forces utilized. The operation would be centered on the use of CIA officers and 300 U.S. Special Operations Forces. On the evening of October 7, the first U.S. attack ensued with cruise missiles and laser-guided bombs. The key targets included military installations and aircraft defense centers. The initial damage was significant, and the administration turned the early bombing into a public relations and media spectacle. The air war was a resounding success, as the Taliban had no way to counter the U.S. onslaught (Burke, 51–52).

The Taliban strength was presumed to be in the ground war. Over 60,000 troops were massed in and around key strategic areas. The forces were supplemented by Pakistani madrassas recruits and Arab volunteers from Al Qaeda and the border regions of Central Asia (most notably the

Islamic Movement of Uzbekistan). In addition, Chechens and Uighurs, most of whom were trained in Al Qaeda facilities over the past decade, were involved in the initial fighting. The logical starting point for the Northern Alliance and the U.S. Special Forces was in northern Afghanistan around Mazar-e-Sharif. The Taliban support was weakest in the non-Pashtun north. As the bombing commenced, it was feared that the regime could fall rapidly, leading to chaos around the capital. Assembling this highly factionalized group of fighters together was a significant challenge.

The majority of the warlords who constituted the bulk of the Northern Alliance were a patchwork of thugs and unsavory characters. Included in this group were Rashid Dostum, Ismail Khan, Abdul Rasul Sayyaf, and Mohammed Fahim. In addition, Burhanuddin Rabbani, the Tajik leader who served as president from 1992 to 1996, also returned from exile. All of the factions were non-Pashtun, a factor that would prove to be of extreme importance as the war progressed. The key to co-opting the Northern Alliance was one thing: money. The first U.S. contingency to arrive two weeks after 9/11 brought bags full of cash in order to buy the loyalty of different factions (Bergen, 55). Fahim was paid $5 million by General Tommy Franks, while the other warlords demanded payment in order to support the U.S. war effort. This strategy of buying allies would be the initial cornerstone of American policy in Afghanistan. Little thought was given to economic development issues, nation building, or advocating civil society. From a cost-benefit analysis, this was prudent; as a long-term rationale policy, it was ill-conceived. The initial cost comparatively speaking was unbelievably low. The long-term damage done by this policy would not be known for some time. The warlords spent lavishly and also were able to build networks of support for illicit activities, such as smuggling and drug running. Several weeks of heavy bombing weakened the Taliban's vulnerable positions in the north. The Americans were concerned that a premature collapse of the regime could lead to chaos, especially if a Pashtun alternative had not been formulated (Burke, 56–57). On November 9, the alliance scored a significant victory, gaining control of Mazar-e-Sharif. Over 8,000 Taliban fighters were captured or killed during the siege as the remaining fighters sought refuge in the Pashtun-dominated city of Kunduz. The capture of Mazar was strategically significant because of its close proximity to Uzbekistan where several thousand U.S. troops were based. Supplying the coalition forces now became a much easier task. In addition, the most charismatic leader of the foreign fighting forces assisting the Taliban, Juma Namangani, was killed in a U.S. bombing operation. Namangani was the leader of the Islamic Movement of Uzbekistan (IMU), a key radical insurgency group operating and training in Afghanistan (Rashid, 82). Within 72 hours of the fall of Mazar-e-Sharif, the vast majority of northern, western, and central Afghanistan was in the hands of the Northern Alliance.

A more pressing concern was how to organize a Pashtun resistance in southern and eastern Afghanistan. The hope was that a general Pashtun uprising would occur, but these efforts may have been undermined by elements within the Pakistani leadership. A group of exiled supporters of the former king Zahir Shah were located in Rome. It was hoped that the different factions could call for a Loya Jirga and unite behind a common leader, but the factionalism of the movements made this virtually impossible. Without a significant Pashtun leadership voice, securing support and achieving a clear victory would be problematic. The first Pashtun leader to enter into the Taliban strongholds was Abdul Haq. A war hero from the Soviet campaigns, Haq had been wounded 16 times and lost a foot during a landmine accident. In the late 1990s, Taliban operatives had assassinated members of his family, including his wife and daughter. Haq tried to persuade exiled tribal elders to support him in an anti-Taliban Pashtun coalition that would include the backing of exiled former king Zahir Shah. Haq firmly believed that factions of the Taliban could be flipped at the appropriate time once the American military pressure increased. After several meetings in Pakistan, Haq made the decision to enter Afghanistan. Both the CIA and ISI as well as Musharraf refused to lend any support to his efforts. Strangely enough, Haq secured the backing of millionaire Chicago businessman Joseph Ritchie. On October 21, Haq entered the country, but within a few days Taliban forces surrounded his entourage. Haq was captured, tortured, and executed by the Taliban. His body was left hanging at the site of a U.S. cruise missile attack that had killed two dozen Pakistani fighters. Some speculate that the ISI had informed the Taliban about Haq's plans (Gall, 28–31). Finding a viable resistance leader to unite the Pashtuns was a crucial concern. The opposition was reeling from the loss of two of the most prominent resistance leaders in Afghanistan. All efforts now turned to the one remaining Pashtun leader capable of leading the efforts: Hamid Karzai.

In the 1980s, Karzai had been involved in the Afghan campaign as part of the Sibghatullah Mojaddedi's mujahideen faction. His easygoing demeanor and desire to find compromise made him a natural politician. Initially, Karzai and his family had been somewhat sympathetic to the Taliban movement, but at some point disagreements emerged between his father and the Taliban leadership that ultimately led to his assassination in Quetta in 1999. Karzai believed the ISI had a role in the death of his father. Following this, Karzai became more closely connected to Massoud and the Northern Alliance. Karzai's tribal connections and Western influence made him an ideal candidate to lead the Pashtun resistance (Schmidt, 131–132). In addition, King Shah was convinced to back Karzai as the best Pashtun alternative. Shortly after the beginning of the American bombing campaign and confident that he could recruit anti-Taliban tribal groups quickly, Karzai and a few loyalists entered Afghanistan from Pakistan. They were able to rally some factions, but everyone he met wanted assurances that the United States would back him. An airdrop of supplies helped him fend off a Taliban attack in late October, but he was forced to be temporarily airlifted out before reentering the country two weeks later on November 14 with American Special Forces. At this point, America was now convinced that Karzai was their man as they began to support him financially and militarily. Pakistani military and intelligence agencies were of course concerned that they were not directing the uprising in the south.

The decisive battle that secured Karzai's position occurred at Tarin Kowt in the important Uruzgan Province. At this point, he was gaining an army that could defeat the remaining Taliban forces and occupy Kandahar. The city had symbolic importance since it was the home of Mullah Omar. Even though the Taliban forces outnumbered Karzai's guerrilla insurgents, the battle was essentially won because of the overwhelming air superiority provided by U.S. forces. The victory convinced many Pashtun tribal leaders to join forces with the resistance (Gall, 207–208). On several occasions, the Taliban forces delayed during the surrender negotiations in order to give Mullah Omar and a number of his key forces time to escape. It was at this time that Mullah Omar made his final decision to abandon Kandahar. Talk of massive Taliban surrenders was underway following the battle.

The Pakistani intelligence community may have been dealing with both sides in the conflict. Ardent supporters of the Taliban regime, including General Mehmood and the ISI, may have wanted the hard-liners in the movement to hold out against the American onslaught. They worried that any moderate elements in the Taliban could make a deal that would harm the long-term strategic interests of Pakistan in the region (Rashid, 77–78). They felt it was best to stay with Mullah Omar, who had proven to be a reliable ally. The Pakistani intelligence community was promising the United States that moderate Taliban elements would eventually emerge. In the past, any sign of opposition to the core leadership would be quickly purged. Many observers were hopeful that a break off group would form, but the loyalty and devoted following of the organization made such a proposition doubtful.

The most embarrassing episode in the period regarding Pakistan occurred when it was discovered that Pakistani fighters were trapped in northern Afghanistan fighting alongside the Taliban forces (Rashid, 91–93). Members of the Frontier Corps had stayed in Afghanistan to help prepare and bolster the defenses. As late as a week before the beginning of the American bombing campaign, Pakistani military personnel were arriving in Afghanistan. Furthermore, ISI trucks and fuel tankers were entering Afghanistan to supply the Taliban fighters. These secret convoys were part of an army-owned trucking company. Members of the Northern Alliance caught wind of this and provided clear evidence to U.S. officials.

To make matters worse, the Pakistani fighters who entered the conflict were not just low-level volunteers but included several high-level officials, including generals. Many were giving advice to the Taliban on how to fortify positions and best prepare their defenses.

Ultimately, the Pakistan gamble ended in disaster as thousands of tribesmen were killed or captured. Many of these forces that escaped would later become members of the Pakistani Taliban splinter organization. A sizeable Pakistani contingent was trapped in Kunduz. This situation had the potential of creating an additional international crisis. General Musharraf made a personal plea to George Bush to temporarily halt the bombing and allow Pakistani forces to airlift members of the ISI and Frontier Corps out of Kunduz. The president approved the bombing pause, and the top-secret mission was undertaken on November 15. It has been speculated by several journalists that not only were Pakistani military withdrawn but also members of the Taliban and Al Qaeda were able to escape via the operation. What was scheduled to be a minor operation ended up being a major airlift that may have evacuated 2,000–3,000 personnel. According to Ahmad Rashid, this "Great Escape (as one Pakistani general called it) would have enormous implications on the subsequent U.S.-led war on terrorism. It is believed that more foreign terrorists escaped from Kunduz than made their escape later from Tora Bora. In both cases, the foreign terrorists were allowed to stay in South and North Waziristan" (93).

As the fighting was coming to an end in northern Afghanistan, a human rights catastrophe ensued. Thousands of prisoners were taken into custody by the Northern Alliance. General Dostum was mostly responsible for the transportation and eventually setting up the CIA interrogation area. A rebellion broke out on November 26, and the subsequent fighting lasted six days. Mike Spann became the first American casualty of the conflict. Over 200 insurgents were killed in the uprising, but the unfortunate aftermath is what shocked the international community. Several hundred prisoners were placed in shipping containers and suffocated in the most horrifying fashion. Later, it became known that some of the containers were left in the desert, where the prisoners were literally baked in the sun. A massive cover up took place, but the media eventually uncovered the story that ended up being one of the worst human rights violations of the entire conflict (Lieven, 409–410).

The Pakistani military and intelligence services were playing a dangerous double game. The irrational belief that a pro-Indian government would be installed in Kabul once the Taliban was vanquished was highly unlikely. Pakistan also feared that once a U.S. victory was secured, the Americans would once again quickly abandon the region. Keeping the Taliban as a viable option remained a security priority for the ISI and select members of the military establishment. This paranoia led Pakistan to continue to secretly support the Taliban against the United States even after the fighting ensued (Hussain, 32).

After the start of the military operations, pressure was placed on Musharraf to make substantive changes in the military and intelligence leadership positions. Musharraf fired three of the key generals who had helped him stage the coup in 1999. The Bush administration was pleased with the move, which showed the general was in clear control of the decision-making process. At this critical juncture, Musharraf convinced Bush of his loyalty for the long haul. The problem, however, could not be solved with changes at the top. A pervasive culture of support for the Taliban had been instilled in the military and ISI for several years. The belief that saving the Taliban was in the best interest in countering possible Indian encroachment was a common view throughout the military. The religious extremism of many members of the officer corps cannot be overstated. Furthermore, Musharraf had to deal with anti-American protests in Pakistan as a result of the bombing raids. Musharraf was hopeful that the changes instituted would lead to the United States consulting with him on any future directives. His initial contact with President Bush was to show his adamant stance that a Northern Alliance-led government in Kabul would not be acceptable to Pakistan. The Pashtuns needed to have a dominant role in the future government (Fair, 77–79). Additional pressure was placed on the United States by the Saudi regime. However, the request by and large was ignored by the Bush team, which would not consult any allies, including NATO, in any decisions regarding the Afghan policy. It became the job of U.S. envoy James Dobbins to quickly organize a gathering to iron out the future political setup in Afghanistan. Dobbins and his team met with key Afghan parties, international organizations, and countries in Bonn, Germany, in the final days of November. The negotiations were aimed at selecting an interim leader for Afghanistan that would be acceptable to all parties involved. The last official president and one of the leaders of the Northern Alliance was the Tajik Burhanuddin Rabbani. At Bonn, it would be essential that Rabbani agree to voluntarily step down as president in order to make the transition legitimate. The 61-year-old Rabbani stated publicly that he would accept the decision made at the conference. He claimed not to have political ambition and that he wanted to do what was best for the country. At times during the negotiations, he made conflicting statements, but ultimately pressure from several of the European powers convinced him to acquiesce to the Karzai selection. The final agreement was broad, gender-sensitive (female representations was mandatory), multiethnic, and fully representative. With the backing of the key regional powers and the former king Zahir Shah, they were able to secure the Northern Alliance factions on the choice of Hamid Karzai as the next leader of Afghanistan. The former king would be granted the title of "father of the nation." The Northern Alliance would be given the key ministerial posts in the new government, including intelligence, foreign affairs, and defense. The issue of reigning in the competing warlord armies was left unanswered. The Pakistani delegation was happy to have a Pashtun leader, but at the same time they did not fully trust Karzai to back Pakistani regional interests. A sign of the impending strain in the relationship between Kabul and Islamabad was apparent early on as Karzai declined an offer to meet up with Musharraf prior to taking the oath of office. The legacy of Pakistani interference in Afghan affairs was well known to the new leader and his team of advisors. It was troubling that no Pashtun delegates from the south or from the Kandahar area were represented. The question of how to deal with the Taliban was problematic. Without the inclusion of the group, implementation on the ground would be difficult if not impossible (Rashid, 103–105). No cease-fire or demobilization was possible without the Taliban. UN negotiator Lakhdar Brahimi believed that the inclusion of the former regime or at least the offer to include them would have given the final accord more credibility. Not all of the diplomats were in agreement on this issue. UN secretary general Kofi Annan believed that any dialogue with the group was impossible at this point in the process. Karzai arrived outside of Kandahar on December 5 to begin discussions on the Taliban surrender. Two days later, the surrender was formalized, and the 43-year-old Karzai was selected as the new leader of Afghanistan. The actually swearing-in ceremony took place in Kabul on December 22.

The burden on the new leader would be tremendous. The capital of Kandahar was becoming chaotic with looting and disorder spreading. Factional rifts were reappearing as a fight over who would control the governorship of Kandahar imploded. Also, the lack of coordination on the part of the Pashtun militia allowed numerous Taliban fighters to escape out of the city and make it to Pakistan. What made this fiasco even more troubling was that the Taliban were never fully defeated. Since the Taliban were offered no seat at the table when the postwar negotiations ensued at Bonn, the movement would continue on as an insurgency operation. This mistake of not attempting to work with factions of the opposition would come back to haunt the United States and future Afghan governments for the next decade and beyond (Khan, 104–105).

Even though the Bush administration clearly stated early objections to the concept of nation building (something he had run against in the 2000 elections), it became clear that the fate of post-Taliban Afghanistan was vital. The main architect of the rebuilding process was foreign policy expert and State Department official Richard Haass. In late September, a group of experts brainstormed about how to deal with the rebuilding of the country. An overwhelming consensus emerged that the United Nations role would be important. The political transition would be coordinated by the UN and eventually UN envoy Lakhdar Brahimi was appointed by Kofi Annan to be the special representative to Afghanistan. The United States utilized James Dobbins as the special envoy dealing with the Afghan opposition. The United States was against a large peacekeeping mission for Afghanistan as the track record for such operations in the 1990s was mixed at best (Bergen, 179). It would become clear that the United States would indeed provide the lion's share of the money, troops, and international planning that Afghanistan required. Eventually, the Bush administration was pushing for the key coalition members to divide up the task of helping in the transition and rebuilding efforts.

MISSED OPPORTUNITIES: TORA BORA AND BEYOND

As the Taliban and Al Qaeda fighters fled toward the mountainous border region between Afghanistan and Pakistan, a sense of frustration and doubt had to engulf the terrorist leaders. The U.S. air campaign had been much more effective than anticipated, and the forces of Al Qaeda had been decimated by the Northern Alliance coalition. On November 11, sources confirmed that bin Laden gathered with local tribal elders and several Taliban leaders to give an emotional speech about the importance of resistance and hand out approximately $100,000 to supporters. The core terrorist fighters departed in a convoy from Jalalabad, heading south to the mountains of Tora Bora just below the White Mountains that delineated the border between Afghanistan and Pakistan. At this juncture in the war, a mass exodus was undertaken out of Afghanistan as thousands of fighters and civilians were fleeing for their lives from the saturated bombing campaign. For the foreign fighters, the escape was more problematic, and several hundred were detained while attempting to cross into Pakistan (Burke, 70–72). For many of the insurgents planning to take a stand at Tora Bora, this was a familiar area because of previous operations in the specific area during the Soviet campaigns of the 1980s. Upon the arrival of the Al Qaeda fighters, tensions arose over operational control between bin Laden's soldiers and some of the tribal militants. From the onset, the operation would be chaotic from both the insurgent and American perspective. Several media reports falsely claimed that the cave structure was extremely elaborate with hydroelectricity, offices, and intricate multilayered tunnels. It was later discovered that this was a gross exaggeration, and the system was much more primitive than reported. The United States was monitoring the area as it had long been anticipated that the Al Qaeda fighters might be heading toward the cave complexes. Once intelligence sources and the military felt a high level of certainty that the Al Qaeda leadership was in Tora Bora, the decision was made to commence with heavy bombing that lasted for 56 straight hours. During the campaign, 1,100 precision-guided smart bombs were dropped on Tora

Bora. During a four-day period, 700,000 American bombs were dropped on the location (Bergen, "Manhunt," 45).

The Al Qaeda resistance was fierce as the fighters held out against the several hundred Northern Alliance troops that laid siege to the area. The militants were further emboldened by the fact that the battle was taking place during the holy month of Ramadan. The situation was problematic because of the multiple escape routes out of the mountain passes with several leading into Pakistan. Very few people, including CIA director George Tenet, believed that the Pakistani military establishment had the ability or even the desire to totally close off the border with Afghanistan. One of the key U.S. operatives on the ground, CIA commander Gary Bernsten, requested that Special Forces be sent in to assault the cave complex and complete the task at hand (Bergen, 70–71). The operation would require several hundred U.S. forces be deployed into the battle. General Tommy Franks made the ultimate decision that the United States would continue with the thus far highly successful "light footprint" strategy and not deploy ground forces into the fray (Gall, 61–63). The decision was based on the fact that it would take too long to deploy the needed troops to the area, and secondly that the current strategy had been so successful in eliminating the Taliban. Franks also naively believed he could rely on the Pakistani troops to cut off the Al Qaeda retreat route. This was problematic for two reasons. First, the lengthy and treacherous border region would be nearly impossible to monitor in any effective way. Second, up to this point the Pakistan military and intelligence community had been unreliable and untrustworthy. The type of operation needed at Tora Bora was of course radically different than what had been utilized against the Taliban fighters. Tora Bora was mountainous and heavily defended, and the expertise of the elite U.S. Rangers would be essential if victory was to be achieved.

Miscalculations occurred from both the Al Qaeda and American decision makers. Bin Laden had assumed that the Americans would land in the Spin Ghar Mountains by helicopter and attack the entrenched fighters. During this operation, the Al Qaeda fighters would inflict heavy losses on the Americans, similar to what had happened with the Soviets in the 1980s. However, the commando operations never materialized as the United States relied on continual heavy bombing to decimate the insurgents (Bergen, "Manhunt," 47–48). Al Qaeda did not have a backup plan, as the fighting on the ground was usually brief skirmishes exclusively with Afghan fighters being paid by the Americans. Eventually, the bombing toll created severe casualties and medical supplies ran out. Furthermore, the Al Qaeda leader was out of cash to pay key warlords and tribal fighters. As the weather conditions worsened, a crucial decision by bin Laden was made to call for an evacuation from the mountainous stronghold. The Al Qaeda leadership contacted the key Afghan warlord Hajji Zaman to call for a cease-fire so that the fighters could prepare to surrender the following morning. This stalling tactic worked and helped bin Laden and his leadership team escape out of the Tora Bora region. Prior to departing, the sheik prepared his last will and testament.

The American situation was also fraught with mismanagement. On top of the decision not to introduce U.S. Rangers, the American military did nothing to secure the escape routes into Pakistan. The overreliance on the Northern Alliance both militarily and politically was a mistake (Rashid, 72–74). The Americans felt that the overwhelming superiority gained by the airpower would offset any potential problems encountered. General Franks and National Security Advisor Condoleezza Rice both stated that the lack of certainty that bin Laden was actually in Tora Bora also played into the decision not to introduce ground forces. The local population, who viewed outsiders with intense distrust, would look upon U.S. soldiers as enemies. Finally, the Bush administration also felt that the American public support for the war effort could decline if casualty rates increased. By mid-December, the Pentagon and Bush team were already planning the next chapter in the war on terror: the invasion of Iraq (Khan, 100–102).

Numerous fighters from Tora Bora were captured after entering Pakistan. The key Al Qaeda leaders were not among them. Bin Laden had shrewdly backtracked to Jalalabad and eventually traveled on horseback to Kunar Province. The president found out in early January that the architect of the 9/11 attacks was still alive. This best chance to kill Osama bin Laden was squandered in December 2001 at Tora Bora. When given the opportunity to finish off Al Qaeda and kill bin Laden, the Bush administration failed to follow through. Bin Laden departed from Tora Bora wounded and anticipating his own death. However, in 2002 the organization would slowly begin to rebuild and expand into new terrain (Burke, 69–71). It would take almost a decade before bin Laden would finally be located and killed in Abbottabad, Pakistan.

The initial military outcome in Afghanistan was victorious for the American policy makers and military, but it would leave Pakistan dealing with the fallout. Social, economic, and political disruptions would plague this already vulnerable country. From 2002 on, Pakistan would be the frontline state on the war on terror. (It could be argued that the epicenter shifted to Syria by 2011, but that is debatable.) Musharraf's policy following the fall of the Taliban was full of contradictions. His military and intelligence operatives pursed foreign fighters and members of Al Qaeda who had crossed into Pakistan in the early part of 2002. Many were rounded up and given to American officials, who would send them to black sites out of U.S. jurisdiction in places like Poland, and Egypt, or they would be sent to the Guantanamo Bay facilities 90 miles off the American coast (Rashid, 224–226). Musharraf refused to dismantle the terrorist network that was very active on Pakistani soil. Many of the groups were connected to the Kashmiri liberation struggle, while others, the Pakistanis believed, would be of assistance in keeping a sympathetic government in place in neighboring Afghanistan. These insurgents were vital to the long-term strategic interest of the Pakistan state. Musharraf informed U.S. officials that Pakistani militants would not be apprehended and were off limits in the war on terror. Some of the key Afghan Taliban leaders (including Mullah Omar) were given sanctuary with the key organization structure being based out of Quetta in Balochistan (Hussain, 67). Several of Musharraf's aides, including retired general Talat Masood, warned him that keeping one set of insurgents alive while trying to apprehend others would be virtually impossible. Musharraf claimed he could compartmentalize the different operations (Gul, 28–32).

Once the chaotic exodus from Afghanistan accelerated, it became virtually impossible to keep any control over the insurgent activities. The border was too porous, and the number of fighters entering the country was far greater than expected. The unintended consequences of the terrorist influx included a growing Talibanization of Pakistan and a shift in the cultural norms of many regions in the country.

With significant sympathy in Pakistan, the Taliban leadership found ample sanctuary. The American war effort in Afghanistan had created a conservative religious revival and tribal unity against the Western efforts. This could be expected with a considerable Pashtun population in both countries. Areas such as Swat under Sufi Mohammad and his Teherik-e-Nefaz-e-Shariat-e-Mohammedi (TNSM) called for a much more rigid form of Islam to be practiced, including the imposition of sharia law. This became typical in many areas of the border region (Yousafzai, 105–106).

The furor over Musharraf's decision to ally with the United States in the war on terror created a political backlash against the government. As the religious movements gained momentum, Qazi Hussain Ahmad, the leader of Jamaat-e-Islami, and Maulana Fazlur Rehman, head of Jamiat Ulema-e-Islam, were detained by authorities but only placed under house arrest. The parties resented the harassment by the Pakistan state and responded by forming a political coalition to oppose Musharraf. Six parties came together to form the Muttahida Majlis-e-Amal or the United Council of Action or MMA. Musharraf may have indirectly supported this coalition, hoping that it would help to keep his more serious rivals in the democratic process on the defensive (Gall, 65–67). The main concern politically for Musharraf was the exiled former leaders Nawaz Sharif of the Pakistan Muslim League and Benazir Bhutto of the Pakistan People's Party (PPP).

The army wanted to alter the constitution, introducing 29 amendments that would further strengthen military rule in Pakistan. Most notably, the position of president would be all-powerful. The military also hoped to ban Sharif and Bhutto from ever becoming leaders in Pakistan. The military wanted to restrict who could serve in government. Bizarre amendments, such as requiring a college degree to run for office, were proposed.

With one of the lowest literacy rates in the world, this was of course far-
cical. A comical side note was that a madrassa certification would hold
the same weight as a university degree. This of course was to strengthen
the mullah's position in politics (International Crisis Group, "Madrasa
Reform," 24–26). These proposed changes were ridiculed by civil society
organizations throughout the country. The media, lawyers, and political
parties all voiced opposition. The ISI intensely vetted the process to see
who would stand with General Musharraf, who was against him, and
who were undecided. Following this process, the intelligence agents set
about harassing and intimidating candidates and their supporters. The
international community was following the preelection activities and was
frustrated by the lack of transparency and accountability. Interestingly
enough, the United States refused to criticize the Musharraf regime out
of fear that it could harm his assistance in conducting the war on terror
(Shah, 189–190). Bush firmly believed that Musharraf was helping to keep
Al Qaeda on the run. To firm up support for the regime, the administration
allocated an additional quarter billion dollars in military aid. The process
was a sham and seemed almost like a throwback to the Cold War policy of
propping up Third World dictatorships. Musharraf issued a Legal Framework Order that extended his presidency for five years.

In the 2002 elections, the citizens were disheartened as rallies and preelection activities were banned. The masses realized that the process was
rigged and the goal was not restoring democracy but solidifying military
rule. It was assumed that the religious parties would always be on board
with the military as a reliable partner. Ultimately, the religious parties
gained control of two border provinces and won a record 68 seats in the
National Assembly. The regime had no problem looking the other way as
the religious coalition promoted their agenda and organized voter registration drives. The turnout and results stunned even the Pakistani intelligence community that had been indirectly backing the religious coalition.
An ISI operative even publicly stated after the election that they were surprised by how successful the MMA coalition was (Gall, 66). The provincial
governments of Balochistan and the Northwest Frontier Province were
now in the religious conservative hands. The Taliban and Pakistan militants looked at the outcome as a significant victory. The electoral outcome
also gave the Taliban more breathing space in the areas where their sympathizers were now in control of the government.

The exodus out of Afghanistan left two options for most of the militants.
The tribal areas of Pakistan would provide ample sanctuary in primitive
conditions that by most accounts were even harsher than what the fighters
had faced in Afghanistan (Jones, 83–84). The second option was to head
toward the densely populated cities of Pakistan such as Karachi, Lahore,
or Islamabad. Many of the Al Qaeda members opted for the urban areas
with Karachi being the main hub for the terrorists. This megacity had been

nearly impossible for the Pakistani authorities to manage with chaos and near anarchy conditions being commonplace. Karachi is a southern coastal city with a notoriously high level of corruption. With easy access and porous borders, the city became one of the cornerstones of terrorist activities in the post-9/11 period. Kashmiri militants, Sunni sectarian fighters, and Al Qaeda all had a major presence in the city. Terrorist bombed the Sheraton hotel and launched multiple attacks against the American consulate. Several kidnappings and murders occurred with the most notable being that of *Wall Street Journal* reporter Daniel Pearl. The tragic abduction and murder of Daniel Pearl was one of the most high-profile events in the early days of the war on terror. Pearl was an American of Jewish ancestry and one of the star reporters for the *Wall Street Journal*. Pearl and his wife were based out of New Delhi and covered events in Asia and the Middle East. Pearl was working on an investigative piece on Jamaat-ul-Fuqra, which was of interest because of its active recruitment of Americans. The shoe bomber Richard Reid was suspected of having ties to the organization. As Pearl reached out to numerous contacts in Pakistan, he eventually ended up connecting with a supposed contact to the group by the name of Omar Sheikh. The last person to see Pearl alive was Jameel Yusuf, who ironically worked on helping to elevate the rash of kidnappings in Pakistan. When the police tracked the last calls to Pearl, the numbers were not traceable (Rashid, 152–154).

The Pearl case was the first act of anti-American terrorism by Al Qaeda since the 9/11 attacks. For the most part, journalists had not been the targets of terrorists in the past, but that would change dramatically in the post-9/11 wars. The abductors demanded the release of several detainees at Guantanamo Bay, but they did not wait long before murdering Pearl. During the first few days of February, three Arab militants decapitated Pearl. The murder was videotaped and released on the Internet. The ISI quickly captured Omar Sheikh, and numerous experts speculate that the Pakistani intelligence community was aware of the situation. The relationship between Sheikh and the ISI was unclear, but they held him for several days prior to his arrest being made public. The police in Karachi did not even know he had been apprehended until the intelligence agents notified them. Originally, it was believed that the kidnappers were part of the Kashmiri militant group Jaish-e-Mohammed, but it was eventually confirmed that Al Qaeda was the mastermind behind the gruesome deed. The Pearl case set off a major outcry from the press. It was uncertain whether he was targeted because he was Jewish, that he worked for a conservative newspaper in America, or maybe that he was digging too deeply into the Pakistani government's connection to the extremists. Pearl's execution was the first murder to be videotaped, and when his remains were recovered, his body had been cut into nine pieces. Even more shocking was the fact that the Al Qaeda's number three, Khalid Sheikh Mohammed known as KSM, took responsibility for the actual beheading. Al Jazeera interviewed KSM several weeks later in which he confirmed his role in the abduction and murder. KSM also reconfirmed the details in a hearing at Guantanamo Bay in March 2007 (Jones, 80–82).

It is apparent that whatever the motivations were for the kidnapping the results were beneficial to the radicals. Musharraf was embarrassed and his credibility severely damaged. Numerous militants were subsequently released from jail, and the government crackdown subsided. U.S. demands for extradition were refused. Sheikh had far too much intel on the ISI connection to terrorist organizations that would have been divulged if extradition had occurred. The cover up in the case was apparent, and numerous members of the cell responsible for the kidnapping and murder were never charged in the case.

As 2002 progressed, the level of violence in Pakistan increased dramatically. Suicide bombers attacked a Protestant church in Islamabad followed by a bombing outside of the U.S. consulate in Karachi. A foiled assassination attempt against President Musharraf also occurred in April. These actions were indications of the terrorist resolve to destabilize Pakistan, adversely impact the economy, ferment sectarian violence internally, and to sow fear into international diplomats stationed in the country. On all four points, the militants were highly successful (Rashid, 154–155). The indiscriminate killings as well as the targeting of groups like physicians, lawyers, journalists, and teachers in Karachi put the region in a state of panic and chaos. Economically, the Karachi stock market plummeted on several occasions because of the growing instability. Sunni extremists connected to Deobandi and Wahhabist factions continually targeted Christian churches as well as Shia and Sufi minorities within the country. The Taliban fighters who had made it across the border after Tora Bora helped to spearhead these attacks and to ferment this radical ideology in Pakistan. The diplomatic core was diminished because of the increased violence. General Tommy Franks and State Department officer Christina Rocca decided to send all nonessential personnel out of the country. Several European embassies followed suit because of the growing danger in the major urban areas. What made the situation even more tense and disheartening was the fact that the Pakistani police believed the ISI was still not cooperating in the investigations. The accusations went even further as claims of the ISI having vital information of militant locations and possible potential attack targets were not shared (Rashid, 220–222).

Musharraf's empty promises about prosecuting the war on terror in Pakistan were wearing thin. His January 12 address to the nation was supposed to be a game changer. Arrests were made usually followed by water-down or dropped charges and militants being released. The Pakistani police released a tiny fraction of the budget allocated toward combating terrorism, even though they would be the targets of attacks more frequently in the early years of the operations. The lion's share of the spending went to the military and intelligence agencies. The lack of equipment, pay, and training for law enforcement made police vulnerable to corruption.

Musharraf's standing at home was also being damaged by the war on terror. The general was perceived as a lap dog of the Americans, and his popularity was declining as he looked like a puppet taking orders from the Western powers. The institutions of the Pakistani state were failing, and civil society was in a free fall. The general would be forced to give up his uniform and govern as a true political leader, a position Musharraf would never be comfortable in (Gall, 88–89). In addition, Musharraf's weaknesses further emboldened the extremist cause as they gained momentum at the ballot box and on the battlefield.

THE SEARCH FOR AL QAEDA IN PAKISTAN

Al Qaeda fighters were forced to flee into Pakistan and did so in subsequent waves (Jones, 82). The preoccupation of the U.S. intelligence community in 2003 was the apprehension of Al Qaeda operatives and leaders living in Pakistan. Several key figures were rumored to be living in the urban centers of Pakistan. Though the whereabouts of the two top leaders, Osama bin Laden and Ayman al-Zawahiri, were not confirmed, the trail of Al Qaeda's number three, Khalid Sheikh Mohammed, picked up momentum. KSM was involved in the planning and implementation of most of Al Qaeda's most spectacular plots, including the 9/11 attacks, the Bali bombings of 2002, and the brutal murder of Daniel Pearl. Agents mapped out a network of close contacts to KSM centered in the area of Rawalpindi, a major urban area approximately 10 miles from the capital of Islamabad. The city's geography with densely populated narrow streets and numerous bazaars made it the prefect location to hide fugitives.

An informant tipped off intelligence authorities about the whereabouts of KSM. The attraction of the $25 million reward was the main factor in the decision to turn on KSM. The fugitive was staying at a two-story complex on Peshawar Road. The Americans and Pakistanis worked together in a joint raid on the complex on March 1. The house where KSM was hiding out in belonged to a member of Jamaat-e-Islami. The successful apprehension of such an important leader of Al Qaeda was probably the most significant intelligence victory in the war on terror. The mission showed once again the importance of human intelligence in combatting terrorism (Bergen, 254).

In assisting the Pakistani government in the apprehension of Al Qaeda fighters, several limitations were placed on the United States. The United States was not allowed to fly over Pakistani nuclear facilities, and Indian military bases were not to be used in the operations against Al Qaeda.

Musharraf granted the U.S. request that most Pakistani bases be open to U.S. military. Finally, extensive (and very expensive) radar facilities were installed by the United States throughout Pakistan. The United States of course increased aid to the regime as an incentive for the regime to help in the efforts to weed out Al Qaeda leaders hiding in the country. The most contentious issue remained was the Pakistani relationship with the Taliban. This was a problem in which very little progress was made toward resolution (Ahmed, 88–89).

Al Qaeda fighters fled to the tribal areas, densely population urban centers, or, in a few cases, Iran. The latter posed serious obstacles because of the strained relations between the United States and Iran that of course meant little to no intelligence was available. The Shia-Sunni divide created some complications for Iran, but they did provide limited sanctuary to some members of the organization. Iran looked at the U.S. military buildup in Afghanistan as a direct security threat. In a short period of time, Iran, tired of the Al Qaeda presence and had most members rounded up and placed under house arrest. It became clear that the fundamental differences between Iran and Al Qaeda created problems and an overall lack of trust was apparent.

The vast majority of operatives sought sanctuary in Pakistan. The United States had to overlook the fact that numerous key Taliban operatives were clearly allowed to live freely in Pakistan without fear of apprehension. Balochistan Province became the hub of Taliban activity as the leadership council eventually reconvened in Quetta. Whenever Pakistani failed to meet U.S. expectations, they simply claimed that it was virtually impossible to control the traffic between the vast Afghan-Pakistan border (Nawaz, 10–11). Conventional forces could not control the border region, and it was apparent that clandestine operations were necessary. This would require special operations and intelligence agents to be an active part of the plan.

The hunt in Pakistan for Abu Zubaydah became the highest priority for intelligence operatives. Zubaydah was obsessed with destroying Israel and the United States, and he ran training camps and guesthouses for Al Qaeda prior to the 9/11 attacks. A close friend and associate of Khalid Sheikh Mohammed, Zubaydah had a role in planning several terrorist operations in the pre-9/11 period. By December, Zubaydah had fled across the Afghan border into Pakistan, settling in Karachi.

U.S. intelligence tracked Zubaydah to 13 safe houses located in the cities of Karachi, Lahore, and Faisalabad. It was decided that a combination of U.S.-Pakistani operatives would raid all locations simultaneously. Zubaydah was seriously wounded, and the CIA went to extraordinary measures to keep him alive, including flying in a surgeon from Johns Hopkins Medical Center to operate on him. The operation was successful, and the raid actually led to the apprehension of nearly two-dozen Al Qaeda members (Jones, 93–94). It became apparent that Al Qaeda had received assistance from the Pakistani-based Lashkar-e-Taiba, a terrorist organization with strong ties to the ISI.

The interrogations of Zubaydah provided a wealth of information about the Al Qaeda network and potential operations being planned. It was also through the process that intelligence operatives discovered that KSM was the actual mastermind of the 9/11 attacks. Through the interrogation process, it became possible to piece together the rationale behind the Al Qaeda movement and recruitment success. The youth bulge in the Middle East and the subsequent economic dislocation of so many young men played roles in the ability of the movement to gain supporters. Furthermore, the excitement and adventure of becoming a radical militant was attractive to youth in the region. Many analysts have drawn the conclusion that religion was secondary and not a significant factor in the draw to Al Qaeda. These findings were surprising and somewhat controversial (Abbas, 156–157).

Zubaydah's case brought attention to the enhanced interrogation techniques being used by the American military at the Guantanamo Bay facility that opened in early 2002. Zubaydah was water boarded 83 times (KSM was water bordered on 183 occasions). Most international experts and legal scholars considered these techniques torture. The problem was that most analysts believe that such techniques were not necessary and that traditional interrogation would have provided similar results. This debate would rage on throughout the war on terror (Jones, 97).

The apprehension of the Yemenis terrorist and Al Qaeda operative Bin al-Shibh in Karachi on September 11, 2002, was one of the highest-profile success stories for counterterrorism efforts. Al-Shibh was part of the Hamburg cell that included several of the 9/11 attackers. He was the main intermediary between the attackers and Al Qaeda.

PAKISTAN-INDIA RELATIONS: 9/11 AND BEYOND

The terrorist attacks of 9/11 complicated and strained the relationship between Pakistan and India. The fact that both countries were strongly allied with the United States in the war on terror did not create a unified effort but probably led to additional tension. The governments of both countries may have thought the Afghanistan campaign would lead to further opportunities to gain the upper hand militarily in the unending Kashmir crisis. Instead of being partners against terroristic elements in South Asia, Pakistan and India seemed closer than ever to engaging in an additional conflict.

Washington's hands-off policy of indifference toward the Kashmir issue (especially following the Cold War) became less tenable after 1998 when both India and Pakistan became official nuclear states. Both the Clinton and Bush administrations were late in implementing sound policies in place to deal with South Asia. The region in general and relations between the two nations specifically became a higher priority (Fair, 157–159). Unfortunately, the U.S. disinterest in the initial post-Cold War period proved costly, as in 1989 Kashmir saw the emergence of a vibrant separatist insurgency that was fueled in part by Islamic radicalism. Financing and training of Kashmiri insurgents was partially funded by Al Qaeda.

After 9/11, Pakistan viewed Afghanistan as key to maintaining a strategic advantage regarding India. The Taliban regime was deposed but Islamabad realized that a friendly regime in Kabul was essential for Pakistan to remain secure. The Northern Alliance success from October to December 2001 was of grave concern for the Musharraf regime and the ISI. It was well known that the Northern Alliance was supported indirectly by all of Pakistan's rivals, including Russia, India, and Iran, and as Kabul fell to the Alliance it was viewed as a strategic defeat for Pakistani interest. As the remnants of the deposed Taliban regime crossed into Pakistan, India took the initiative and established a strong presence in Kabul under the Karzai administration. It seemed that a new battlefront in South Asia had now opened up (Rashid, 248–249).

At first, the Kashmir militia groups were more secular and nationalistic in nature. This changed as the regional dynamic was altered by the rise of Islamic movements during the anti-Soviet campaigns in the 1980s. The first wave of Islamic groups was more moderate and inspired by the model established by the Muslim Brotherhood. The Kashmiri insurgency shifted in a more radicalized direction by the mid-1990s as the Deobandi and Wahhabi influence increased and attempts to Islamize Kashmir were apparent. Pakistan intelligence and military elements felt they could control the movement since it was essential to the overall foreign policy of Pakistan. Ultimately, the All Parties Hurriyat Conference (APHC) became the group organizing the Kashmiri militants. The population was becoming more engaged in protests and actions against the Indian authorities in response to human rights violations and general repression, including extrajudicial killings, torture, and rape (Weaver, 262–264).

From the perspective of the Pakistani military, the Kashmir insurgency afforded it the opportunity to divert thousands of Indian troops for long periods of time. This took pressure off the Pakistan military, which allowed it to promote efforts and further engage in the Afghan situation. Musharraf had a history of aggression toward the Indians dating back to his involvement as a soldier in earlier conflicts as well as his direct action in the Kargil fiasco of 1999 that ultimately catapulted him to power.

The main terrorist group that coalesced in Kashmir was the Harkat ul-Mujahideen. The group had been a key ally of the Taliban and had a strong backing from the ISI. The group was heavily involved in running training camps across the border in Afghanistan. The U.S. military targeted Harkat in 1998 after the embassy bombing in Africa and again in October 2001.

Harkat had become a global entity with networks established in Chechnya, Somalia, and Central Asia. The group leadership had ordered the hijacking of an Indian airliner in December 1999 and later was responsible for the kidnapping and murder of Daniel Pearl. Several key leaders of Harkat had been imprisoned including Masud Azhar and Ahmed Omar Sheikh. Both were subsequently released as a result of the hijacking of the Indian airliner. The Indian government was convinced that Pakistani intelligence agents were involved in the hijacking, which further strained relations between the countries. Once released, the charismatic Azhar helped to establish a new terrorist group in Kashmir Jaish-e-Mohammed. The radical nature of the group was evident when they attempted to assassinate President Musharraf in 2004 (Gall, 84–85). Jaish also introduced the tactic of suicide bombings into Pakistan. This high-profile terrorist action by Jaish led to Indian demands for Pakistan to be labeled a terrorist state by the international community. Efforts to achieve this were unsuccessful, but India-Pakistan relations were severely strained by 2000. The United States showed growing concern as CIA intelligence reports put the potential for conflict at an unacceptably high level.

Attempts by Indian prime minister Vajpayee to start negotiations with Musharraf in May 2001 ended in complete failure. The quick embrace of Pakistan by the United States following the 9/11 attacks angered the Indian authorities. U.S. tolerance for terrorist attacks originating out of Kashmir would be low as the Bush administration took a somewhat different tone with Musharraf on the matter of the Kashmiri insurgency. As stated earlier, the Pakistani military and intelligence community had no intention of reeling in the extremist groups in the disputed region. Tensions reached a critical point when Pakistani militants stormed the Indian parliament on December 13, 2001, killing 14 people. India engaged in large-scale troop deployments, and war seemed like a distinct possibility. The timing of the crisis could not have come at a worse time. This was the crucial month when the hunt for Osama bin Laden was taking place, and Pakistan made the decision to redeploy troops toward the Indian border and away from the Afghan border area (Hiro, 147–149). The United States tried to pressure General Musharraf to reign in jihadist activity against India and to take much stronger measures to eliminate extremist elements in proximity to India. Musharraf was forced to make a public address to the nation on January 12, 2002, proclaiming that Pakistan would not allow its territory to be used for terrorist activities and that no organizations promoting terrorism or jihad would be allowed to function within the country. Within the speech, the general mentioned Kashmiri terrorists' activity specifically, but he also said that Pakistan "would never surrender its claim to Kashmir because it runs in our blood." Several groups were banned from the country, and numerous militants were arrested (Rashid, 117).

As had been the case in the past, the words and actions of the Pakistani leadership did not match. It was clear by March that General Musharraf had no intention to fulfill his promises from January. Militants were freed and banned organizations simply changed their names. The Bush administration was reluctant to apply too much pressure for fear of harming the U.S. efforts in Afghanistan and also endangering the viability of the Musharraf regime. The negotiations between the parties were difficult as India continued to take a hard-line stance, and Pakistani efforts to curb extremist activity seemed insincere as India pointed to renewed Kashmiri insurgency activities in July 2002.

Escalation was heightened over the fear that nuclear weapons may have been acquired by Al Qaeda or another militant jihadist group. Bin Laden had stated back in 1998 that the acquisition of a nuclear weapon was a religious duty. A fear that a 9/11 follow-up might include nuclear weapons was a grave possibility to U.S. intelligence experts. The fear intensified when it was discovered that two Pakistani nuclear scientists, Sultan Bashiruddin Mahmood and Abdul Majid, had worked with the notorious Abdul Qadeer Khan and had secret meetings with Osama bin Laden and Ayman al-Zawahiri. No confirmation of any serious action was uncovered, but this discovery once again led America to push the Pakistani regime to further purge extremist elements out of the government (Fair, 208–210).

With continued U.S. pressure, Pakistan and India agreed to de-escalate regional hostilities. It had taken nearly three years after 9/11 to see substantial progress in improving the diplomatic relations in South Asia. After so many false promises by the Musharraf regime and with only marginal progress being made in the hunt for terrorist sanctuaries and a realization that India was a serious global power, the United States made a decision to secure New Delhi as the main geostrategic partner in the region. Even though George Bush had a close relationship with General Musharraf, he had proven to be opportunistic and dangerous by most of the key advisors to the president. Even though the relationship with Pakistan was strained, aid would continue to flow and mishaps by the regime would be overlooked.

CHAPTER 4

The Ungovernable Tribal Region: Post-9/11 Centerpiece

Once the operation at Tora Bora came to a close, the focus of the U.S. efforts in the war on terrorism should have shifted to the east and the tribal region bordering Afghanistan and Pakistan. It was well known that the majority of fighters fleeing the American bombing efforts were heading to the protection provided by the terrain and tribal sanctuary in the border areas. Numerous armed groups were engaged in the region in the post-9/11 conflict, including the Afghan Taliban, the Pakistan Taliban, Al Qaeda, a patchwork of international terrorist groups, tribal militias, and the Pakistan armed forces. Osama bin Laden found the FATA region to be the best location available in order to try and regroup his depleted Al Qaeda organization. The shift into Pakistan would ultimately alter the culture and social fabric of the tribal societies infiltrated by a mix of militants from Central Asia, Africa, China, Kashmir, Chechnya, and numerous Arab countries. The area would be labeled "terrorist central" and the "world's most dangerous place" by pundits, political commentators, as well as chief executives. Before analyzing the changing nature of the war on terror as if shifted to the tribal region, it is important to understand the background and makeup of this volatile area.

TRIBAL PAKISTAN: HISTORY AND SIGNIFICANCE

The Federally Administered Tribal Area (FATA) of Pakistan and the adjacent Northwest Frontier Province (NWFP) are exclusively Pashtun areas with approximately 40 million inhabitants. FATA is a territory covering 10,000 to 11,000 square miles resting on the border between Pakistan's

NWFP and southern Afghanistan. The Durand Line is the division between Pakistan and Afghanistan. Approximately 3 to 4 million Pashtuns reside in the FATA region in addition to the 1.5 million refugees from Afghanistan (Norell, 27–30).

The Pashtuns are fiercely independent and take immense pride in having maintained their independence for most of history. The number of Pashtun tribes is open to interpretation, but approximately 60 actual tribes along with an additional 400 subclans are known to exist. The largest groups include the Afrid, Achakzais, Bangash, Durrani, Khattak, Mehsuds, Mohammadzai, Mohmand, Orakzai, Shinwari, Yusufzai, and Waziri. The pre-Islamic tribal code of *pashtunwali* is the most significant aspect of Pashtun culture and has regulated society for centuries (Nawaz, 1–2). Pashtunwali is based on the absolute obligation of hospitality, sanctuary, and revenge. Honor and chivalry are key aspects of this tradition.

The contemporary historical period was filled with intrigue and uncertainty. In 1947, Pashtun leader Abdul Ghaffar Khan rejected incorporation into Pakistan because of his initial alliance with the Indian National Congress (INC). Meetings between the INC leadership and the Pashtuns did not go well, and the cultural disconnect was very apparent. The Pashtun leadership was hoping that during the electoral process the option of an independent Pashtunistan would be on the table, but this did not occur. The choice was basic: India or Pakistan. The election was boycotted by a large segment of the Pashtuns in the NWFP. Approximately half of the population was involved in the vote with a sizable majority voting to join Pakistan. Khan took the oath of allegiance in February 1948. However, on numerous occasions Khan made public statements supporting opponents of the Pakistan state. These pronouncements ended up landing him in jail several times over the next decade. By the 1960s, he was living in exile in Afghanistan. Many elites within the Pashtun hierarchy, including Khan's son Wali Khan, had leftist leanings, but the political leadership was continually beset with factionalism as pro-Chinese and pro-Soviet groups emerged. Numerous coalitions formed with many of the movements advocating a nationalist agenda. Compared to other anti-Pakistani nationalistic movements such as Balochs, Bengalis, and Sindhis, the Pashtuns were more moderate. Part of this can probably be explained by the Pashtun inclusion in the Pakistan military (Ghufran, 1099–1101). Their dominant role is exemplified by the fact that over 40 percent of the highest ranking officers in the late 1960s were of Pashtun origin, including two of the first military leaders of the government, Ayub Khan and Yayha Khan. Within the Pashtun regions, the main political party was the National Awami League (NAP).

By the 1970s, religious parties were starting to garner more political momentum, most notably the Deobandi influenced Jamiat-e-Ulema (JUI). Another burst of nationalist fervor emerged in 1973 inspired by the

Pashtuns in neighboring Afghanistan led by Muhammad Daoud. The timing of this push may have been motivated by the events of 1971 as Bangladesh gained independence from Pakistan. Daoud wanted to use this
as a model for the creation of an independent Pashtunistan. Later in the
decade, two trends dissipated the nationalist push. First, the economic situation for a portion of the population improved because of the oil boom
in the Gulf States. Many Pashtuns went to the region as guest workers and
sent remittance back home to Pakistan. Second, the war in Afghanistan
and the massive refugee influx into the Pashtun region diminished the
irredentist rhetoric. Many claimed that the changing demographics had
created a de facto Pashtunistan in Pakistan. The most serious ramifica-
tion of the Soviet war was the change in the Pashtun region from an ethic
emphasis to one of religious fundamentalism.

Administratively, FATA is divided into seven agencies: Khyber, Kurram,
Orakzai, Mohmand, Bajaur, North Waziristan, and South Waziristan. The
Khyber Agency is the most important link between Pakistan and Afghanistan. The agency is named for the famous pass that runs through the two
countries. The population is approximately half a million and is inhabited
by the Afridis and Shinwaris tribes. The Afridis are one of the more tolerant tribal groups, as they are known to respect the Sufi traditions and have
a long tradition of literary accomplishments. The Afridis oppose some of
the ultraconservative views of the Deobandi school of thought. The Shinwaris are highly involved in business endeavors in the tribal region, but
tend to have more influence on the Afghan side of the border. The Khyber
Agency saw increased militancy and had been the hub for rogue radio
broadcast that promoted pro-Pakistani Taliban rhetoric (Norell, 37–38).

The second tribal area with a population of 450,000 is the Kurram
Agency. The two main tribal groups are the Turi and Bangash. This area
has some pro-Shia elements from both the tribal groups. Kurram is also
in the agency with the strongest connection to the Northern Alliance in
Afghanistan (Bergen, "Talibanization," 363–364). The region has some
significant opposition to the Taliban, but over a period of time this has
diminished.

The Bajaur Agency is the smallest region and very inaccessible. The
population is approximately 600,000 and the agency borders the Kunar
Province of Afghanistan, which has been a Taliban stronghold. The largest
tribal presence is the Tarkani and Utman Khel. Both Al Qaeda and Taliban
fighters fled to this area following the fall of the government in Afghanistan. The region is one of the more politically active with the Muttahida
Majlis-e-Aman (MMA) coalition prominent throughout. This region has
been a centerpiece of the U.S. drone campaign that intensified during the
first Obama administration.

The Mohmand Agency is named after the main tribe that constitutes the
majority of the population. This region of approximately 350,000 is known

as the heart and soul of guerrilla activity. This was the main area of insurgency efforts against the British historically. The agency opposed efforts by the Pakistani state to unify tribal areas together. Religious leaders have always played a more prominent role in this agency.

The Orakzai Agency is the smallest region with a population of roughly 240,000. The two prominent tribes are the Orakzai and the Daulatzai. The inhabitants of the area include both Sunni and Shia Muslims. Sectarian violence has become more prevalent in recent years. Several members of the Pakistani government hail from the region, giving it more clout nationally. The agency made news by banning international health-care workers and halting vaccination programs.

North Waziristan is the second largest agency geographically and is mostly inhabited by the Wazir and Dawar tribal groups. The population of 375,000 has always been a centerpiece of radicalism and rebellion. The agency promotes the concept of Pashtunistan as an independent entity. Regional transportation is the economic mainstay of the area. Waziristan received global attention for the kidnapping industry (including the high-profile apprehension of *New York Times* reporter David Roede) that has flourished in recent years. The tribal customs of the region, including music and dancing, have put the agency at odds with the Taliban's harsh policies against these forms of entertainment. Even with this cultural rift, the Pakistani Taliban has established formal offices in the area and a strong presence overall.

The final agency and largest in size is South Waziristan. The Mehsud and Wazir tribes dominate the area that has approximately 425,000 inhabitants. The tribesmen from the area are proudly independent. The area is known for its skilled fighters and warriors. The region has the highest literacy rates and also a significant percentage of civil servants in the Pakistani government. Conservative Mullahs hold sway over the vast majority of the population and even hold office in the National Assembly. During the past decade, insurgents from neighboring countries, including Uzbekistan, have moved into the area. The first leader of the Pakistani Taliban, Nek Mohammad, was from the region.

Militancy in the tribal region of Pakistan is a significant part of the historical narrative. The tribal groups are fiercely independent and protective. The decision by the British to allow the region to be maintained as a buffer zone along the western frontier of the empire adjacent to Afghanistan was in many ways an admission of defeat. The overwhelming British military superiority and abundance of resources did not lead to total victory in the tribal belt (Abbas, 19–21). A long protracted war against the Wazirs and Mehsuds (along with a number of smaller tribal entities) never led to long-term peace and colonial control. Local autonomy for the most part remained in place. Communities controlled aspects of law enforcement and the judiciary. Traditional assemblies known as *jirgas* were vital in maintaining order in tribal societies.

During times of volatility, the British launched sporadic campaigns into the region that they considered the furthest extreme of the empire. Occasionally, the conflicts ended in stalemate, while in other cases, such as during the operations undertaken during 1839 and 1878, British forces were ultimately defeated. The British official in charge of the region was known as a political agent. This operative of the colonial administration was able to provide incentives in order to maintain control over tribal areas. At numerous times, major deployments of British military personnel would take place to quell uprisings. The origins of tribal uprisings were varied from outright anti-colonial movements to quasi-religious rebellions and in defense of Pashtun culture.

In analyzing the particular case of Waziristan, scholars point to the development of a model of how authority is centered. Akbar Ahmed states, "the sources of authority stem from three distinct, overlapping, and in some ways mutually interdependent, though often in opposition, sources of authority: the tribal elder, or malik; the religious leader, or mullah; and the political agent representing the central government" (Ahmed, 49). Historically, the jirga system or council of elders was extremely important in tribal decision making. As noted earlier, the code of Pashtunwali was vital in tribal society. The second source of authority resting with the mullahs was subservient to the tribal leaders because they had the ability to appoint the religious leaders. The key to understanding this dynamic was that the mullahs were usually outsiders brought in to provide religious education at the madrassas. The political agents were originally part of the colonial structure, so even in its contemporary form there was bound to be tension with the first two sources of authority. This authority structure provided continuity through most of modern tribal history. This was to be shattered as the war on terror engulfed the Waziristan region.

Traditional society was usually controlled by the major tribal groupings. A careful balance was maintained between tribes and religion. Scholars or the *ulema*, along with the feudal landowners or *khans*, and finally the tribal elders or *maliks*, received patronage in political undertakings. Central to all of the undertakings was the concept of *pashtunwali* or way of the Pashtuns.

This historical structural arrangement would be severely challenged during the turbulence of the 1970s and 1980s (Hilton, 65–66). Most significant have been the disruptions caused by forced relocation of populations into refugee or IDPs camps and subsequently the loss of traditional identities. Filling the void, of course, has been a radical brand of Deobandi Islam imported mostly from Saudi Arabia. The economic vulnerability of the tribal regions made the Saudi financial backing of conservative Islam even more appealing. This new wealth impacted Pashtun culture in numerous ways. Many Pashtuns had started working in the Gulf States during the boom of the 1970s. In addition, the anti-Soviet campaign led to massive aid money entering the area. The dark side of this economic change would include the emergence of arms trafficking, the proliferation of the drug trade (including opium and hashish), and the general breakdown of the traditional social order. Local patronage networks that had been in place historically were challenged and replaced by a new system (Bergen, 28–29). The political agency system that had emerged during colonial times and continued in the period after Pakistani independence was acquired and also deemed redundant and obsolete.

This transformation would not have been possible without the influence from General Zia during his leadership tenure from 1977 to 1988. Since the tribal areas already tended to lean toward a more conservative outlook regarding religion, the promotion of Deobandi Islam was a reinforcement of values already in place in many of the areas. The change did threaten the tradition societal framework in the region, especially the influence on local religious leaders. By the late 1990s, the first references to the Talibanization of the region were mentioned. A more assertive and at times aggressive form of Islam was promoted as music and dance were outlawed, the wearing of beards for men was mandated, and beauty parlors and shops were shut down if deemed morally corrupting. This anti-Western campaign was similar to what had transpired in neighboring Afghanistan a few years earlier.

THE INFLUENCE OF MADRASSAS

The move toward a more conservative, radical version of Islam would not have been possible without the reforms that took place in the madrassa system in Pakistan. The process took over during the Islamization policy of General Zia. Changes were instituted in the legal system with the establishment of sharia courts to try cases under Islamic law. Within the legislative realm, steps were taken to Islamize the economy by eliminating interest in the banking industry and requiring national banks to deduct a zakat from deposits. The Islamization process was also promoted through the media, including radio, television, and the mosques. The goal of the regime was to promote Islamization in education, the armed forces, the civil service, and any endeavors remotely connected to the government. The overall impact of this policy change was to heighten divisions in society and increasing sectarian conflict (International Crisis Group, 10–13).

The program also helped to marginalize Zia's political opponents. The more secular segments of society were put on the defensive as the Islamic agenda permeated all aspects of public life. The regime even used religious texts to justify domestic policy decisions. The directional shift won overwhelming approval from the religious seminaries. Money flowed into this sector with a goal set in 1979 of funding 5,000 religious schools into the system.

A key component in the overall scheme was modernizing the madrassa system so that the religious schools and formal education systems could be integrated. The plan laid out in the Halepota Report was ensuring the autonomy of the religious sector. Part of the proposed plan was to implement a financial assistance program for students and create job training for madrassa graduates. A final step that was pushed hard by the Zia administration was to update the status of the madrassa degree (International Crisis Group, 25–27).

For the most part, two types of madrassas emerged from the Zia campaign. The first type produced jihadi literature, mobilized public opinion, and recruited and trained fighters. The second type was more independent with support from JUI. They tended to have problems with the Zia administration but still were aggressively involved in the anti-Soviet campaign of the 1980s. The ISI provided money and helped with the training of the students that emerged from these madrassas that were located in the Pakistani tribal areas and camps along the Afghan border (Schmidle, 58–60).

Most of the Pashtun madrassas in the NWFP and Balochistan were guided by the Deobandi sect of Islam, and they aggressively supported the jihad concept. As the Soviet campaign intensified and the refugee problem increased, the madrassas were flourishing. The influence of funding from the Gulf States as well as the United States helped to keep the system functioning. The rapid increase in the madrassa system was due to the influx of refugees entering the tribal areas of Pakistan. This population would be hardened and ready to engage in jihad whenever called upon to do so.

The operational aspect of the madrassa system varied depending on location and time. At first, the main priority was to provide volunteers to help the mujahideen in Afghanistan. Later on, the madrassas would have jihad networks in urban areas within Pakistan, such as Karachi. The Haqqani network and the JUI under Fazlur Rahman helped to funnel support into the schools and place volunteers wherever needed. These fighters would be invaluable to the American and ISI efforts against the USSR and later would form the core of what would become the Taliban movement. The jihadists trained in the camps would end up taking up the fight against India, Russia, and the United States. The Pakistani intelligence bureaucracy felt that the madrassa system could be highly effective in the struggle over Kashmir (Rashid, 235–236). It was no coincidence that immediately following the end of the Soviet campaign the Kashmir struggle accelerated. Most troubling from the Pakistani perspective was the internal strife created out of the madrassa system. The most negative consequence of the proliferation of the madrassas was the increased sectarian violence that engulfed Pakistan for over a decade. Tragically, the madrassas in place for most of Pakistani history did not promote religious divisions that are the cornerstone of the movement today (Templin, 4–5).

The government has yet to find an effective way to deal with this growing crisis.

The importance of Saudi money and influence on the madrassa problem cannot be overstated. The Salafis/Wahhabis influence is blatantly anti-Shia. This increasing level of hostility has caused a violent backlash from Shia organizations and madrassas within Pakistan. Iran noted the victimization of the Shia in Pakistan and increased funding to militant sects to counter these attacks (Ispahani, 152–153).

Additionally, numerous political parties with overt sectarian agendas emerged as a result of the growth of the madrassa system. Some of the movements were formed during the Zia years, while other groups organized as offshoots of the mainstream parties. Other groups reinvented themselves during Musharraf's tenure. Sipah-e-Sahaba, Sipah-e-Mohammed, and Lashkar-e-Jhangvi are three examples of parties fermenting sectarian violence that were formed as a result of the growth of madrassas. Mainstream political parties in Pakistan have been quick to blame the United States for the growth of sectarianism. The ISI shoulders part of the blame for fermenting the growth of extremism.

CULTURAL CHANGES IN THE TRIBAL REGION OF PAKISTAN

The most significant legacy of the proliferation of the madrassa system may have been the alteration of culture of Pakistan. The initial push in the madrassas was anti-communist in nature, as the main enemy of Islam was perceived to be the godless USSR. The target audience of the jihadist rhetoric was refugees entering the camps from Afghanistan. The propaganda was amply funded by the Saudis and other Gulf States with a clear message that all Muslims were obligated to partake in Holy War against the enemies of Islam. Part of the jihadist rhetoric was to indoctrinate the impressionable youth about the plight of Muslims in areas like Palestine, Chechnya, and Kashmir. The emphasis on the obligation to help financially, verbally, and physically was stressed. The moderate elements within the Pakistan educational structure were at a distinct disadvantage, as they had to counter Gulf States funding as well as support and assistance from the U.S. government. An additional source of funding came from NGOs in many of the Gulf countries.

The madrassas promoted intolerance towards other sects within Islam as well as other faiths in general. After the initial public relations component was up and running, the jihadists quickly learned the trade and were able to run it independently after help from outside entities ended. The propaganda emphasized the importance of families sending their children to the madrassas. Catchy phrases, like "Jihad is the shortest route to paradise," were aggressively promoted. When fighters were martyred, the families of the fighters were taken care of financially, giving an added economic benefit to justify the system. In addition to the radicalization of education, Pakistan saw an increase of extremism within the mosque structure (Rashid, 235–236). Once again, this policy dates back to the period of Zia's rule. It became commonplace and expected for citizens to financially support the religious schools and the mosques. In the post-Soviet period, 94 percent of all charitable donations made by Pakistani citizens went to religious institutions. Ultimately, the exact economic situation of the madrassas and mosques is difficult to ascertain because this information is not public record. The government does financially help the madrassas indirectly through donations of land and at times selective monetary donations. In many ways, this can be looked upon as the state promoting the jihadist culture.

Later attempts to reel in the madrassa activities were met with significant backlash. Furthermore, easy-to-navigate loopholes were created by the Pakistani bureaucracy. Musharraf proclaimed publicly his intent to defeat extremism by reforming the madrassa system. The administration banned eight militant groups, froze their assets, and arrested thousands of members. Studies conducted internally found over 700 extremist madrassas in the Punjab province alone. The sincerity of these efforts could be called into question as the general may simply have been paying lip service to the international powers in the aftermath of the 9/11 attacks. Opportunities to accelerate the crackdown were rejected and in some cases the ISI may have assisted jihadist organizations to strengthen their position. For example, no attempt was made to stop the thousands of madrassa volunteers from crossing into Afghanistan to fight in the Taliban campaign during October and November 2001. Estimates of 10,000 jihadists crossing into Afghanistan from Pakistan were noted by U.S. intelligence services. This episode did not end well for the Pakistani administration as most of the young jihadist volunteers were killed or captured during the subsequent bombing campaign with blame being placed on the regime for allowing this movement to occur. Ultimately, Sufi Mohammed, the leader of the Tehreek-e-Nafaz-e-Shariat-e-Mohammadi (TNSM), who facilitated the cross-border operation, was arrested and imprisoned, as he became the scapegoat for the botched mission (Schmidt, 115–117). Musharraf would act in whatever way that enhanced his chances of survival. Shortly after his address to the nation in January 2002, several schools were shut down but quietly reopened shortly afterward partially because the students literally had no place to go. Essentially, the operation of the madrassas became more low-key for a brief time until public pressure dissipated. It was also very apparent that any crackdown would not be done using military force or excessive violence. Arrests were made but mostly for minor charges with quick release dates. Many militants expressed unity with the military and the ISI (Gul, 15–17). The enemy was not Pakistan, but India and international forces trying to weaken or destroy the state. Many jihadists expressed displeasure with Musharraf after his pro-American statements, but they felt that the state was still supportive of their objectives and agenda. The militants were always on the back burner as they played into Musharraf's anti-democratic agenda. This would change as the war on terror progressed and militant organizations became much more anti-Pakistan in their rhetoric and actions.

One of the most common funding mechanisms that emerged was through the transfer of revenue established for humanitarian or educational projects to charities that diverted to jihadist causes. Several jihadist groups had changed their names or moved locations, but the purpose and goal remained steadfast. This attempt at regulation by the Pakistani government was most pronounced during Musharraf's tenure in the post-9/11 years. In the end, the changes were cosmetic as frozen accounts were opened. Unquestionably, the area most impacted by the proliferation of the madrassas was the tribal region bordering Afghanistan.

One of the more troubling aspects of the madrassa growth was the foreign influence in Pakistan. This phenomenon dates back to the Soviet war as jihadist fighters took up refuge in Pakistan. Many of the students worked with Islamic charities or NGOs. During the initial surge of madrassas, the attendees were allowed to travel very freely in Pakistan (Bergen, "Talibanization," 165–166). Registration and accountability were lax as the entire madrassa system was rather chaotic. Many gravitated to the large urban madrassas in Karachi, Islamabad, and Faisalabad; others settled in the more remote tribal regions. The end result is that the foreign influence permeated the entire country. The foreign students living in Pakistan of course faced numerous obstacles. First was the obvious language barrier, which made associating with the local population nearly impossible. Second, the foreigners, especially the Arab students, tended to be more rigid and conservative in their views and lifestyles. Some of the foreign fighters ended up assisting the Taliban movement in their takeover of Afghanistan in the mid-1990s. Close to 90 percent of all militants apprehended have been international. The regime usually has an easier time controlling the homegrown militants than the organizations run by Arabs or Afghanis. At least in the initial years of the war on terror, the indigenous groups did not challenge the government. They supported a nationalistic anti-Indian policy, which was in tune with the Musharraf administration. A significant problem was that the foreign-born residents who have gone through the madrassa system would not be welcomed back in their country of origin. Of course, the militants would not want to return to their country of origins for fear of persecution or imprisonment. Madrassa students from countries such as Yemen, Egypt, Jordan, and Algeria would have good reasons to fear for their safety since these countries have abysmal human rights records.

Another policy attempted by the Pakistani government in 2002 was to create "model madrassas" to help raise the educational standards. The purpose was also to contain the militancy coming from so many of the schools. The educational institution itself needed to be reformed as well as a significant overhaul of the curriculum. The tricky part of the process was always how to maintain some oversight without intruding on the autonomy of the madrassas. Prior to the crackdown of the system following the war on terror, Pakistan was attempting to set up a model madrassa system in Islamabad, Karachi, and Sukkur (Rashid, 272–273). The plan was to keep the administration very loose and informal, as not one school of Islamic thought would be prioritized. The madrassa union's known as *wafaqs* would be part of the governing board, but opposition from the group occurred as many did not approve of any regulatory body administering the system. They felt that this was an attempt to undermine religious education in Pakistan. Previous efforts by several leaders had failed in this capacity. An agreement in late March 2002 officially established the reforms, which gave the madrassa leadership more flexibility in the content taught. In a telling statement from Abdul Malik, one of the wafaqs leaders, "real modern knowledge cannot override divine knowledge." He further stated that "secular and atheistic views cannot enter the madrasa." For much of the religious community, the government reforms and the development of "model madrassas" had little relevance on the day-to-day operations in place.

The biggest challenge that occurred at this juncture was the proposed regulation and financial transparency of the madrassas proposed by Musharraf in his address to the nation in January 2002. This was quickly met with hostility and uproar. Most commentators believed that neither the government nor the religious community had any intention on actually implementing serious change. This was seen as rhetoric on the part of Musharraf to appease the United States and the international community. Proposed penalties that could be imposed for noncompliance were in fact not very serious. Withdrawal of *zakat* payments was one of the penalties but only a minor part of the funding actually had anything to do with the tax. The government also stated the desire for all madrassa funding from abroad to be channeled through the Pakistani bureaucracy. This monitoring of the funding was ridiculous and could never be implemented. The high level of corruption within the state meant that no entities would allow this to become standard practice. The rationale behind this was that most of the madrassa funding came from private sources from abroad. A further clause mandated foreign students studying in Pakistan to go through official registration with the government. This was also unenforceable, as it would take a tremendous amount of resources to monitor the thousands of foreign students entering Pakistan on a regular basis.

The government hoped that the incentives proposed by the government could help to alter the madrassa culture over time. Grant money would help with the distribution of free books to over 10,000 schools and was earmarked for the hiring and training of over 16,000 teachers. Over $230 million was allocated for curriculum development and registration purposes (International Crisis Group, 24–27). This plan sounded wonderful on paper and in press releases to Western media and the United Nations, but the actual implementation was nearly impossible. The majority of madrassas were not registered because they do not want any governmental or bureaucratic meddling. Also, plans for the certification of instructors were open to significant interpretation. The idea of putting madrassa instructors on parity with the teaching in public education was flawed and grossly unfair.

THE PAKISTAN TRIBAL REGION POST-9/11: THE WORLD'S MOST DANGEROUS PLACE

As the Taliban regime collapsed in November 2001, the only alternative to secure survival was to head into the tribal regions of Pakistan. Senior officials and fighters were given sanctuary with the approval of the ISI and Pakistani military. For all of their flaws and mishaps, the Taliban was still the best available alternative to promote Pakistani interests in Afghanistan. The rationale was that the United States was expected to exit the region relatively quickly, and Pakistan needed to be prepared for the aftermath of this inevitable withdrawal. Having a proxy in place was in the long-term interest of the Musharraf regime. The exodus across the border was by all accounts an intentional policy. Claims from Pakistani officials that the disorder and chaos were uncontrollable are somewhat misleading.

The two key objectives for Pakistan were to secure strategic depth and to guarantee a pro-Islamabad regime in Kabul as quickly as possible (Kapur, 103–106). The Pakistani government was adamant that it has a proxy in place, similar to the situation in the 1980s, because the Western interest in the area would wane quickly. It was considered vital to the interests of Pakistan to help keep the Taliban as a viable option in the region. The maneuvering to accomplish this would need to be as covert as possible. The situation in tribal Pakistan was considerably different than during the anti-Soviet campaign nearly two decades earlier. The population had grown dramatically, and the proliferation of weapons was much greater. The religious organizations and parties were much better organized and assertive, and there was a substantial increase in the madrassas and anti-Western sentiments. By 2002, areas in close proximity to FATA, including Balochistan and the NWFP, were run by Deobandi organizations associated with Jamaat Islami and the Jamaat Ulema Islami Party. The region in general began to aggressively promote sharia law. Furthermore, a number of Western influences, such as music and advertising, were banned. In the government, female bureaucrats were fired, making the system dangerously close to what had been imposed in Taliban-run Afghanistan in the late 1990s.

History will look at 2002 as a watershed year for Pakistan as it became the centerpiece in the war on terror. The Musharraf regime was in a difficult situation as it was being pressured by the United States and Western allies to aggressively pursue the terrorists who had sought sanctuary in Pakistan. Some of the militants had taken refuge in the remote tribal regions of the country (at first mostly in South Waziristan), while others were suspected to be in the densely populated urban centers, such as Karachi and Rawalpindi.

The militants who entered Pakistan established bases and restarted military operations. Part of what transpired was economic in nature. Impoverished tribesmen helped provide sanctuary and safe passage out of Afghanistan became wealthy from this business venture. Many of these tribal guides would later become members of the Pakistani Taliban organization. South Waziristan's geographic diversity and intense terrain made counterterrorism incursions into the region very problematic. The high mountains, steep slopes, deep ravines, and thick forests provided the optimal hideout for the militants. Much of South Waziristan was easy to defend and remained inaccessible to outsiders. It was estimated that by the summer of 2002, 3,500 foreign fighters had taken refuge in the area. As the Americans gathered more intelligence, this lack of effort on the part of Pakistan became a major point of contention (Khalid, 567–568). Al Qaeda's first reformed base for operations was Angur Adda in South Waziristan. This base was used to facilitate attacks against U.S. military positions in Afghanistan. The United States was suspicious that Al Qaeda may have not only received intelligence on American positions, but that the Pakistani Frontier Corps may have even provided cover for the militants attacks (Rashid, 269). This situation was reminiscent to the U.S. predicament in the Vietnam War when communist insurgents would cross from neutral Cambodia and attack American positions in South Vietnam. The contemporary situation was even more shocking because unlike Cambodia, Pakistan was actually an ally of the United States in the war on terror. It is also well documented that Pakistani intelligence operatives and members of the ISI assisted the Taliban fighters as well as members of Gulbuddin Hekmatyar's Hizb-e-Islami Party. The latter group had recently reemerged to help defeat the Americans in Afghanistan, but they were forced to quickly flee across the border into Pakistan. Hekmatyar had been pressured to leave Afghanistan once the Taliban regime gained power in 1996. He had spent the past several years in exile in Iran but returned to try and help the greater cause of global jihad. The most dangerous force was undoubtedly the Haqqani network, which had a strong presence in both Afghanistan and Pakistan. The financial strength of the network along with its tight connections to the tribal groups made the Haqqanis difficult to combat or control. These militant organizations were perceived to be in the ISI camp. They would be helpful to Pakistan's goal of maintaining strategic depth regionally.

Other groups did not fit as neatly into the overall scheme. The Islamic Movement of Uzbekistan (IMU) and Al Qaeda were more problematic to deal with. According to journalist Ahmed Rashid, "To maintain its influence among the Taliban and Afghan Pashtuns, the ISI developed a two-track policy of protecting the Taliban while handing over Al Qaeda Arabs and other non-Afghans to the United States" (Rashid, 221). Ultimately, the ISI was forced to create new covert organizations in order to help guide Taliban policy. The bureau would be organized and run by retired ISI and military officials, who would be contracted out in many cases through the less suspicious Frontier Corps. These agents would be located in key areas in proximity to the Taliban leaders, such as Quetta and Peshawar. They would have jobs within the community in order to conceal their involvement. Many of these agents had forged bonds with the Taliban back in the 1990s. Several operatives within the Pakistan establishment worked tirelessly to ensure that the Taliban would be looked upon in a positive light in Pakistani society.

This departure in Pakistani policy was partially due to the fact that the United States was becoming more engaged with the Pakistani intelligence community. The U.S. military and intelligence agents remained suspicious of the ISI, but still provided new equipment, technology, and training. The frustration level on behalf of the alliance fighting in the war on terror increased as Taliban attacks became more frequent by 2003. The Bush administration naively trusted Musharraf, believing that the assistance to the Taliban within Pakistan was coming from rogue elements in the intelligence sector. Over an extended period of time, it would become more apparent that the support of the Taliban was indeed coming from the highest level of the Pakistani state. It was uncovered that the ISI had set up training facilities in Quetta and that military procurements were arriving from the Gulf States. It was also suspected that military support was provided to Taliban fighters heading back into Afghanistan and that medical teams were set up to assist with the wounded once they returned across the border. The Taliban fighters were indigenous to the Afghanistan-Pakistan region. The use of Arab or other foreign fighters would have been extremely dangerous and could have very well altered the American policy on Pakistan (Abbas, 108). This was a line the Pakistani authorities did not want to cross.

The continued cross-border attacks emanating out of the South Waziristan region and FATA in general eventually put American military leaders in a situation where they informed Genera Musharraf to either put troops in the region to deal with the insurgency or the U.S. forces would take unilateral action. The Pakistani policy under General Ali Jan Orakzai was to do the bare minimum to appease the United States. The balancing act that Pakistan was playing was becoming more difficult as domestic elements within the country wanted to ensure that the resettlement of the militants in FATA would not be hampered by any military operations. A pro-Taliban policy was a high priority in Pakistan and was considered vital in countering the inevitable India encroachment into the region. The government continually denied the presence of any militants in Pakistan. Several sources, however, confirmed not only the presence of militants but also that those elite members of the ISI had frequent meetings with key leaders, such as Jalaluddin Haqqani, as well as Tahir Yuldashev of the IMU. The insurgency position was solid, and they began to take control of the political dealings in the region disrupting the traditional norms of tribal control. Through the use of terror, intimidation, and murder, the insurgency created a sort of Talibanization in the tribal region. This precarious situation put pressure on the Karzai administration, as well as the American military operations. This consolidation of radical control in the Pakistan tribal region continued unabated from 2002 into 2004 (Burke, 370–373).

THE IMPLOSION OF THE TRIBAL REGION: GROWING TENSION IN FATA AND BEYOND

For reasons not entirely certain, the militants decided to turn on General Musharraf. Possibly his continued support for the American war effort in neighboring Afghanistan or the militants' anticipation of a more aggressive stance against the insurgency might have led to the change. On two separate occasions in December 2003, insurgents with ties to the Taliban living in the tribal regions attempted to assassinate Musharraf. He narrowly escaped assassination when militants tried to blow up his motorcade near his military headquarters in Rawalpindi. The first attempt included a bomb located under a bridge that he was passing over. Two suicide bombers driving a truck full of explosives launched the second attack 11 days later. In both cases, advanced technology given by the Americans, including electronic jamming devices, were used to thwart the attacks. The general also benefitted from the armored plated vehicles he always traveled in. Evidence was uncovered that the suicide attackers were Libyan and trained in the newly opened bases in South Waziristan. Al Qaeda was adamant in wanting to bring down the Musharraf regime and to kill the general because of his support for the American war effort. Alarming intelligence data also showed that Al Qaeda had active supporters working within the Pakistan military, an alarming point on numerous levels as the Pakistan nuclear arsenal could be compromised. It was also apparent that Al Qaeda had maintained its ability to operate effectively as the missions against Musharraf were well planned and decentralized (Gall, 85). Upping the rhetoric further was a fatwa issued by Ayman Zawahiri calling for the death of Musharraf. In addition, Al Qaeda released video footage of bin Laden and Zawahiri in what was assumed South Waziristan discussing the futility of the American war effort. This propaganda stunt on the second anniversary of the 9/11 attacks further embarrassed the Pakistani regime. The thought that the world's most wanted criminal was living freely and roaming about Pakistan infuriated the Bush administration and U.S. military leaders. Tensions were also running high between Pakistan and Afghanistan, and several border skirmishes occurred in 2003. Occasional brief and usually minor Pakistani military incursions into the tribal regions occurred, but they were usually insignificant and probably done for public relations rather than actual military objectives (Hussain, 37–39).

Musharraf ordered the first significant military operation to destroy the militants. The operation covered a 50 square mile area of South Waziristan. This decision in many ways changed the nature and the role that Pakistan played in the war on terror. In early March 2004, troops from the Frontier Corps entered the village of Kalosha in the Wana region of South Waziristan. The goal of the operation was to flush out and defeat foreign fighters who had taken refuge in the region. Most of the fighters located in the village were Al Qaeda fighters from Arab countries and members of the Islamic Movement of Uzbekistan led by Tahir Yuldashev. Initially, 2,000 troops entered the region to conduct a sweep and root out the foreign fighters located there. The Pakistani scouts that moved into the Wana valley were hoping to surround the area where the suspected militants were hiding and then solicit help from the local villagers in negotiating their surrender. Instead, the insurgents broke out of the weak encirclement that was set by the military. To make matters worse, the local tribesmen rallied behind the militants, who had been given protection by the villagers. The militants were well prepared and had fortified key positions prior to the arrival of the military contingent (Rashid, 270–271). Trenches and tunnels were dug, and the militants set up a sound communications system to coordinate the counterattacks. Supply convoys and helicopter reinforcements were called in but decimated. It was apparent that the insurgents had set a trap as the Pakistani contingent was obliterated and 8,000 regular army reinforcement forces were sent in to halt the carnage. It was later confirmed that many of the fighters were seasoned veterans of Yuldashev's IMU. It is interesting to note that Yuldashev had become a key religious leader in the region upon his arrival in the post-9/11 retreat. His inspirational sermons and ability to connect with the tribal elders made him a trusted ally and partner (Bergen, 322–323). Yuldashev was wounded in the fighting, which probably garnered more sympathy for the rebels. In the ensuing clash, members of the Frontier Corp were scattered, and numerous were taken hostage. After weeks of bloodshed, the insurgents were defeated, but the area was devastated with massive population displacement and civilian deaths. This became an unfortunately common pattern in the tribal areas. The insurgent forces would retreat, and the brunt of the damage was to the civilian population, which further radicalized the region. Following the operation, Ayman al-Zawahiri issued a message on Al Jazeera calling on the Pakistani military to turn on Musharraf and refuse to spill the blood of their countrymen.

The overall assessment of the operation was that the Pakistani military was unprepared for the confrontation. The troops that entered the tribal region were ill-equipped and poorly trained. Very little intelligence was utilized prior to the engagement and thus the Frontier Corps took heavy losses. The militants were not only heavily armed, but they had the strategic high ground and were dug in and well prepared for the coming confrontation. The most alarming aspect was the suspicion that the ISI had given the militants key intelligence information about the upcoming attack. The idea that the Pakistani intelligence community would act in a manner that could deliberately endanger the lives of members of their own military is difficult to comprehend. General Musharraf claimed that 46 soldiers were killed, but unofficial sources stated it was over 200. It was also publicly stated that the main target in the operation was indeed Al Qaeda's number two, Ayman al-Zawahiri (Gall, 87–89). As would be the case in so many controversies in Pakistan, no formal inquiry took place, and many speculated about an internal cover up. A demoralized military suffered desertions, as many soldiers did not want to engage militarily against fellow countrymen. Many members of the Frontier Corps were also concerned about retribution from the well-connected militant network.

From a public relations perspective, this was a disaster for the Pakistani military. The tribal insurgents under the leadership of Nek Mohammed were looked upon as standing up against unjust aggression. Mohammed's family had gained fame as tenacious fighters in the Afghan war against the Soviet Union. The fighters upheld the *pashtunwali* code of honor by protecting groups, such as the IMU and some members of the Arab factions that had sought sanctuary in South Waziristan. The tribes were indirectly connected to Al Qaeda and undoubtedly provided assistance to the group at times in the post-9/11 period. Nek Mohammed had heroically helped Tahir Yuldashev escape from the grasp of the Frontier Corps. Following the debacle, the Pakistani government decided to sue for peace and withdraw its forces in order to secure the release of several soldiers still being held hostage (Abbas, 108–109). This started a pattern in which the military

would sign a peace accord with the militants in the tribal regions in order
to regroup and evaluate the merits of future operations. During the official
treaty signing at Shakai in late April 2004, it was the militants who operated from a position of power. At the actual signing, hundreds of tribesmen attended, cheering on Nek Mohammed in what was by all accounts a
capitulation by the Musharraf regime. General Safdar Hussain negotiated
the terms, which stated that the government would require foreign militants to register within a week, and the leaders of the insurgents operating in Waziristan were pardoned. The terms were unenforceable, and the
agreement broke down within a few weeks.

An additional military operation was launched in the early summer as
a blockade was implemented to stop goods and supplies from entering
at the key location of Wana. The militants sustained the most significant
blow in late June when Nek Mohammed was killed by a U.S. drone strike.
The region was reaching a boiling point. The population was incensed
as the Americans were directly involved in killing Pakistanis on Pakistani soil. The influx of foreign fighters preaching a Salafist brand of Islam
made the region more volatile (Norell, 80–82). The Al Qaeda goal was
simply to have the region as a zone in which they could train militants
and plan future operations. It became increasingly difficult to convince
fellow Pakistanis serving in the military and security sector that it was
vital for them to risk their lives to confront fellow countrymen in Pakistan.
There was really no love lost between the Pakistan military and the United
States as many key leaders made it clear that they hoped to see the Americans bogged down in a quagmire in neighboring Afghanistan. In addition,
the tribal regions felt that their economic needs were still being neglected,
even though millions of dollars of aid was being infused into the country
because of the war on terror. With a per capita income of fewer than $500,
the citizens clearly realized they were second-class citizens in the country.
Also, with the literacy rate hovering around 17 percent and female literacy
at an abysmal 3 percent, the tribal population had legitimate grievances.
The lack of educational opportunities also played into the thriving success of the madrassas. The health-care system was in dire need of help
with slightly over 500 physicians for the entire FATA region. The infrastructure was totally neglected, and the people felt the region was simply being used as a staging ground for cross-border attacks against fellow
Pashtuns in Afghanistan (Nawaz, 13–15). The resources provided for the
region were used almost exclusively for military activities.

It was apparent that General Musharraf's situation was fragile. Pakistan was the recipient of $26 billion in American aid during the period
2001 to 2013 but internally the country seemed to be tinkering on the brink
of civil war. Discontent within the military was growing, and religious
parties and organizations felt that the general's pro-American policies

had weakened the country. Throughout Pakistan, it was believed that the cost of being an American puppet had weakened Pakistan in regard to its regional place vis-à-vis Afghanistan. The despised Northern Alliance had a strong foothold within the Karzai administration in Kabul. The reality in Afghanistan was that the ethnic factions of the Northern Alliance and not the Pashtuns maintained the military power within the army. The Taliban regime was the prefect proxy for Pakistan, and their demise damaged Pakistan's ability to control and manage regional affairs. This turn of events was considered tragic for the long-term security interests of Pakistan, and it reversed the gains that had been achieved regionally dating back to the late 1970s.

To complicate the situation further, America was quickly turning its attention toward the situation in Iraq. The fear among the elites in Pakistan was that an American departure was eminent. This concern led the Pakistani military and intelligence apparatus to double down on helping with the resurrection of the Taliban in Afghanistan. The regime turned to a pro-Taliban general to head the ISI. Lieutenant General Ashfaq Parvez Kayani, who previously worked on Taliban strategic initiatives, was now one of the three most powerful individuals in Pakistan. The Americans believed that he was trustworthy due to the fact that he was trained at the U.S. Army Staff College at Fort Leavenworth. This would be an ill-fated decision, as Kayani proved to be one of the most aggressive Taliban supporters in contemporary Pakistani history. His pro-Taliban maneuvering would severely damage U.S. interests in the region for close to a decade (Goldberg, 58–59).

The Pakistani rhetoric on the policy was simple: the Taliban was a reality, and the regime had to find a way to deal with them to promote what was in the best interests of Pakistan. Cloaking this in nationalist terms made it much easier to sell to the key decision makers within society. As the tension became more severe between Musharraf and Afghan leader Hamid Karzai, siding with the Taliban became easier to justify. As the general progressed toward his final years at the helm, he came to view the Taliban support as an absolute necessity.

How much of this support for the Taliban was equated with indirect support for Al Qaeda is difficult to ascertain. Some analysts speculate that Ayman al-Zawahiri was given sanctuary in a Pakistan government guesthouse in 2005. This double-dealing pattern in the relationship of Pakistan and Al Qaeda was troubling for U.S. intelligence officials. Some of the information about Al Qaeda operatives being given safe passage or sanctuary came from supporters of the militants in the tribal region. Zawahiri was secured in a safe house in Kohat, staying at the home of one of the provincial governors (Gall, 90). Many of these reports of Al Qaeda whereabouts were not fully corroborated at the time and were not released by reporters and journalists. After the death of Osama bin Laden, it was confirmed that he had indeed lived in the tribal areas for three years prior to eventually moving to Abbottabad. Several accounts from militants confirmed that bin Laden was in North Waziristan in 2003. Reports corroborate that he moved frequently through the tribal region for most of the three years after his escape from Tora Bora. In this initial period, the Pakistan officials were turning a blind eye to the Al Qaeda activities in the region, and the tribal population for the most part remained silent and refused to relinquish his whereabouts. It was actually when the military operations in the tribal regions intensified with increasing drone strikes and the killing of Nek Mohammad that bin Laden fled the Waziristan area and his trail went cold. It became known that bin Laden actually moved to the Swat valley and then to Haripur for two years prior to making his way to his final destination of Abbottabad. It is still difficult to fathom that the Musharraf government did not possess some intelligence about the whereabouts of the world's most wanted fugitive (Gall, 92).

The ensuing chaos in the FATA region played into the hands of the militants. As the population continued to be exploited and traumatized by the conflict, Al Qaeda and the Taliban stepped in with plans to reform the area. The region was renamed the "Islamic Emirate of Waziristan," and a conservative social structure was implemented regionally. In this process, the social dynamic of the region was altered in a significant way. Tribal elders were marginalized or intimidated by the Taliban, and Al Qaeda and the military seemed to lack the resolve to take significant action. Aid that was infused in the region was squandered by the military and not used to improve the economic conditions of the population. With no accountability in place, the situation played into the hands of the conservative religious elements and their supporters. This void occurred because the population of the tribal region felt neglected by the government that continued to make false promises about infusing the area with economic aid. Little assistance reached the region, and desperately needed political reform was stalled. Nothing risky would be attempted, as this could possibly undermine the Musharraf regime. The Bush administration lacked expertise in the area, and as attention turned more and more toward Iraq, the region was neglected (Bergen, 147–149). Numerous scholars believe the growth of Taliban support was directly related to the U.S. mishandling of the FATA policy. No political or economic reforms were implemented, as the policy was simply one of a basic military solution to the problem. New weapon systems were given to Pakistan, and the United States amped up missile attacks that turned the society against the United States. The technology acquired by the Pakistani military to fight the insurgents in the tribal regions was actually used to combat the insurrection on Balochistan and to help aid the Kashmir resistance.

THE EROSION OF MUSHARRAF'S LEGITIMACY AND
THE EMERGENCE OF CIVIL SOCIETY

Through the chaos and turmoil of the past decade, a bright spot for Pakistan has been the development of civil society that has best been exemplified by the Lawyer's Movement of 2007. Musharraf 's grip on power was tenuous as pressure was mounting on him to share power, relinquish his military role, and allow legitimate free and fair elections. The general continued to take steps to ensure that he maintained control of the political situation in Pakistan. However, the situation on the ground was changing. The population and most notably the elites were ready to take action to ensure accountability and progress toward a more legitimate and transparent democracy.

By the spring of 2007, Musharraf did not face any substantial opposition to his rule. The two key figures in modern Pakistani political history were both living in exile outside of the country. The parties competing in Pakistan were beset with factionalization and petty bickering. No serious mass mobilization efforts seemed to be on the horizon. The economic situation in Pakistan was stable with a steady growth rate hovering around 7 percent. In addition, Musharraf had the luxury of having the full support of the Bush administration, since the Americans looked at him as a key ally in the war on terror (Jalal, 327).

The threat to Musharraf came from an unlikely place: the judiciary. In mid-2005, Iftikhar Chaudhry was appointed as chief justice to the Pakistani Supreme Court. Throughout Pakistani history, the judiciary had been docile and mostly fell in line behind the dictates of the generals who ruled the country. The idea of an impartial independent judiciary was foreign to Pakistan.

Chaudhry discussed with his fellow justices the idea of being proactive and moving in an activist direction to support civil rights and rule of law. The court began taking a more assertive role in issues such as police abuse, torture, gender discrimination, forced marriages, unjust rape laws, and environmental protection (Constable, 218–220). These bold and aggressive moves on the part of the court alienated several key groups in Pakistani society. The military was angered because some of the environmental decisions would hurt their private investments. Religious conservatives were upset by rulings favoring gender empowerment.

The most controversial stance taken by the court was on issues regarding human rights, most notably the issue of illegal detainments and torture. The military establishment and especially the ISI were guilty of massive amounts of questionable detentions, widespread torture, and hundreds of disappearances ("Pakistan: 2008 Country Reports on Human Rights Practices," February 25, 2009). It was common that prisoners were not brought to trial after being apprehended. The intelligence establishment covered up the disappearances and obvious human rights violations. After the Supreme Court started to request information and demand accountability, several hundred detainees were released by the security personal. President Musharraf complained to the United States that many of the released prisoners were affiliated with Al Qaeda and that their release would endanger the security of Pakistan and make the war on terror more difficult. Further investigations showed that Musharraf's claim was unfounded and that indeed most of the detainees were political prisoners who opposed the regime's policies in places like Balochistan and Sindh (Rashid, 380).

Musharraf and his allies in the military were angry and frustrated with the new activism of the Supreme Court and Chaudhry. Worries that the court could invalidate a second Musharraf term were a serious concern. In what may have been an overreaction by some of the general's more aggressive supporters, on March 9 Musharraf suspended the chief justice on charges of corruption and misuse of authority. Chaudhry was placed under house arrest after being roughed up by the security personal. The image of such an important public figure being treated in a demeaning manner only helped to fuel the movement that was about to envelope the nation.

Within 24 hours, lawyers gathered in bar associations throughout the country to protest the treatment of Chief Justice Chaudhry. Strikes were called in numerous cities that halted legal proceedings nationwide. The Lawyers Movement would be broadened to include numerous segments of society, including journalists, urban professionals, NGOs, and women activists. The protesters and strikers demanded the release of Chaudhry, the resignation of Musharraf, and the holding of free and fair elections. The protests posed a significant danger to Musharraf because of the middle-class nature of the emerging movement (Lieven, 114–116). Many of the activists may have noticed the trends toward the demise of authoritarianism and military rule globally and desired a similar fate for Pakistan. The key senior military advisors told Musharraf that the protests would be short lived but the reality of the situation was much more dire. The rapid escalation of the protests endangered the ability of the regime to govern effectively. During a hearing to determine whether Chaudhry would be permanently removed from the bench, thousands of attorneys showed up to accompany him to the courthouse. The protest turned bloody and violent as police battled the protesters.

Over the coming months, Chaudhry became the spokesperson and champion of the Lawyers Movement that promoted rule of law, constitutional foundations, and true democratization. The movement was a significant challenge to the military in Pakistan. During his speaking tour, thousands of supporters appeared at every location. His motorcade was inundated with cheering crowds that were eager for a change in the system. The government response was to set up counterprotesters, who were supposedly opposed to the chief justice. These counterprotesters were paid by the military to create chaos and incite violent clashes with Chaudhry supporters. In one instance during early May, 50 citizens were killed in Karachi during the protests. As the situation continued, thousands of supporters were jailed, and the police suppression continually worsened. Excessive police brutality became the norm at virtually every location. TV broadcast was forbidden, and press censorship was rigidly enforced (Schmidle, 124–125). By late July, the Supreme Court ruled in favor of Chaudhry reinstating him to the court as the chief justice. This democratic victory seemed to be a watershed event for Pakistan. Musharraf's troubles were mounting, however, as a more ominous situation was escalating involving the issue of growing militancy in the nation's capital.

THE TURNING POINT: THE SIEGE OF LAL MASJID

The seminal event that intensified the conflict between the Pakistani government of Pervez Musharraf and militants in the tribal regions was the siege of the Lal Masjid or the Red Mosque in Islamabad. The madrassas located on the site were ultraconservative including the controversial all-female Jamia Hafsa. The students studying at the madrassas were predominately from the tribal regions and the NWFP and were aggressively advocating for the implementation of sharia across all of Pakistan.

The founder and organizing force behind the mosque was Maulana Abdullah. He had organized mujahideen in the conflict against the USSR in the 1980s. The mosque was a transitional stopping point for many of the jihadist fighters heading off to the war. Abdullah forged close ties with Harakat ul-Jihadi (HUJI) and its leader Qari Saifullah Akhtar. Interestingly, Lal Masjid was the first mosque built in Islamabad following the decision to move the capital in the 1960s. At the time of the crisis, the individuals in charge of Lal Masjid were Maulana Abdullah's sons, Abdul Rashid Ghazi, and his brother, Abdul Aziz. They controlled all decision making at the location (Lieven, 157–159). Ghazi was more acclimated to Western ways, having attended English schools and obtained a master's degree in International Relations. He had spent time in both the jihadist and Western worlds and seemed early on to have a somewhat torn identity. He worked for the United Nations Children's Fund (UNICEF) and spent time vacationing in areas frequented by Westerns. For Ghazi, the turning point occurred when family friend Qari Saifullah Akhtar introduced Maulana and Ghazi to Osama bin Laden on a trip to Kandahar in 1998. After spending a short time with bin Laden, Ghazi was convinced of the righteousness of his struggle against the West (Siddique, 11–13). The experience for both father and son changed the direction and role of the Red Mosque. Within

a few months, however, an assassin, the family suspected was an operative of the ISI, would gun down Maulana Abdullah on the premises of the
Red Mosque. Following this tragic event, Ghazi decided to move into a
permanent role of helping his brother run the Red Mosque. Ghazi knew
his brother was somewhat provincial and did not understand how the
world of politics worked. Aziz had simply attended a madrassa in Karachi. The introverted Aziz had been the apparent heir to run the facility by
his father, but Ghazi's personality seemed to fit much better in the role of
leader. Aziz was reluctant to give interviews and shunned the limelight.
The brothers were in favor of establishing an Islamic State in Pakistan similar to what Mullah Omar had in Afghanistan, and they spoke openly of
their disdain for democracy.

The first salvo in the ensuing dispute occurred when several hundred
female students occupied a children's library in Islamabad close to the
Red Mosque and declared it to be ruled under sharia. Ghazi was known
to have called the female students at his madrassa his female commandos (Schmidle, 131). The public relations campaign intensified in the early
part of 2007 as the militants in the Red Mosque launched a campaign promoting virtue and attacking vice in the Pakistani capital in a Taliban-style
manner. One of the more fascinating aspects regarding the Red Mosque
was that many of the citizens attending the mosque were from a middle-
class background, which was an unusual phenomenon for such a militant
establishment.

Soon the rhetoric was followed by action as sharia courts were established within the mosque. It is interesting to note that many of the new
breed jihadists were literate products of the madrassas and had more formal education, with many obtaining university degrees prior to joining
up with jihadist cells. Within the next few weeks, brothel owners were
kidnapped, and storeowners selling DVDs were pressured to close. Supporters of Ghazi organized a bonfire burning CDs and DVDs that were
deemed offensive. The militants even apprehended several security officials who were patrolling too close to the mosque entrance. They were
later released, but it was apparent that the students were becoming more
emboldened as time progressed. Many of the hardened militants who
stayed through the entire ordeal were members of several notorious terrorist organizations, including Sipah-e-Sahaba, Jaish-e-Mohammad, and
HUJI. Rumors of students intimidating females not to drive and threatening others to dress in a more modest fashion became common. Journalists and pundits were commenting on the "Talibanization" of the capital
(Khan, 254–255). Part of this was undoubtedly hype, but, as time progressed, the situation became more untenable. The location of the Red
Mosque in the center of the nation's capital and bureaucratic center made
the ordeal even more surreal.

The Pakistani government was dealing with multiple complex issues, including an increasingly volatile situation with the Balochistan insurgency and pressure from opposition parties to allow the two former leaders of Pakistan, Nawaz Sharif and Benazir Bhutto, to once again return to Pakistan to vie for political office. In addition, increasing terrorist activities were threatening the peace and order within the urban areas. Finally, a very impressive civil society movement was emerging within the middle class in Pakistan led by the lawyer's movement, who wanted to see the chief justice of the Supreme Court, Mohammad Chaudhry, reinstated to his previous position. In plain terms, Musharraf was reeling and seemed on the ropes. The general was becoming more isolated and trusted fewer and fewer of his closest confidents who had been with him over the years.

Ghazi and his associates seized on the vulnerably of the Musharraf regime, calling for an Islamic Revolution. He demanded changes from the government, and the militants seemed ready to engage in armed insurrection as they stockpiled arms and claimed to be ready for martyrdom. The militants took the bold step of kidnapping Chinese sex workers, which incensed the Chinese government and pressured Musharraf to take action against the militants at the Red Mosque. The large-scale investment from China over the past decade made the relationship of vital importance to Pakistani officials. Infrastructural development for highways and port areas cost China hundreds of millions of dollars.

In early July, police and paramilitary rangers surrounded the Red Mosque. Gunfire was exchanged with militants, as a major confrontation seemed evitable. Many citizens with indirect ties to the mosque came out in support of the student militants (Siddique, 34–35). Pakistani Rangers took fire from inside the structure as they attempted to cordon off the areas surrounding the complex. In the initial confrontation, one Ranger died. The militants had been preparing for what they considered an inevitable clash for months. They had ammunition vests, gas masks, and Kalashnikovs. They quickly took up key strategic positions in the area adjacent to the Red Mosque.

The clerics in charge urged the students to wage jihad against the Pakistani authorities. As the key leader, Ghazi relied on his charismatic personality to secure the loyalty of his followers, who were at times fanatical in their support of the cause and their leader. The youth were inspired and eagerly waged jihad. They encouraged everyone to join in the fight against the corrupt Musharraf regime. The students damaged and looted several locations close to the Red Mosque, including the Ministry of the Environment. Several casualties were reported in the first hours of fighting, and the situation became a public relations disaster for the government as reports of young girls being wounded and killed in the fighting started to circulate (Siddique, 14–15).

As the crisis intensified, many of the organized religious parties in Pakistan began to distance themselves from what they perceived as Ghazi's radicalism. The MMA coalition that had several seats in the Pakistani Parliament condemned some of the actions of the militants. The former instructor of Aziz denounced him for occupying the children's library close to the mosque location.

By the end of the first day of fighting, the government decided to cut the power to the neighborhood where the Red Mosque was located. A strict curfew was also imposed as Musharraf and his aides hatched a plan of attack to end the standoff. In what would be an ominous sign of what was to come, the militants patrolling the area in front of the complex stated, "We are ready for suicide attacks. The blood of our martyrs will not go to waste" (Schmidle, 137). Ghazi was sequestered inside the complex, fearful of an impending arrest if he dared to venture out. The leadership was convinced that Musharraf wanted them eliminated.

By the second day, the panic level was intensifying as Ghazi seemed open to cutting a deal with the Musharraf government. The militants may have expected that such a deal would be worked out since the precedent of the regime making deals with militants was established as early as 2003 and had become a common occurrence during the war on terror. During the evening hours of day two, Ghazi's brother Aziz was captured trying to escape from the complex disguised as a women dressed in a black abaya. The authorities went to great lengths to publicly humiliate Aziz on television. As the military moved closer to taking action, a general amnesty deal was offered to any of the fighters wishing to surrender. Over a thousand fighters or supporters inside the complex did surrender with a promise of financial payment for surrendering. Ghazi was left with close to a thousand fanatical fighters located inside the complex with him.

The siege conditions were also problematic for the adjacent neighbors that were left without power and thus no air conditioning. Food shortages were also a growing concern. The military needed to act relatively quickly. The propaganda machine was in full force as Ghazi was demonized as an irrational zealot who was harboring foreign terrorists within the complex. Ultimately, the militants had no way to negotiate any sort of acceptable conditions, and a violent ending was inevitable.

The regime launched Operation Silence and instituted a media blackout of coverage. Phase one lasted a week and eventually commandos detonated explosives in order to destroy the walls leading into the complex. Intense fighting lasted 18 hours with Ghazi and his followers fighting to the bitter end. The death toll estimates range from the 4 to 500 mark (Fair, 190).

The aftermath of the siege gave militants within Pakistan a momentum boost. The Pakistani Taliban and other militant groups within the tribal region spoke of revenge against Musharraf. After the demolition of the historic Amir Hamza mosque, Hamna Abdullah made a speech in front of thousands of female activists stating, "our bodies will fall, but mosques will stand. Rivers of our blood will flow, but we will not let the greatness of Islam be harmed." The mosques and seminaries were referred to as "Islam's forts" and "God's house" (Sheikh, 130). Terrorists intensified their attacks including an increase in suicide bombings, roadside attacks, and ambushes against military forces. Al Qaeda leaders used the event to promote the idea of overthrowing the Musharraf regime with Ayman al-Zawahiri releasing video footage condemning the operation. The media used the phrase "massacre" to describe the fighting. The sophisticated tunnel system the authorities claimed existed was not found, and neither was any sign of foreign "high-value" terrorists. The authorities quickly tried to cleanup the situation, but by all accounts they would suffer fallout from storming the Red Mosque.

EXTREMISM EMBOLDENED: THE POST-LAL MASJID FALLOUT

In the aftermath of the siege of the Red Mosque, Pakistani intelligence confirmed that the militants at Lal Masjid had been forging closer ties to several extremist groups within the country. Most noteworthy were Baitullah Mehsud in South Waziristan and Mullah Fazlullah in the Swat region. Many of the students studying at the madrassa were from the tribal region, making the tragedy hit even closer to home. The militants responded quickly and violently. Fazlullah declared a jihad against the regime. Convoys were ambushed, and several soldiers were killed. Roadside bombs were also being readily used with the militants learning the tactics that had been enormously successful in Iraq. Most lethal were the suicide attacks, a tactic unheard of in Pakistan previously. In the years following the Red Mosque incident, the number of suicide attacks aimed at the Pakistani army or government representatives also increased significantly, both in the tribal regions and in large Pakistani cities such as Lahore, Islamabad, and Karachi (Sheikh, 87).

The militants' most successful operation was the capture of approximately 250 soldiers in the Mehsud region of South Waziristan in late August 2007. Early on, the militants started to focus on more coordinated operations led by recently released Guantanamo Bay detainee Abdullah Mehsud. However, in the previous year, Mehsud committed suicide during a military attack in the Balochistan region, and the leadership mantle was placed in the hands of Baitullah Mehsud. The final decision to officially form the Teherik-e-Taliban was announced in December. Interestingly, a decade earlier, Mohammad Rahim had formed a similar organization to try and galvanize the former fighters from the Afghan war who were living in Pakistan.

One of the women from a village in Azad Kashmir collects water from glacier runoff. (Photo by Kristin Topich)

A woman in traditional Pakistani clothes carries water back home in Azad Kashmir. The water is collected from glacier runoff. (Photo by Kristin Topich)

Roadside in Muzaffarabad, the capital of Azad Kashmir. (Photo by Kristin Topich)

Pakistani family working in a field in northern Pakistan. (Photo by Kristin Topich)

Tribal region of Pakistan. (Photo by Kristin Topich)

Tribal region of Pakistan. (Photo by Kristin Topich)

Remote region of northern Pakistan. (Photo by Kristin Topich)

Marketplace graffiti in the tribal region of Pakistan. (Photo by Kristin Topich)

The Rakaposhi Mountain in northern Pakistan. (Photo by Kristin Topich)

The inhospitable mountains of northern Pakistan. (Photo by Kristin Topich)

Housing development outside the Baltit Fort in the Hunza valley. (Photo by Kristin Topich)

The picturesque Karakoram, Himalayan, and Hindu Kush Mountain ranges converge in the Hunza valley. (Photo by Kristin Topich)

Agricultural life in northern Pakistan. (Photo by Kristin Topich)

CHAPTER 5

The Talibanization of Pakistan

The troubled tribal region and the continuing disruption in Pakistan led to a monumental decision that would alter the direction of the conflict. At a gathering on December 14 in South Waziristan, approximately 40 tribal leaders made the decision to pull their resources and forces together to form the Tehrik-e-Taliban Pakistan (TTP). This umbrella organization constituted dozens of Taliban-affiliated groups from throughout Pakistan.

Numerous factors helped to unify the tribes into formulating the TTP. The Pakistani military decision to launch several incursions into the Waziristan region was a prominent factor. (Most notably, Operation al-Mizan sent 70,000 to 80,000 troops into the tribal region for the first time in Pakistani history.) The operations by the military and the influx of foreign militants contributed to the collapse of the local political systems in significant portions of the tribal areas (Sheikh, 23). The conflict shifted into a religious struggle and not just a fight against the Pakistani military. In addition, the militants were motivated to take action by the growing presence of America in Pakistan. Evidence of this was the expansion of the U.S. embassy in Islamabad, the proliferation of private U.S. security firms like Blackwater into Pakistan, and the passage of the Kerry-Lugar aid bill, which was touted in the media as a way to diminish Pakistani sovereignty. The militants began to receive mainstream support within the country. The media was covering more controversial issues like the Cartoon Crisis, the mistreatment of detainees at Guantanamo Bay and Abu Ghraib, and the detention of Pakistani citizens at the hands of the United States. It was obvious that the disastrous ending of the siege of Lal Masjid played prominently into this decision. The perceived disregard for life and the aggressive nature of what the militants believed was a merciless operation inspired the decision to unite.

The Pakistani Taliban is highly decentralized with supporters being divided into three levels: core members, affiliate members, and sympathizers. When the groups converged, the overwhelming choice for the leadership position was Baitullah Mehsud. Several members of the Wazir tribe who had long-standing disputes with Mehsud attended the meeting and reconciled with their former advisory. Hafiz Gul Bahadur from North Waziristan was elected first deputy chief, or amir, while Maulana Fazlullah, head of the Taliban in the Swat region of the Northwest Frontier Province (now known as Khyber-Pukhtunkhwa), was elected general secretary. Several other former enemies of Baitullah Mehsud, including Malwi Nazir from South Waziristan and Faqir Mohammed from Bajaur, were represented at the initial meeting (Bergen, *Talibanistan*, 151–152). In addition, leaders from all seven agencies were in attendance. Representatives from the Northwest Frontier Province, including Swat, Malakand Buner, and Dera Ismail Khan, were also present. The regions were represented in a TTP shura, or council, located in Miram Shah, the administrative headquarters of North Waziristan (Norell, 36–40).

The TTP was by its very nature fragmented. The dynamics of tribal politics in Pakistan have always been factionalized. Rifts and disagreements that would hamper its effectiveness would emerge from the start. As early as 2008, factions led by Hafiz Gul Bahadur and Mullah Nazir broke with the main alliance only to reform with them again in 2009 (Sheikh, 25). Early on, the main points of contention were whether the group should attack Pakistani military and government targets and what relationship the group should have with foreign fighters. Some experts have coined the terms "good" and "bad" Taliban to designate whether the factions attempt to harm Pakistani interests. The disagreements between the factions would dominate the TTP for the foreseeable future.

THE IDEOLOGY OF THE PAKISTAN TALIBAN

The narrative put forth by representatives of the TTP is one of Islam being attacked by a hostile enemy. The duty of the Pakistani Taliban members is to protect God and his laws and defend sharia. In Mona Kanwal Sheikh's groundbreaking book *Guardians of God*, she outlines the ideological views of the TTP based on interview data gathered during the period 2007–2011. The concept of Islam being under attack was a constant narrative put forth by the TTP representatives. The conflict waged by the Taliban was perceived as defensive in nature as Muslims were attacked by the West and the Pakistani regime that was complicit in waging war against Islam. The jihad being waged was best explained as a war of reciprocity against the actions of the enemies of Islam.

According to Matiul Haq, a high-level TTP operative, in order to achieve a truly Islamic system, three conditions had to be met: "Muslims must unite against their enemy, they must boycott foreign systems, and initiate jihad against those who are trying to prevent it" (Sheikh, *Guardians of God*, 77). The current regime had to be defeated in order for Islam to flourish in Pakistan. Sheikh's interviews showed the intense admiration that the TTP had for the Afghan Taliban regime when they ruled from 1996 to 2001.

The leaders and followers interviewed believed that an unholy alliance of the unbelievers, the Jews, and the Christians were acting to destroy Islam. American aggression had ideological and doctrinal roots. The use of the term "crusade" by President Bush was used as a reference to validate the point. The militants interviewed stated that the defense of the madrassa system was vital. Several TTP backers stated that the destruction of the seminaries were a main focus of the American attacks. The paranoia of the militants was also witnessed in the fear of the immunization program sponsored by the Western interests. The Taliban believed that rather than eradicating polio the program was meant to make Pakistanis infertile. Western influence on areas like culture and education are also prominent attempts to weaken Islam.

The data collected by Professor Sheikh showed the wide gap between Pakistani Taliban perspectives on the West and the West perspective of the TTP. The view of the United States in the Muslim world in general and Pakistan in particular has only grown worse during the long and drawn out war on terror. It is also apparent that Western views of Islam in general and Pakistan specifically have deteriorated.

MILITANCY IN SWAT: THE SPREADING OF TALIBANIZATION

Swat is one of the seven divisions in the Malakand region in the Khyber-Pakhtunkhwa Province. The region is one of the main gateways into Afghanistan as well as being one of the most scenic and majestic areas in all of South Asia. Numerous commentators refer to it as the "Switzerland of Asia." Swat was an independent state under a prince or wali until the merger with Pakistan in 1969. In the subsequent two decades after decolonization, Swat saw infrastructural improvements, and the region remained peaceful and stable. Though geographically close to Afghanistan, Swat did not suffer any fallout from the Soviet campaign during the 1980s. Once the Taliban gained power in Afghanistan in 1996, many residents of Swat supported the movement, believing the regime to be freedom fighters who supported swift justice (Bergen, 289–291).

The Islamist party Jamaat-e-Islami (JI) emerged in the late 1980s in the Maidan area. Sufi Muhammad was an original supporter of the JI but broke with the group to form the Tehrik Nifaz-e-Shariat-e-Muhammadi or TNSM. Eventually, Muhammad began preaching for the imposition of sharia across the Swat valley, but the organization became more radical as it was clear that the Pakistani state would not respond to any of the militant's demands. In the militant stronghold of Malakand, the chant of sharia or martyrdom became commonplace. Eventually, the TNSM militants began blocking roads, and by 1994 clashes with the military became common. By the end of the year, the militants secured an agreement with authorities, stating that a justice-based system was allowed in Malakand, which the TNSM interpreted to mean sharia. This was perceived as a victory for Sufi Muhammad and the TNSM.

Following this victory, Sufi Muhammad saw his popularity decline. Numerous fighters had been killed in the clashes with the government, and shortly after the agreement was signed Muhammad went into hiding. Eventually, the success of the Taliban in Afghanistan rehabilitated his image among the Pashtuns in Swat. Pro-Taliban propaganda advocating an Islamic revolution streamed into Pakistan on a regular basis.

The monumental events of September 11 would alter the situation in Swat. Sufi Muhammad's status was elevated, and he quickly galvanized supporters into a tribal militia to assist the Taliban and Al Qaeda in Afghanistan against the American forces. Over 10,000 fighters from Swat, Buner, Dir, Shangla, and the tribal agencies of Mohmand and Bajaur entered the conflict in 2001. The militants were decimated, suffering tremendous casualties. As the remaining fighters attempted to cross back into Pakistan, Sufi Muhammad was arrested and imprisoned for seven years (Gall, 64–65). The TNSM was outlawed as militancy, at least temporarily, subsided.

The American-led war on terror with the full backing of the Musharraf regime meant that the Swat region would not calm for very long. A new leader for the militancy emerged in Sufi Muhammad's son-in-law, Maulana Fazlullah. A local cleric lacking serious religious credentials, Fazlullah started out as a Quantic instructor at the Mam Dheri mosque. By 2004, the dynamic in the region was changing, and Fazlullah began advocating threats against anyone not supporting the full implementation of sharia. His notoriety increased dramatically when he launched an unauthorized FM radio channel to spread his jihadist message across the region. His conservative rhetoric became popular with the Pashtun population in the border area, and he quickly became known as "Maulana Radio." His message was a combination of Salafis ideology and rabid anti-Americanism. Using the Taliban playbook from Afghanistan, Fazlullah discouraged families from sending female children to school and banned television watching and listening to music (Yousafzai, 115–117). Fazlullah burned TV sets, computers, and video cameras on the grounds that they encourage sin. He attempted to destroy Buddha relics and historic rock carvings in the Swat valley (again following the Afghan Taliban lead). One of the most notorious campaigns championed by the radical cleric was the attack of polio vaccinations in the Swat area. He called the operation a "conspiracy of the Jews and Christians to stunt the population growth of Muslims."

This once tranquil area became one of the most dangerous places in Pakistan during the subsequent years of the war on terror as the militants established multiple bases of support in the region. Violence became commonplace as random killings, kidnappings, and general brutality accelerated. The spreading chaos led to the displacement of thousands of citizens destroying the social fabric and economic well-being of the area.

The problems in the Swat area were multifaceted and grievances against the authorities were significant. Most notable was the corrupt justice system that failed to work in the interest of the citizens. Historically, the region was ruled by a wali system that was known for honesty and speedy justice for all citizens. Most disputes were settled in a matter of weeks, while under the Pakistan administration, litigation could drag on for years (Soherwordi & Khattak, 291–292). Legal procedures were beset with long delays, expectations of bribery, and a general decline of citizens' confidence in the system. One of the promises from the militants in Swat that was so appealing was a swift judicial system similar to what had been installed in Afghanistan under the Taliban regime. Clerics such as Maulana Fazlullah were able to deliver in this particular area.

In addition, the Pakistani authorities continued to make concessions to the militants during the first few years of the war on terror. By acting in a weakened and vulnerable state, the government strengthened the position of the TNSM and later Fazlullah's militant factions. Confidence in the state plummeted, and this, coupled with growing economic problems, gave the militants an opening that could be exploited. Instead of intervening to help the population in Swat, the Musharraf government made concessions and cut deals with extremists.

The social conditions in Swat were also stagnant as infrastructure and education development was stalled. Only five secondary schools were operational in 1969 when the population was approximately 200,000. Swat's population is now at two million, and no additional facilities have been constructed since (Khattak, 292). In addition, unemployment has continued to rise and land loss in a pervasive problem. The main base of recruitment for Maulana Fazlullah included the youth, the growing unemployed population, and landless tenants. It was neglect from both the government and the coalition of religious parties known as the MMA that also fed into the anger and eventual turn to militancy.

Segments of the population were attracted to the fiery rhetoric of clerics like Fazlullah, while others were persuaded that the foreign forces in Afghanistan posed an existential threat to Islam. The dire social and economic conditions also played into the extremists gaining support. The crisis at the Red Mosque during the summer of 2007 further helped to embolden the cause.

Some commentators believe that intimidation and fear played a major role in the radicalization of Swat. Maulana Fazlullah was skillful at co-opting criminals and thugs into his movement. This provided needed muscle for the cause, and the criminals were able to gain power and to further exploit the citizenry to maintain their activities. At no time did Fazlullah's fighters exceed the total of 5,000.

Following the Red Mosque disaster, Fazlullah gained more exposure, and his organization increased attacks against the Pakistani authorities as revenge for what happened at the Red Mosque. By late October 2007, the Musharraf government announced the first major operation to destroy Fazlullah's base in Swat, known as Operation Rah-e-Haq or "Just Path." Initially, the militants had control over 59 villages that were run in a Taliban-style fashion (Siddique, 32–35). Fazlullah's men controlled the government structure and police force. Initial attempts to capture the fighters failed, and many of the Pakistani soldiers sent to Swat deserted. The military changed tactics and started employing heavy artillery attacks that subsequently led the rebel forces to abandon facilities, and they withdrew to the mountains by the end of December.

As pressure intensified, Fazlullah fled into western Afghanistan. From this location, his fighters were able to successfully mount hit-and-run operations against Pakistani forces. By February 2008, the violence was taking a toll in the region. Several hundred people had been killed, including over 80 Pakistani soldiers. In addition, the fighting had displaced over 600,000 civilians. The conflict in Swat was now being labeled as the "Talibanization of Pakistan."

By the spring, negotiations between the militants and the Awami National Party (ANP) were underway. The recent provincial elections that had secured the ANP as the government in the region were viewed as a positive sign for peace prospects in the area. A first step toward peace was when the provincial authorities secured the release of Sufi Muhammad from prison after serving a seven-year stint. By late May, an accord was reached between the government and militants, which allowed for the implementation of Islamic law in Swat in exchange for the cessation of hostilities against agents of the state.

Both sides claimed victory, but the peace would be short lived. Within a month, Fazlullah demanded the withdrawal of Pakistani forces from Swat prior to his fighters disarming. This standoff led to Fazlullah renouncing the agreement. Skirmishes took place, and the Taliban fighters killed several ISI agents. The conflict resumed during the summer. Pakistani forces attacked Kabal, Matta, Bara, Bandai, Kooza Bandai, Khwazakhela, and several other towns in the Swat region. The Taliban intensified targeted killings of military personnel and destroyed the last remaining ski resort, located in the city of Malam Jabba.

The next year witnessed some of the most violent episodes in the history of Swat. Nearly two million citizens were forced to flee Swat for cities such as Islamabad and Peshawar. Numerous schools were burned down, shaving of beards was strictly forbidden, and music was banned from the area (Abbas, 150–151). With the exception of the town of Mingora, the Pakistani Taliban controlled all of Swat. The regional authorities attempted to negotiate with Sufi Muhammad, who in reality no longer commanded the respect of the militants. It was Maulana Fazlullah who controlled the fighters in the area.

Another temporary peace accord was signed in February 2009. The militants secured the implementation of sharia in Malakand. Shortly after the signing, Fazlullah complained of unwarranted harassment by the Pakistani authorities. Soon, several government officials and police officers were killed, and the Pakistani Taliban had moved into the Buner area, a mere 70 miles from the capital of Islamabad. As the militants continued to advance, taking the town of Daggar, they may have finally overextended their reach.

THE DEMISE OF MILITANCY IN THE SWAT REGION

Further negotiations aimed at convincing the militants to vacate areas where they had consolidated control in, such as Swat, Buner, and Dir, proved unsuccessful. Alarm both within Pakistan and from abroad led to a policy change by the Musharraf regime. By April 2009, the Pakistani military decided to launch their most ambitious operation thus far. Civilians were evacuated in advance with approximately 2.5 million people leaving the area close to militant control (Khattak, 289–290).

In the subsequent fighting from April to July 2009, the Pakistani military achieved substantial gains across the region. Numerous Taliban commanders were killed, along with approximately 1,300 fighters. In addition, hundreds of militants were arrested, including Taliban spokesman Muslim Khan. A large storage depot of arms was discovered at the recently captured town of Piochar. The militants were forced to flee from virtually all of the captured territories. Local fighters took up arms against the militants in support of the Pakistani operation. In numerous towns, including Mingora, Kanjoo, Matta, Kalam, Manglawar, and Khwazakhela, the bodies of dead militants were left in plain sight as a warning to potential Taliban recruits. As 2009 progressed, the violence subsided but sporadic attacks and occasional suicide missions did occur.

By the end of 2009, it was apparent that a significant shift away from the Pakistani Taliban in Swat had taken place. The brutal tactics of the Taliban militants, including the targeting of civilians and public executions, played a role in turning the population against the extremists (Khattak, 306–308). Polling data gathered in the region stated that less than 10 percent of the population was in favor of a Taliban-style governing structure.

In addition, the Pakistani military made a more sincere effort to sweep the Taliban out of the region. This was really the first time that the government forces entered an area with few restrictions placed on them. The entire Swat region was attacked during the operation putting the militants on the defensive very quickly. Civilians were given fair warning and had the opportunity to clear out of the area prior to the launching of the full-scale military operations.

The Awami National Party took power in the region during 2008 and failed to secure any concessions from the Pakistani Taliban. This sign of weakness only emboldened the militants and may have made them overconfident. More daring attacks were staged, and high-profile operations were undertaken. The growing concern from the ANP gave the military a clear green light to take more aggressive action in the area.

Following the Pakistani military success in Swat, the remaining Pakistani Taliban leadership fled to neighboring Afghanistan to seek sanctuary. Fazlullah promised renewed military operations in the Swat region. Many of his commanders were killed in the operation or imprisoned. Once the region was firmly under government control, it was a return to the status quo. The regime continually neglects the region, failing to provide for the basic needs of the citizens. Education is underfunded and the economy is in shambles from several years of intense fighting (Yousafzai, 194–196). Unemployment hit record levels, and the once prosperous tourist industry is nonexistent. These numerous problems continually plaguing the area make the population vulnerable to renewed extremist rhetoric.

SUICIDE ATTACKS AND SECTARIAN VIOLENCE: A NEW LEVEL OF TERROR EMERGES

One of the alarming side effects from the Swat operation was the exodus of militants out of the region and into the Punjab area. What eventually occurs was an outgrowth of the TTP into a regional faction known as the Punjabi Taliban. The most obvious difference was that the movement was Punjabi rather than Pashtun. These ethnically delineated lines are of course easily crossed and significant misperceptions can be drawn if the reader is not careful. The movements most commonly associated with the Punjabi Taliban include Sipah-e-Sahaba Pakistan (SSP), Lashkar Jhangvi (LeJ), and Jaish-e-Mohammad (JeM). It is worth noting that sectarian tensions are not new to Pakistan as numerous groups opposing the Shia and Sufi movements have been active since the 1980s to 1990s. This was a result of concerns over the impact the Khomeini Revolution in Iran would have on the South Asian region. For example, the roots of the SSP were centered in the anti-Iran hysterical following the rise of Khomeini. Confronting militants in this area was difficult as groups morph into new entities and changes were frequent. Ideologically, some of the terror groups were sectarian, while others had a regional emphasis or were more global in nature (International Crisis Group Report, May 2016, 3). As tension and violence in the region accelerated, many of these subgroups jumped on the TTP bandwagon. In Punjab, sectarian violence and the ultimate destruction of the Shia was the centerpiece of the ideology. LeJ was the most notorious anti-Shia faction and was involved in high-profile attacks, such as the bombing of the Karachi Sheraton Hotel in May 2002. The JeM was more centered on the Kashmiri struggle but also targeted Westerners and was responsible for the Daniel Pearl execution in 2002. Many of the organizations collaborated with Al Qaeda at times in planning and carrying out missions against Western targets.

The concept of suicide bombing was something previously unheard of in Pakistan. The first suicide attack actually dates back to 1995, when a truck bomb was rammed into the Egyptian embassy in Islamabad, killing 14 people. It was not until the ouster of the Taliban in late 2001 that the tactic would be implemented on a periodic basis in the Afghanistan-Pakistan theater of the war on terror.

With the undertaking of full-fledged war in Afghanistan and Pakistan, many Islamic militants perceived the engagement as a civilizational battle for the survival of the faith. Mark Juergensmeyer coined this definition as a classic case of cosmic war: a struggle for the defense of a specific identity that can only be won in a different time period because of the perceptible disadvantage on the battle field. "To the Taliban dogma, western presence in both Afghanistan and Pakistan is likely to be considered a threat to the Islamic identity" (Lanche, 2). In such a struggle, the terrorists rationalize the use of suicide missions as justifiable. Jihadist rhetoric states that anything representing or helping the enemy can be targeted, including NATO convoys, civilians, moderate clerics, and agents of the government. An additional troubling trend is when the targets and the attackers share the same faith. This is more commonplace as the Pakistani violence has become much more sectarian in nature. Religion is usually coupled with other societal ills, such as frustration, helplessness, or personal grievances, to create a breeding ground for extremist action, such as suicide missions (Khan, "Analyzing Suicide Attacks in Pakistan," 2).

The goal is still to a significant degree to use suicide attacks to gain the attention of the population, government, and media. When the images of death and destruction become a regular occurrence because of suicide missions, the society is put into a perpetual state of fear and anxiety. As the military responds in a harsh way, the population will eventually no longer trust their leaders and the goals they pursue.

During the first few years of the war on terror, suicide missions in Pakistan were rare, with the first episode occurring in Karachi in 2002. With the revival of the Taliban movement in 2004, the numbers started to increase. In 2005, 136 attacks occurred, while 137 missions were carried out in 2007. The casualty account was 1,100 in 2006, but rose to 1,730 by 2007. By this time, conventional means of combatting Western forces had been for the most part futile. According to the theory of Mia Bloom, suicide bombing only occurs during the second phase of a conflict after the insurgents have unsuccessfully engaged more conventional means (Lanche, 4). Many scholars claim that by 2007 the Pakistani state had shifted from a country suffering increasing terrorist attacks to a country in a state of civil war (University of Chicago Database on Suicide Attacks).

With numerous extremist organizations in competition with each other, suicide bombing became a sort of competition of factions trying to outdo one another (Lanche, 4). Rival Pakistani Taliban factions were engaged in assassinations and random acts of violence against each other. Another devastating aspect of this acceleration of violence was a tendency to target clerics, who opposed the use of suicide missions, as well as tribal leaders, who spoke out against the tactic.

Pakistani Taliban leader Baitullah Mehsud was adamant in stating the importance of suicide bombers, sometimes referred to as fidayeen. Mehsud stated that suicide bombers could never be defeated. According to Imtiaz Gul, "When these fidayeen are told that hoors (beautiful girls) are waiting, looking out of the window in paradise to embrace them, these youngsters (became so impatient) they all clamor to be the first to go on a mission. They want to see how many "hoors" out there are really waiting for them in paradise (Gul, "The Al Qaeda Connection," 136). Mehsud had stated the suicide bombers were the TTP's atom bombs. Clear evidence emerged that suicide bomb factories were present in the South Waziristan city of Spinkai. Children as young as nine years of age were recruited by the TTP to be martyrs in suicide missions. Film footage recovered by the Pakistani military showed children being instructed in suicide training. Extensive brainwashing of the young students occurred while they were at the rural madrassas. According to the account from one would-be recruit, "My teacher told me I would rocket into paradise once I press the button" (Gul, 137). TTP leader Mullah Fazlullah spoke to supporters stating the option to sacrifice oneself as a blessing from God and those conducting the sacrifices as especially pious. Fazlullah elaborated, "the willingness to die—sacrifice oneself—is interpreted as evidence of true devotion" (Sheikh, 148). The martyrdom concept became the ultimate sacrifice to fight against satanic powers and unbelief. The human sacrifice of suicide is considered more powerful than the enemies' use of weaponry, according to TTP spokesperson Azam Tariq.

Militant leaders interviewed about the role of suicide tactics explained the justification of such missions. Muslim Khan, the infamous "Butcher of Swat," claimed in a conversation with political scientist Mona Sheikh that "he had no doubt that they were legitimate means not only in a situation of desperation but also in other non-defensive situations, so long as they were accompanied by the right intention (*niyat*): to fight along the path of God and pave the way for His system" (Sheikh, 73). He further elaborated that "extraordinary measures such as suicide or self-sacrifice primarily by linking them to the importance of defending the Islamic system" (74).

Professor Sheikh also interviewed Matiul Haq, the son of Sufi Muhammad, who was the founder of the TNSM in the Swat valley. He was adamant that the Pakistani Taliban missions were not suicide but self-sacrifice. This point of clarity was significant because suicide is forbidden in Islam. If the intent of the operation is to fight the enemies of God, then it is considered legitimate. During Sheikh's interview with Haq, he stated: "Fidayeen attacks against the *kafir* are completely legal, not only legal in Islam but also dominant in Islam. But when Muslims use this method against other Muslims, then it is haram. I am saying that in a confrontation with a kafir, you cannot call these suicide attacks. When Muslims attach bombs to their bodies and go to the kuffar, then we call it fidayeen in our language. This is completely justified in the Quran and the Hadith . . ." (76).

Sheikh also interviewed Khalifa Qayum, a senior member of the anti-Shia SSP. He rejected suicide operations as unlawful according to Islam, but also stated that if your life is over anyway, you might as well take the enemy with you. He further stated that if one is cornered like a desperate cat, this would not be categorized as suicide (113).

Finally, Professor Sheikh interviewed Muhammad Yahya Mujahid, a member of Lashkar-e-Taiba (LeT). He stated that the legitimacy of suicide attacks depended on the location of the attack. His view was that if a person blows himself up in a military installation, the case is different from a person who blows himself up among civilians. Mujahid also stated that attacks in Muslim countries should not target other Muslims.

For the most part, two elements were important in suicide training: jackets for suicide strikes and IEDs. Most of the expert trainers were members of Al Qaeda. The apparent success of such tactics in the Iraq war probably impacted the decision to begin utilization of suicide missions in both Afghanistan and Pakistan.

The success of suicide attacks has led to the tactic being utilized countrywide. It is now common to hear of attacks in remote tribal regions and major urban centers throughout Pakistan. The porous borders and lack of effective police and security personal make it nearly impossible to combat suicide missions. The main center of this violence still occurs in the NWFP, which has approximately 40 percent of all attacks, followed by the Punjab region with slightly over 20 percent. The FATA region is the third most prominent region with 15 percent. More recently, urban centers have become more serious targets for suicide attacks.

Overall, suicide missions focus on the Pakistani state, the U.S. presence in the region, or sectarian opposition to the militants. Terrorist groups perceive the Pakistani state as aggressively pursuing militants because more substantial military operations have been conducted in recent years. The lethal nature of the drone operations makes the United States an obvious target for suicide attacks. The most alarming recent trend has been in the realm of sectarian attacks, which seem to be the most indiscriminate (Khan, 3–4). Martyrdom missions have become more attractive to the younger cohort, especially following high-profile events like the massacre by the Pakistani military at the Lal Masjid compound.

THE RETURN OF BENAZIR BHUTTO

The volatile year of 2007 provided the conditions in which the iconic two-time leader of Pakistan, Benazir Bhutto, could make a move toward returning to power in Pakistan. Her Pakistan People's Party (PPP) did the best job of any movement in Pakistani history of espousing a democratic political culture. The PPP was in reality the only national party in Pakistani history consistently garnering the support of one-third of the electorate. Bhutto's continuous battles with the military and intelligence establishment hampered her throughout her political career and would eventually prove deadly.

Bhutto would attempt to reenter the scene in Pakistan at one of the most chaotic times in the country's history. The regime of Pervez Musharraf continued to lose legitimacy, and Islamic militancy was at an all-time high. Bhutto's platform included a return to true democratic principles and civil society (including civilian rule), as well as halting Pakistan's drift toward state failure. She claimed to have learned from past blunders, and her troubles with endemic corruption and mismanagement seemed to be ancient history. The ground swell of support for her return was significant (Gall, 174–175).

The Bhutto family has endured tragedy and heartbreak for decades. First, the patriarch of the family, Zulfikar Ali Bhutto, was executed on trumped-up charges at the hands of Zia-ul-Haq in 1979. Following this was the mysterious poisoning death of Benazir's youngest brother Shahnawaz in 1985. Finally, 11 years later, Murtaza was killed in a police shootout in Karachi in what seemed to be a set-up assassination. The family it seemed could not escape death and despair.

The United States had put a tremendous amount of effort behind President Musharraf and deliberately ignored any overtures from Bhutto or her representatives. However, sometime in 2006, the Bush administration started to cautiously reevaluate Pakistani policy. The idea of a

Musharraf-Bhutto coalition of some sorts was in the works. The British government was involved in the negotiations that would allow Bhutto to return to Pakistan with all corruption charges being dropped. Furthermore, she could compete in the next election cycle, but, if victorious, would share power with Musharraf. The goal of the policy change was to try and rehabilitate the regime and give the government a boost of needed legitimacy. Western powers also believed this would strengthen Pakistan in the fight against terrorism and possibly help to mobilize mass support. The Taliban's signs of strength undoubtedly played into this decision.

Once details of the negotiations were released, several parties involved were clearly frustrated. Members of Bhutto's PPP believed that dealing with the reprehensible Musharraf was bad politically and also dangerous. Bhutto's contemporary rival, Nawaz Sharif, was also dismayed over the deal because it became clear that he and his party would be the odd man out. Sharif believed that Bhutto was going to build a united front with him to topple the highly unpopular general. Critics in the media and amongst civil society organizations wondered whether Bhutto was willing to do anything to gain a final chance of regaining power. In reality, this was probably the last best chance for Benazir Bhutto to regain her political footing inside of Pakistan. Her image would be vastly improved in the international community and, by working with Musharraf, she might be in a better strategic position with the military. Ultimately, America's support for Musharraf made this the only viable option for Bhutto.

Musharraf was walking a tightrope, and this was the best move for him to extend his time as a leader. A major part of the rehabilitation that Musharraf was undertaking was the decision to shed his uniform and become a truly civilian leader. Agreeing to free and fair elections was the next step in the process. Finally, by sharing power with parliament and the prime minister, he could strengthen his legitimacy and subsequently guarantee his survival (Rashid, 386–387).

Benazir Bhutto's triumphant return to Pakistan occurred on October 18, 2007. Her plane landed at Jinnah International Airport in Karachi. The lengthy caravan would take nine hours to travel less than six miles. The atmosphere was jubilant as citizens felt hope for Pakistan's future for the first time in several years (Rashid, 37–38). Power outages along the caravan route were suspicious and later an investigation confirmed that this was a malicious attempt to keep Benazir from getting too much exposure in the media. More damaging was the fact that jammers designed to block cell phone signals that could detonate a bomb from a remote location were not functioning properly.

The worst fears of Bhutto's security team rang true as suicide attacks struck the convoy. Bhutto was in her vehicle at the time of the detonation and protected by two cordons of security personal. The outer core was breached, but the inner core remained intact. The impact was devastating, and the carnage unspeakable. Three police vans were totally destroyed and over twenty officers killed on impact. In all, 139 people were killed with a high proportion of the dead being security and law enforcement personal. In addition, over 500 people were wounded in what would be labeled the worst terrorist attacks in the nation's history (Farwell, 124). Bhutto's team quickly rushed her to the Bhutto residence, Bilawal House.

Suspicion quickly turned to the Pakistan Taliban leader Baitullah Mehsud. He had previously threatened Bhutto if she attempted to return to Pakistan. Mehsud was quick to deny responsibility for the carnage and subsequently sent several follow-up messages to Bhutto proclaiming his innocence. Other Pakistan government officials were more generic, blaming the militancy. Benazir's husband told reporters from Dubai that Musharraf's intelligence agents bore responsibility for the violence. Musharraf quickly condemned the attack, promising to launch a thorough investigation.

Bhutto's perspective was on the mark. She proclaimed that this was an attack on democracy. Her condemnation targeted Al Qaeda, but she also criticized the government for not taking the proper steps to secure the safety of her entourage. Any trust between the two was shattered at that moment.

To complicate the situation further, the two-time former prime minister Nawaz Sharif returned to the country on November 25 after a seven-year exile. The former leader had been refused entry into Pakistan earlier in the year and remained in Saudi Arabia. Musharraf had privately met with King Abdullah, pleading with him to not allow Sharif to leave the emirate. The Saudi monarch refused the request and Sharif was now returning to politics (Fair, 114).

The investigation uncovered that there were two probable attackers who used explosives and ball bearings associated more with security personal rather than militants. It pointed to a carefully laid out plan with organizational involvement. The financial resources needed for such an attack eliminated the possibility of a solo lone wolf operative. Indian security expert Bahukutumbi Raman speculates that the bombers may have even been part of the security team guarding Bhutto (Farwell, 125).

Bhutto's team quickly asserted that several current and former members of Musharraf's government should be investigated in regard to the attack. Former ISI head Hamid Gul, retired general Ejaz Shah, and Musharraf political ally Chaudhry Pervez Elahi were all publicly named as individuals of interest by Bhutto's investigation team. Criticism was also leveled at Musharraf because of his refusal to allow private cars or vehicles equipped with tinted windows. In addition, the regime did not provide the jammers that could have proven invaluable in countering remote control devices so common in suicide missions. Although with the slow pace of the convoy, it is actually unlikely that jammers could have helped stop this particular attack. Bhutto's team may have been thinking about preventative measures to counter future attacks. It is worth noting that jamming technology used by Musharraf back in 2003 probably saved his life when suicide attackers attempted to blow up his vehicle on two separate occasions. Many argue that the fact that not only would Musharraf not provide such technology for Bhutto, but he would not even allow it to be purchased privately makes him complacent in her death two months later. The Musharraf regime also denied visas for security firms that Bhutto wanted to hire for protection. Both Blackwater as well as ArmorGroup (a London-based firm) had significant experience in protecting VIPs and diplomats. No reason was given by the government as to why the visas were denied. Undoubtedly, the failure to acquire jammers was the most vital mistake made by the Bhutto security team. Bhutto eventually turned to the Iraqi president to acquire the jamming devices. By all accounts, the Pakistani government failed miserably in its efforts to protect the former head of state. This mistake would ultimately prove fatal for Bhutto and would also cost Musharraf any future role in the Pakistani government. Members of Bhutto's entourage also stated that intelligence provided by the United Arab Emirates pointed to several potential plots to assassinate her. This information had been passed on to Musharraf but no action was taken.

Ultimately, Musharraf's Machiavellian ways eventually emerged as he attempted to double cross the United States and Benazir Bhutto. The leaders had met face-to-face in London and Dubai, and several stipulations were laid out with American approval. Musharraf decided to renege on several key parts, including the appointment of a neutral government, the appointment of an independent electoral commission, and the disbanding of local government officials that were partial to the general (Rashid, 377). The U.S. position was problematic. Musharraf was extremely vital in the continued war on terror, and the Bush administration made the decision not to amp up additional pressure on Musharraf. According to some aids close to Bhutto, U.S. vice president Dick Cheney was adamant that Bhutto make further concessions and that Musharraf's position was to be maintained. The State Department uncovered evidence that Musharraf was planning to rig the elections with the help of the ISI. High-level meetings and calls to Bhutto encouraged her to continue on the path of collaboration with Musharraf. The State Department South Asian Head Richard Boucher and U.S. deputy secretary of state John Negroponte both held private meetings in Islamabad encouraging Bhutto's cooperation.

From the time of Bhutto's arrival back in Pakistan until her tragic assassination, danger and death hounded her. Journalist Christina Lamb was the correspondent most closely connected to Bhutto. She stated that Bhutto knew the apparent dangers, but the crowds of cheering women and children who had come out from all over Pakistan to attend her rallies inspired her to continue and, at times, take unwise risks. She was determined and refused to use the bulletproof shield that could have been placed around her vehicle to provide added protection. Some commentators believed she put an undue burden on those close to her by not taking the precautious. Musharraf claimed to have warned Bhutto to avoid public rallies and appearances. Critics claim Musharraf was simply trying to derail her growing momentum leading up to the elections.

Bhutto's political consultant Siegel was gravely concerned for her safety. The intense level of animosity regarding the former leader was high in some circles. He advised Bhutto to wage the campaign without putting herself in harm's way; this was not Benazir's style. She loved being with the people, and the energy level and excitement surrounding her campaign appearances was unbelievable. Everyone around her knew that this life and death struggle was about something bigger than individual safety; it was about the future of democracy in Pakistan (Farwell, 127–128). It is still worth noting that after the Karachi attack in October, she should have known how serious the threats would be. Many argue for the sake of Pakistan's future, she should have been more cautious in her campaigning.

Musharraf was concerned that the situation was spiraling out of control. On November 3, he delivered a national address in which he announced the suspension of the Pakistani Constitution. He claimed that the threat from Islamic extremism was growing and that action needed to be taken. A provisional constitutional order was put into place to guarantee the security and stability of the state. Later statements by Musharraf that he had consulted with and received the approval of key military leaders, cabinet officials, and the hierarchy of the ISI were rebuffed by nearly everyone he claimed to have solicited advice from. Musharraf was clearly unable to articulate the rationale behind this move, and his public relations campaign to secure support behind the decision was a disaster. Journalist Gretchen Peters stated, "the general had strayed into the twilight zone." He had written his own speech, which shifted from Urdu to English for no apparent reason. During his address, he viciously attacked the judiciary that had become his most formidable enemy in the past year (Farwell, 132). Musharraf had twice fired chief justice Chaudhry, and he took this opportunity to denounce the judiciary for its corruption, abuse, and failure to help in the fight against extremism. The general went into an offensive mode, compiling an enemy list and surrounding key governmental buildings, including the judicial offices, with security personnel. Individuals suspected of opposing Musharraf were detained without formal charges being brought. Even though he tried to deny it, Musharraf had in fact declared martial law.

Opposition mounted quickly as lawyers took to the streets again by the thousands. Several key newspapers and media outlets expressed shock and disbelief that such actions were taken by Musharraf without any serious crisis underway. The police used harsh methods to violently suppress the mounting protesters. Human rights activist Asma Jehangir, political opposition leaders, and celebrity Imran Khan were among those detained by authorities. Key members of the judiciary refused to acknowledge the validity of Musharraf's declaration of a national emergency (Shah, 219–220). Numerous supporters began to distance themselves from the general, who seemed to be losing his grip on reality. The refusal of the media to side with Musharraf was especially damaging. Musharraf made the monumental move of handing the military reins over to General Ashfaq Kayani on December 3. This ended a 46-year military career. He hoped that no matter what his former comrade-in-arms would stand by him, but this was not to be the case later on. Anti-Musharraf elements went as far as setting up alternative transmissions from Dubai. The civil society movement that had emerged earlier in the year remained relevant and was eager to act when needed.

For her part, Benazir Bhutto handled the crisis in a calm and composed manner. She quickly requested the lifting of the state of emergency, and she stayed focused and on message. She sensed that public opinion was clearly shifting away from Musharraf, but her moves were calculated and rational and made her look like a candidate ready to regain the reins of power. The strategy of shifting momentum in her direction along with capitalizing on favorable public opinion trends was a winning combination. Musharraf's blunder took a situation in which Bhutto was a potential coalition partner and turned it into an adversarial crisis situation (Gall, 177–178).

Bhutto decided to challenge the general, calling on him to lift the media bans, restore the constitution, and resign from the army. A deadline was set for November 15. Furthermore, elections were to be held by January 15 or a 220-mile long march would be orchestrated from Lahore to Islamabad. This statement issued at a press conference meant that Bhutto was planning a popular uprising against the regime. Following the press conference, Musharraf retaliated by placing her under house arrest. She was forbidden from holding any further press conferences, and the neighborhood surrounding her house was cordoned off.

Several individuals working with Benazir Bhutto claim she was securing evidence about the potential electoral fraud in the time leading up to her death. She believed that the ruling Pakistan Muslim League or the Qaid-e-Azam faction was being set up to secure the victory. She had left a letter stating that if she died, Musharraf was to blame for refusing to provide adequate security for her team, while she was on the election trail. As the campaign progressed, she spoke more openly and aggressively about the electoral plans being orchestrated by Musharraf. Bhutto's meeting with Afghan president Hamid Karzai the morning of her assassination was dominated by her frustration over the rigging of the electoral process.

She had been told repeatedly that the ISI had definitive plans to do whatever was necessary to ensure that a free and fair process did not occur. Karzai greatly admired Bhutto, and her death dealt a devastating blow to cooperation between the two countries.

THE DEATH OF AN ICON

On December 27, Benazir Bhutto addressed a crowd of 5,000-8,000 supporters at the Liaquat Bagh in Rawalpindi. Ironically, the location was named after Pakistan's first prime minister, who had been killed by an assassin in the same location in 1951. This is also the location that houses the Pakistan Army Headquarters. The local police had a plan to form a box formation around her vehicle to protect against an attack, but that plan for some unknown reason was not carried out. The security detail was supposed to include close to 1,400 police officers and everything from rooftop snipers to elaborate metal detectors. The area had been swept for explosives the morning of her scheduled speech.

During the event, the security focus seemed to be on crowd control rather than protection. It was clearly apparent that the number of police and the roles they would play were much different than promised. Toward the end of the event, the majority of the security team disappeared, leaving the former prime minister vulnerable. Her small security team of 14 was the main line of protection by the time of the attack. In Bhutto's final speech, she deplored the violence that was engulfing her country and pleaded with the citizens to reject extremism. She said that only the democratic process could save the nation (Jalal, 349). Prior to the event, the Pakistani ISI general Nadeem Taj had warned her to cancel the speech for fear of a potential attack. Bhutto's security advisor Rehman Malik did not take the warning seriously and no additional precautious were put into place.

As the event came to a close, Bhutto loaded into her armored Toyota Land Cruiser and attempted to drive through the crowded area. Police had blocked an expected left hand turn, forcing the vehicle to veer right. As the path forward was blocked to a near standstill, she decided to lift her head out of the sunroof to wave to supporters. The police watched passively, while the crowd pushed forward toward Bhutto's vehicle. It is still uncertain as to who prevented the Cruiser from moving forward, but the result was tragic. A large group of supporters gathered around the vehicle when a clean-shaven young man wearing a white shirt, a sleeveless dark waistcoat, and rimless dark sunglasses edged his way closer to the Toyota. "He was described as having a normal haircut, and it was speculated that his age was between twenty two and twenty five" (Farwell, 139). Released footage from the BBC shows the gunman quickly opening fire in the direction of the Cruiser, sending three shots at Bhutto. Seconds later, a suicide bomber detonated a charge, creating mass carnage and chaos.

The explosive weighed four to five kilograms and was wrapped with hundreds of ball bearings. Over one hundred people were wounded, and the death toll was 28. Bhutto was rushed to Rawalpindi General Hospital approximately two miles from the location of the attack where she was pronounced dead by a team of attending physicians. The Pakistani Information Ministry quickly identified Benazir's cause of death as a wound to the neck. Within a few hours, the story had changed with officials claiming she had hit her head against the lever of her vehicle's sunroof while attempting to duck. The Pakistani officials changed their story for the third time, later claiming that shrapnel had caused her death. Unbelievably, a fourth account was issued, stating that the skull fracture was sustained by either the fall against the sunroof or when she ducked. The PPP information secretary claimed that there were clear bullet injuries to the head.

Conspiracy theories abound about multiple sharpshooters, but no clear evidence collaborates this assertion. What is certain is that the government destroyed forensic evidence by hosing down the blast scene. Furthermore, according to the findings of an inquiry conducted by the United Nations that were released in April 2010, which stated, "The collection of 23 pieces of evidence was manifestly inadequate in a case that should have resulted in thousands . . . it also found that City Police Chief Saud Aziz impeded investigators from conducting on-site investigations until two full days after the assassination" (UN News Centre—"UN report on Bhutto Murder finds Pakistani officials failed profoundly" 1). In addition, the decision by Aziz not to conduct an autopsy (something that is usually legally mandatory) raised further suspicion. No forensic pathologist signed the final medical report following her death. Ultimately, it is not certain whether a bullet or the bomb blast caused her death.

Anger in Pakistan over the assassination was intense. Musharraf's initial response was callous, stating that he had warned her not to go to Rawalpindi because of intelligence reports from what he called "friends in the Gulf States" (supposedly Saudi Arabia and the United Arab Emirates) that certain groups were planning action against her. Musharraf also claimed that his security personal had specifically warned her not to expose herself by standing through her armored car's escape hatch to wave to crowds. Hoping to calm emotions, Musharraf declared a three-day period of mourning. His tactic became one of trying to coup Bhutto's goals of fighting terrorism and promoting democracy. This ploy did not work. Grief and suspicion turned to rage as the authorities quickly and haphazardly cleared the bombing site of any potential evidence by thoroughly hosing down the venue and destroying evidence. The authorities claimed that this was necessary because vultures and crows were gathering around the location. Eyewitness accounts during the aftermath did not corroborate the government's story. When earlier assassination attempts were carried out against Musharraf, the crime scene was sealed and combed for clues. The situation was very different with the Bhutto case. Few photos were taken, and all of the routine practices usually carried out at such a crime scene were ignored. Additionally, physicians at the hospital were instructed to change statements after being briefed by government officials. (Later authorities from Scotland Yard were brought in, but given limited latitude in the investigation.) Musharraf failed to ensure a comprehensive security plan to protect his rival, which in turn led her to depend on the PPP for her protection. The party did have a group of enthusiastic volunteers known as Jaan Nisaar Benazir or "those willing to give their lives for Benazir." Unfortunately, they were poorly trained and disorganized, lacking the expertise needed to help prevent the tragedy from unfolding. Ultimately, the government's failure helped to erode Musharraf's credibility after the assassination.

For several days following the assassination, chaos engulfed the region as government offices, banks, railway stations, and container trucks were burned and destroyed. Several dozen people were killed in the mayhem. Musharraf decided to temporary push back the election until February 18. The government was quick to blame the Pakistani Taliban leadership for the assassination. In particular, Baitullah Mehsud was labeled as the mastermind behind Bhutto's death, and the authorities released a telephone transcript that provided evidence of his involvement. Several experts doubt the authenticity of the transcript, and the later to-be-released conversations. Over 400 security personnel had been killed by suicide bombings in 2007 alone, and not one person had been captured or charged for the bombings. Now, as journalist Ahmed Rashid states, "the public was expected to believe that the military had resolved the Bhutto murder in a couple of days, blaming the very man with whom the ISI had struck a peace deal earlier in the year. Reinforcing this sense of disbelief and anger at the government was Musharraf's failure to show any remorse over Bhutto's death" (379). Eventually, a young teen boy was detained by authorities near the Afghan border, and he confessed to the authorities that Mehsud was the person responsible for the attack, which was planned in South Waziristan.

In the days following the assassination, Musharraf seemed to become unraveled. He believed his connection with the military, along with support of the religious community and his independence from the United States, made him the right man to continue to take on terrorism in Pakistan. The news for Musharraf went from bad to worse as an e-mail written by Benazir stating that Musharraf should be held responsible should she be assassinated. The general was surprised and struggled with formulating an adequate response. Musharraf became more isolated from his advisors and was turning to a smaller cohort of mostly current or former military aides rather than individuals who could help in the realm of political affairs. The longer he stayed in power, the more convinced he became about it being God's destiny that he lead Pakistan. By the time of Benazir Bhutto's assassination, the general had been in power for eight years. Musharraf's limited attempts to mobilize support in the post-assassination period show that his grip on reality might have been slipping.

The narrative conveyed by the Pakistani authorities stressed that the country was the real victim with Bhutto's assassination. The violent extremism was attacking the country, and the Musharraf regime would tackle the problem while continuing to promote democracy. Finally, the perpetrators would be tracked down, and justice would be served. In addition, the regime claimed that they did not know about the security shortcomings because the line of communication between the Bhutto team and the government was inadequate. This narrative was of course problematic because it was clearly evident that Bhutto had been pleading with the authorities to increase security virtually from the day she arrived back in Pakistan in late October.

Musharraf needed to desperately deflect the blame from him. He did not grasp that the assassination had severely harmed his credibility. Key leaders in the PPP and numerous commentators and journalists suspected that either Musharraf directly or some of his key advisors were involved in the assassination plot. By late January, close to two-thirds of Pakistani citizens believed the government had a role in the death of Benazir Bhutto. Not surprisingly, the job approval rating for Musharraf hit an all-time low as over 70 percent of the citizens polled had an unfavorable view of Musharraf (Abbas, 136–137).

Musharraf's political future sustained a fatal wound with the assassination of Benazir Bhutto. The general seemed uncertain as to what direction to take, and this political paralysis led to growing paranoia and isolation. Numerous journalists and PPP members believed that the ISI and the Muslim League had planned to manipulate the upcoming elections. The assassination of Bhutto made such rigging virtually impossible. After his party was overwhelmingly defeated in the February elections, Musharraf seemed totally surprised. He did not understand the magnitude of the assassination. The general had a small inner circle dominated by yes men who showered him with praise and good news. This is a characteristic of politicians who believe themselves to be too self-important.

General Cheema branded the assassination an "act of terrorism" and not just a normal criminal case. The military quickly labeled Al Qaeda and their associates, the Pakistani Taliban. The names of Baitullah Mehsud and Maulana Fazlullah were quickly targeted as the main conspirators. The 34-year-old Mehsud was selected as the leader of the TTP in late 2007. The Pakistani authorities released a purported interception of a conversation between Mehsud and one of his associates. During the press conference, the authorities claimed to have "irrefutable evidence that al-Qaeda, its network, and its cohorts are trying to destabilize Pakistan which is in the forefront of war against terrorism. They are systematically targeting our state institutions in order to destabilize the country" (Farwell, 178). The government never released an authenticated tape of the conversation, raising doubts about the authenticity. Journalists questioned how the call had been taped, which was answered that it was a "secret technical matter." Further doubt about the credibility of this narrative was raised because of how scripted the conversation sounded. The final shadow of doubt was cast when a Pakistani journalist traveled to Makeen, South Waziristan, to see if the story could be checked out, only to find that the town had no phone service (Schmidle, 212–213). It is not certain that the conversation ever took place.

The public relations campaign launched against the TTP and Mehsud was one of the earliest attempts by the Pakistani authorities to call out the militants in such specific terms. The Tehrik-i-Taliban-Pakistan (TTP) was a known entity, and a scenario in which they would have attempted to assassinate Bhutto seemed very plausible. Investigations into terrorist attacks during 2007 found that youngsters from the Mehsud tribe of Waziristan carried out the vast majority of suicide attacks (Hussain, 141–142). This evidence would make it much easier to pursue Baitullah Mehsud in connection to the Bhutto assassination.

It was hoped that this explanation could help strengthen Musharraf's position with the Pakistani public. The vast terrorist conspiracy attempting to bring down the Pakistani state would enforce his hard-line stance in the fight against extremism. The TTP in collusion with Al Qaeda would not stop its relentless attacks against Pakistan. The authorities claimed that Bhutto was near the top of the Al Qaeda hit list. The emphasis on the foreign connection was played up in this narrative. Linking Mehsud to the assassination was an effective strategy in theory because giving a target a specific enemy usually resonates with the public. Part of the problem with the story was that if the government could effectively intercept and record a conversation with Mehsud so quickly, why could they not apprehend him? It was also confirmed that Mehsud had at times worked with the Pakistani military authorities (*Dawn*, January 14, 2008). Furthermore, during the recording, Bhutto is never mentioned by name, and Mehsud did not seem to know that his men were involved (even having to ask their names). Authorities claim Mehsud had met with the assassin Saeed Alias Bilal. If that were the case, he would have known more of the details and of course would have known his name. The United Nations Commission also threw doubt about whether Mehsud was involved. Musharraf seemed to want to treat Mehsud as a political figure to be dealt with rather than a criminal and terrorist. Reports of Mehsud using children as young as 11 for suicide attacks and his policy of buying and selling children should have been played up more effectively in the media. A clear antiterrorism campaign with the TTP and Mehsud on center stage should have been utilized after the death of Bhutto. Critics argue that a much more intense multimedia campaign was needed to discredit the extremist and rally support behind Musharraf. It would take until March 2008 for authorities to formally charge Mehsud with planning the attack on Bhutto. The formal process of charging the leader of the TTP did not lead to an intense attempt to apprehend him. Mehsud denied any involvement in the assassination plot. According to a close associate of the TTP leader, he is reported to have said, "Why on earth would we kill her? We had no enmity with her and more importantly she has done no wrong to us." In a bizarre turn of events, the authorities actually negotiated a peace agreement with him in order to secure the release of hostages that were being held in the tribal region (Woods, 156). However, these attacks against the TTP and Mehsud had limited success. Too much doubt and suspicion was raised about Musharraf's intentions. It did not help matters that the United States came out very quickly and supported the Pakistani government's story line. Experts from Homeland Security, the Brookings Institute, and close regional advisors to President Obama fell in line to back the standard view from the Pakistani administration. In addition, Musharraf did not show any humility in discussing the death of the former prime minister. When interviewed in Western media regarding the Bhutto assassination, Musharraf went to the extreme of blaming her for partaking in reckless behavior.

The e-mail message written by Bhutto that blamed Musharraf if she was to be killed was damaging beyond repair. The fact that the government did not show good faith in trying to provide adequate security for Benazir once she returned in October also helped to fuel that speculation. Additionally, Musharraf's public relations team did not put together a coherent strategy to counter the accusations about the regime's role in the assassination. Instead of investigating any potential ties between the assassins, the military, and the intelligence community in Pakistan, Musharraf chose to defend and shield them from any blame. Bhutto had laid the groundwork for a lengthy report condemning the regime and the ISI that was to be released to key American politicians with close connections to U.S.-Pakistani relations.

The investigation into the assassination was controversial. The Pakistani government wanted Scotland Yard to lead the inquiry, while the PPP wanted the United Nations. Musharraf was also adamant that only the cause of Bhutto's death and not the circumstances surrounding it would be analyzed. The Pakistani media and opposition parties were critical of Musharraf's decision, claiming that he was trying to whitewash the investigation. Leading international figures, including then senator Hillary Clinton, called for an international investigation. Her statement was highly critical of the Musharraf administration that she claimed lacked any credibility (Farwell, 158). Legal experts in Pakistan demanded an independent investigation chaired by deposed Supreme Court justice Iftikhar Chaudhry. This request was ignored. The Scotland Yard investigation was limited by the Pakistani Interior Ministry, so that all the team was able to do was to use the evidence already compiled by the Pakistani authorities. Ultimately, the Scotland Yard report was released, which claimed a single assailant. The narrow focus of the Scotland Yard report made no mention of how the government agencies had collected the evidence, and it contradicted eyewitness reports from the crime scene. In addition, the immediate events after the assassination seem to validate the charges of a potential cover up. The authorities claimed to have a large security contingent present at the time of the rally, but this was not confirmed by any of the video footage from the event. The Pakistani authorities stated that crowd control was a major concern, but this is not clear from the evidence presented. These contradictions led to the conclusion that a cover up was taking place. The government either wanted to avoid criticism over the failure to provide adequate security or possibly conceal the role that some members of the security team may have played in Bhutto's assassination.

Musharraf was in damage control in early 2008. He tried to portray the image of being a confident leader by meeting with U.S. secretary of state Condoleezza Rice at the World Economic Forum in January. The message from the West was still consistent that Musharraf was on the frontline in the global war on terror. Musharraf's attempt at rebuilding his image in the media was a disaster. In an interview with Fareed Zakaria, he once again seemed to blame Bhutto for being careless in her decisions to make campaign stops in areas where danger was imminent.

THE ELECTIONS OF 2008

Bhutto's husband, Asif Ali Zardari, produced Benazir's will, which declared that he should lead the party in the event she was killed. Little opposition in the party ranks appeared, and he quickly assumed the leadership mantle of the PPP. In the parliamentary elections in February, the PPP won overwhelming victories in what many believed was a sympathy vote (especially since Zardari had such a tarnished reputation). Circumstances were ripe for change to occur during the 2008 elections. Several of the smaller parties boycotted the elections, and growing security concerns led to a lower than expected voter turnout of only 44 percent. The PPP garnered 31 percent of the popular vote and 121 seats in the national assembly. The PML-N came in second with 91 seats, while Musharraf's PML-Q garnered a mere 54 seats. A coalition government was formed, and the agreement quickly restored the judges dismissed by Musharraf in November 2007. Eventually, the new coalition started to investigate the possibility of bringing impeachment proceedings against Musharraf. It was also clear that Musharraf's former allies in the army would not continue to back him (Jalal, 352). General Ashfaq Kayani was no longer in the general's corner as the military was receiving increased criticism for perceiving to protect him. Political operatives convinced Kayani to meet with Musharraf to convey the message that the situation was no longer tenable. In a monumental move, the former general gave a long, emotional televised speech opting to resign from office on August 18, 2008. The citizens of Pakistan were overwhelmingly in favor of this move as Musharraf had been totally discredited. Celebrations occurred nationwide. Soon afterward, the PML-N withdrew from the coalition government. Zardari had made it clear that he wanted to assume the presidency. He indicated months earlier to U.S. officials his intention to secure the top job. Sources confirm that even though the United States remained neutral during the campaign, Zardari had the blessing of the Bush administration. Several officials, most notably Pakistani ambassador Anne Paterson, actually believed he would be a more cooperative ally than Benazir. The messy corruption charges against Zardari had been cleared up, but he still faced money-laundering charges in Switzerland. International pressure, mostly from the United States, helped to negotiate the charges being dropped (Markey, 32). In addition, over $60 million frozen since the 1990s was subsequently released. When elections were held on September 6, the PPP under Asif Zardari scored a comfortable victory, and he became the new president of Pakistan.

The idea that a man with such a tarnished history who had been imprisoned multiple times could ascend to the highest office in the country was remarkable. The tragedy of Benazir's death coupled with the total implosion of the Musharraf administration allowed this strange transition to take place.

CHAPTER 6

Pakistan on the Brink

As the transition to Asif Ali Zardari took place, Pakistan entered a new phase of uncertainty. The final months of Musharraf's tenure were bleak. The regime was discredited, and the lame duck period of 2008 was filled with anxiety as the economy suffered and the state structures seemed paralyzed. The population looked at the military as a major part of the problem, and thus the idea of intervention seemed very remote.

Zardari guided the Pakistan People's Party in part because his son Bilawal Bhutto was still in college and considered too young to take over the mantle in such a dangerously tense time. Zardari's tainted history of corruption, mismanagement, and general hedonism created obvious anxiety within Pakistan. He had spent 11 years in jail and a considerable amount of time in exile. His reemergence following Benazir's assassination in December 2007 had in many ways gone better than expected. He cobbled together a five-party coalition, which was a first in Pakistani history. The Islamic fundamentalist parties along with Musharraf's party were left out of the coalition. The new prime minister was Syed Yousuf Raza Gilani, a PPP operative who had been imprisoned by Musharraf. Nawaz Sharif's Muslim League was offered the key economic and financial ministries (Craig, 3–4).

The new government decided to try and tackle the growing terrorism problem. Zardari pledged to hold talks with the Pakistani Taliban and other groups that had taken up arms against the state, such as the Baloch insurgents. General Kayani was the main military advisor to the new administration, and he strongly encouraged Zardari and Gilani to put a high priority on the terrorism problem. The Americans were optimistic that this fresh start for Pakistan was a positive development and consequently sent a high-level delegation to Islamabad to help plan the future course of relations between the countries.

The past year had been one of the most tumultuous in Pakistani history. A growing problem with internally displaced persons (IDPs) due to terrorist violence, harsh weather conditions, and natural disasters plagued the country. Soaring food prices and electricity shortages made life for the average citizen difficult. The backlog of court cases due to the lawyer's movement and the unaccounted political prisoners nationwide caused frustration and anxiety. The Pakistani Taliban had just officially coalesced in late 2007, and they continued to make gains in the tribal regions. The state was still feeling the fallout from the Red Mosque disaster of 2007. Finally, the security situation was tense because of the new problem of suicide attacks (Khan, 1–3).

The United States had growing concerns that the Pakistani eagerness to make peace deals with the insurgents showed weakness and vulnerability. From a strategic point it allowed the Taliban to move across the border into Afghanistan, where they could launch further attacks against American military personal. The focus of the terrorism problem was to shift within a few months after Zardari took the helm. The November 26 attack in Mumbai put a new and, in some ways, more dangerous twist to the Pakistan terrorist situation.

LASHKAR-E-TAIBA AND THE TERRORISM ATTACK IN MUMBAI

Lashkar-e-Taiba (LeT), which translates as "Army of Pure," is the name of the armed wing of the radical Islamic organization Markaz Daawat ul Irshad (MDI) located in the Muridke near the bustling city of Lahore. The organization was officially formed in 1990, but the evolution of the group dates back to the mid-1980s. The University of Engineering and Technology in Lahore was the birthplace of the movement. A missionary group known as Ahl-e-Hadith (a sect closely related to Wahhabism) led by Professors Hafiz Mohammed Saeed and Zafar Iqbal organized the group. Saeed traveled to Saudi Arabia in the 1980s, where he received religious training by Wahhabi clerics. He emerged as the most prominent leader in the group based on his charismatic sermons and ability to gain converts. Saeed and LeT promoted the importance of reestablishing the Muslim Caliphate and the inevitable destruction of India. Saeed's rhetoric was filled with references to the Mughal Dynasty in India and the desire to see Muslims once again in control of the Indian subcontinent. LeT advocates that preaching da'wa is as important as jihad in promoting Islam (Fair, 3–5). This mentality has allowed the group to build a solid foundation and grassroots movement that is sustainable for the long haul. In terms of recruitment and outreach, LeT is more successful than most militant organizations.

After the end of the Soviet occupation of Afghanistan, the Pakistani Intelligence Agency, the ISI, backed LeT as a way to promote the insurgency in Kashmir. They were eager to gain control of the newly revitalized Kashmiri insurgency movement. Within the security community it was perceived that Pakistan looked at LeT as an essential buffer against further Indian encroachment into Kashmir. LeT plays the role of proxy in order to keep the Pakistani government and military distanced from direct hostilities with India (Clarke, 1–3). The LeT operations were almost exclusively restricted to Kashmir as the group focused on guerilla-style commando raids.

In the aftermath of 9/11 and the terrorist attack on the Indian Parliament on December 13, 2001, the United States designated LeT as a Foreign Terrorist Organization. This policy change is not surprising considering that many experts believe that LeT is the most lethal terrorist group operating from South Asia (Fair, 1). The LeT leadership was forewarned by the ISI of the status change, which helped the organization elude sanctions and also allowed them to move key assets before the change was finalized. Because of the growing pressure from the Western powers, LeT continually goes through name changes and reorganization in order to avoid being targeted. Even though LeT has been seen as a local actor predominately dealing with the Kashmir issue, the group has always aspired to have more of a global reach. The unrealistic goal of achieving a victory in Kashmir would, according to LeT rhetoric, eventually lead to the defeat of India and the reestablishment of Muslim rule over all of South Asia (Tankel, 2–3).

The success of LeT can be attributed to their ability to organize at the local level, assisting in grassroots social service work that benefits the population in need. For example, LeT raised significant funds for the victims of the Indian Ocean tsunami in 2005 and later for earthquake relief in Kashmir. This prominent humanitarian focus has further enhanced the reputation of LeT (Tellis, 12–13). Furthermore, the organization successfully established a sophisticated infrastructure with the dual purpose of missionary work and military training. LeT has a vast network of facilities that are at times protected by the Pakistani military. Since LeT does not attack Pakistani security forces and they partner with the regime in the objective of gaining back Kashmir, they are basically untouched by the authorities. The group maintains a vast compound in Muridke, near Lahore, that includes offices, schools, dormitories, a garment factory, and an iron foundry (Riedel, 117). Since LeT is centered in the Punjabi region of Pakistan, they recruit in the same general area as the Pakistani military and security personal. This factor makes the group more difficult to combat, and tactics used against groups like the Taliban are not as applicable to LeT. Unlike several terrorist organizations in South Asia, such as the Pakistan Taliban, LeT does not recruit extensively in madrassas. The LeT fighters tend to be slightly older and better educated than most terrorist recruits in the region. Georgetown University professor Christine Fair states that most recruits have attended secondary school and even college (Fair, "Insights from a Database of Lashkar," 20–22). This valuing of education might stem from the fact that the original leadership and founders were professors with many holding advanced degrees.

Even though LeT was founded from the Ahl-e-Hadith theological tradition, they tend to recruit mostly from the Deobandi and Barelvis schools of thought. Originally, LeT had ties to Al Qaeda, but this connection has been less significant in the past decade or so, and some scholars believe the ties between the organizations were always quite tenuous. They did provide sanctuary for members of Al Qaeda following the U.S. invasion of Afghanistan. Several important operatives, including Al Qaeda number three Abu Zubaydah, were captured in LeT safe houses. The key to LeT's longevity has been the loyalty it has shown to the government in Islamabad. The group has also maintained a consistent leadership structure from the time of the group's founding. Additionally, LeT has never contemplated an attack on a target in the West. Finally, LeT operates outside of Pakistan, with most of the activity centered in Kashmir and to a lesser extent Afghanistan.

THE MUMBAI ATTACK: INDIA'S 9/11

One of the most successful attacks in the history of terrorism occurred in late November 2008 when commandos from Pakistan trained by Lashkar-e-Taiba launched a three-day siege of several keys locations in Mumbai, India. The attack's main targets—India's financial capital, Westerners on vacation, Israelis and Jews and local bystanders—have been the same targets of the global Islamic jihadist movement (Riedel, 13). The attack was skillfully prepared and included in-depth reconnaissance and thorough planning. The organizers were able to use the element of surprise in creating confusion within the India security officers, leading to a catastrophe.

The 10 attackers' point of departure was the seaport city of Karachi, where the militants left on a cargo vessel. The attackers later confiscated an Indian fishing boat that took them to a close enough proximity in which to use inflatable boats to finally make it to the shoreline of Mumbai. The terrorists murdered the crew upon taking the vessel and beheaded the captain prior to departing the fishing boat.

The operation was carefully planned, and the attackers had detailed diagrams of the locations they were entering. Exact routes and locations were mapped out from the point of landing to the final objective. The surviving attacker, Mohammed Ajmal Amir Qasab, verified communications with key leaders of LeT. The 10 terrorists were heavily armed with assault rifles, machine guns, pistols, and an abundance of ammunition, hand grenades, improvised explosive devices, and digital timers in order to place bombs at key locations to maximize the chaos.

Mobility was essential for the success of the operation. Multiple teams attacked several locations simultaneously. The teams wreaked havoc on the urban population by staging armed assaults, carjackings, targeted killings, hostage taking, building takeovers, and placement of IEDs (Rabasa, 5). From the standpoint of trying to maximize the death toll, these tactics were probably not the most productive. The common terrorist strategy of suicide bombings had become the norm for the better part of the past decade. In fact, the Mumbai attack was somewhat of a throwback to the terrorist actions of the 1970s and early 1980s. What made Mumbai unique was the combination of numerous tactics, which in reality garnered a tremendous amount of exposure for the operation, by far surpassing what most suicide attacks would receive.

The terrorists were able to confuse the authorities by moving from target to target. All of the selected locations were deemed soft and unguarded, making them vulnerable to attack. This led authorities to believe that the number of attackers was much greater than 10. In addition, the use of timers on explosive devices further complicated and confused counterterrorism measures. Once security authorities arrived at a location, the outmanned group of three or four attackers would move to another location. Both the media and law enforcement agencies grossly overestimated the number of terrorists, making countermeasures problematic (Brenner, 132–134).

The four teams included one team of four and three teams of two. The Chhatrapati Shivaji Terminus (Mumbai's main train station) was the first target. This target seemed more random as average middle-class Indian citizens bore the brunt of the attack. The objective of spreading fear in the minds of ordinary citizens was the main goal. After departing the train station, they moved to the Cama & Albless Hospital, where they once again killed in a horrific and random manner. The final location was scheduled to be the Trident-Oberoi Hotel, but security teams intercepted the duo en route, killing one and wounding the other.

The other teams and locations were being more targeted. The second group headed to the Nariman House, a complex run by members of the Jewish Chabad Lubavich movement. Several hostages were taken and later killed as the assailants viciously tortured the hostages by stabbing them in the genitals. The number killed by this group was by far the lowest.

The third team headed directly to the Trident-Oberoi Hotel, where the killing was once again random. This team would hold hostages for over 17 hours before being killed. They phoned the media and tried to negotiate demands, which in reality was a tactic used to stall security forces.

The final group included two teams of two attackers, and they headed to the famous Taj Mahal Palace Hotel. The attackers entered through the Leopold Café and the rear of the hotel. The terrorists swept through numerous floors of the complex, killing innocent civilians and setting fires in strategic locations. The tactics delayed action by the Indian authorities. The siege of the Taj lasted over 60 hours and gave the group enormous exposure in the national and international media. All told, 172 people were killed in the attacks, which would quickly be labeled as "India's 9/11" (Rabasa, 1–2).

It is clear that maximizing the death toll was a top objective of the operation, but previous attacks that relied solely on explosives created a higher death toll. LeT also prefers fidayeen (high risk) style commando raids to the suicide operations carried out by groups such as Al Qaeda and ISIS. The militants can kill as many targets as possible before succumbing to enemy operations (Fair, 5). The attack revealed a level of sophistication that is not standard for terrorist operations in the region. This is evident in the planning and coordination of the mission, as well as the ability of LeT to take advantage of the propaganda benefits. For policy experts, the most ominous aspect of the Mumbai operation was that the Pakistani terrorist network had extended its reach beyond Kashmir, showing the regional danger of this growing menace.

In a strange twist, it was discovered that one of the main masterminds of the operation was David Headley, an American-Pakistani who at one point had worked as a drug informant for the Drug Enforcement Agency (DEA). Headley's mother was a Philadelphia socialite, and his father was a noted Pakistani poet and diplomat. Headley went to boarding school in the Philadelphia area but eventually dropped out. After a series of arrests for everything from drug trafficking to domestic violence, Headley eventually became radicalized by the ideology of LeT. He became estranged from his mother and her Western lifestyle and turned toward trying to help further the goals of LeT. Unbeknownst to U.S. authorities, Headley helped to organize the Mumbai attack and later was instrumental in attempting to plan a similar terrorist plot in the Netherlands. After Headley was apprehended and convicted, he provided intelligence to the United States and India about the work of LeT and other terrorist cells in Pakistan (Tankel, 5–6). In 2010, he was sentenced to 35 years in prison.

In the aftermath of the attack, criticism of Pakistani involvement was quick and overwhelming. The Indian government blamed the Pakistani government for turning a blind eye to the activities of LeT. Clear ties between the ISI and LeT are well known throughout the intelligence community. Some within the Indian establishment wanted a military response in retaliation for Mumbai. The communication links between the attackers and the ISI were clear, but it was uncertain how high up within the intelligence community this went. Ultimately, India displayed remarkable restraint and took a more moderate approach to dealing with the aftermath of the attack. It was calculated that the high risk of military action in the long run would not harm LeT in any significant way.

The problem that Pakistan encounters is more fundamental. The government has very little control over the actions of the military or ISI, who operate without any impunity. The civilian government of President Zardari cannot reel in or hold the intelligence apparatus to any sort of accountability in matters related to the support of militants like LeT. Analysts believe that if too much external pressure is applied to Pakistan, the democratic gains made in recent years could be eliminated. From the perspective of the Pakistani intelligence community, the choice to partake in the Mumbai event is disturbing. The decision may have been part of a plan to derail any potential peace accords between India and Pakistan (Riedel, 120). Since a deal between the countries was close to being finalized in late 2007 and early 2008, the intelligence community may have felt the need to destabilize an impending peace deal. The Pakistani support of LeT in Mumbai may also have strained relations with the United States. This sort of brazen move could cause eruptible damage in the relationship that could also harm the policy in neighboring Afghanistan. Finally, this event shows that members of the Pakistani military and intelligence community will go to extreme lengths to achieve the ultimate goal of weakening India in whatever way possible. Rapprochement with the Hindu-dominated nation is not acceptable to some within the Pakistani establishment.

The actions taken by the Pakistan government in the aftermath of the attack was minimal. Pakistan initially denied involvement in the attack, claiming that the terrorists were not Pakistani and that the attack did not emanate from Karachi. Later, the regime moderated its tone and placed LeT leader Hafiz Muhammad Saeed under house arrest, and several offices used by the militant operations were closed. Saeed, however, was released in June 2009, as he seems to be an untouchable figure in the Pakistani militant community. There has been no real crackdown on LeT's ability to function effectively within Pakistan. Simply put, LeT is considered valuable to numerous officials in the military and intelligence communities, and protests from India or the United States do not seem to matter (Rabasa, 15–17).

As authorities tried to piece together the lessons of Mumbai, Indian officials received considerable criticism. One of the key controversies centered on whether authorities should have been better prepared for the ensuing attack. In early 2008, a terrorist suspect was arrested with diagrams and drawings of several key locations in and around Mumbai. The one attacker that survived the November operation told Indian authorities that reconnaissance had begun in mid- to late 2007. This sort of intelligence failure may make the state more susceptible to future attacks. In addition, Indian security personnel were slow to respond, which some commentators blame on the rigid bureaucratic structure of the state. Security officials involved on the ground said they were following orders by not sending police to engage the terrorists. According to Marie Brenner in *Anatomy of a Siege*, "India is a top-down society of entrenched bureaucrats, with appallingly inadequate communication among agencies" (Brenner, 126). The decision was made to wait on army contingents that arrived nearly five hours after the attack started. Special elite response teams did not appear for several additional hours. Dozens of victims could have been saved had police engaged the attackers in a more aggressive fashion at the Taj Hotel instead of waiting for the elite units to arrive from New Delhi.

It remains to be seen if Lashkar-e-Taiba will remain a serious threat to staging future Mumbai-style operations outside of the Kashmir area. The group faced minimal backlash following Mumbai, which could be perceived as a sign of weakness from both India and Pakistan. The group has distinct advantages that make it a more long-term regional threat in South Asia.

LeT has an extensive network of support that includes funding from numerous nations and diaspora communities. In addition, LeT has proven to be very sophisticated in providing a social service network that helps win over converts from the impoverished communities in Pakistan. LeT also has a well-organized and hierarchical leadership apparatus in place, which manages operations and the propaganda/public relations work of the group. Finally, LeT's close connection to the Pakistani military and intelligence communities means that protection from the state is virtually guaranteed.

COUNTERTERRORISM GOES HIGH TECH: THE DRONE POLICY IN PAKISTAN

During the war on terror, no issue has been as controversial as the use of predator and reaper drones by the United States. The volume of literature on the drone policy is significant, as supporters justify its use as a way to minimize U.S. casualties and avoid "boots on the ground." Critics of the policy point to the collateral damage inflicted, and the loss of innocent lives, and the possibility of creating more enemy combatants (Ahmed, 1–4).

Prior to the attacks of 9/11, the United States had never used armed drones in combat. Within the first two months of combat, operations in Afghanistan drone attacks were used to target members of Al Qaeda. Mohammed Atef, the military commander of Al Qaeda, was killed in November in what would be the first use of a drone in the context of combat. The rationale for the use of drones was that this was a continuation of the global war on terrorism and absolutely necessary in order to eradicate

Al Qaeda and its allies in South Asia. This was a clear and precise way to decimate our adversary in a war that had no limitations.

Ultimately, the frontline of the drone campaign would be in Pakistan. By the end of 2014, over 400 strikes had occurred in Pakistan, killing an estimated 2,400 people (Jones, 93). Intelligence estimates that this is the longest sustained covert bombing campaign in U.S. history. The main target area of this campaign would be the tribal area of South and North Waziristan with a total population of 800,000 that was overwhelmingly civilian. The lethal nature of the attacks coupled with the total lack of accountability would prove troubling for all observers of the war on terror. Over the course of his two terms in office, George Bush launched 48 drone strikes in Pakistan (Bergen, 8). The reasons behind the minimum use of drones can be explained in several ways. The technology was still being developed and mastered, and the uncertainty of the effectiveness of drone usage might have played a role. The legal ramifications might have possibly influenced the decision regarding the lethal use of drones. Staging attacks on a country in which the United States was allied with and was a partner in the war on terror would be a risky endeavor since the United States was worried about the vulnerability of Musharraf. Finally, the intelligence regarding the number of potential suspects and targets residing in Pakistan may have been unclear, especially in the early stages of the Bush administration.

The main target in the early stages of the drone campaign was Nek Mohammad, the 29-year-old tribal leader from South Waziristan. His desire was to galvanize the tribal regions together to combat the United States. Nek Mohammad had experience fighting with the Taliban in Afghanistan. He was closely tied to the notorious IMU that had been on the frontline in the initial operations against the American fighters in the last two months of 2001. The IMU sustained heavy losses, including the death of their legendary leader Juma Namangani. The remnants of the IMU fled across the border into the tribal region, where Nek Mohammad helped to find them sanctuary in order to regroup (Rashid, 271–272). This assistance gave immense power to Mohammad, the IMU cadres, and their leader Tahir Yuldashev. The group was dedicated to helping him with future militant operations. Initially, the militants staged several cross-border raids into Afghanistan, where they targeted American fighters around the Shkin area.

The Pakistan military decided to engage the militants in the spring of 2004 in order to decimate the foreign presence in the tribal areas. Furthermore, the operation was seeking revenge on the militants as they had targeted President Pervez Musharraf for assassination on multiple occasions. The Pakistan operation ended in abysmal failure as the militants were not defeated, civilian casualties were significant, and the operation was both a public relations and military failure. A peace agreement was negotiated between the military and Nek Mohammad during April. The peace agreement did not hold up very long and fighting resumed within a few weeks. This was when the decision to utilize the drone technology was made. On June 17, a predator drone landed a direct hit against Mohammad in Wana, killing several combatants and their children. Nek Mohammad was among the dead. The international press reported the story, as this was noteworthy for being the first use of drones for the purpose of assassination of an enemy combatant. U.S. officials denied responsibility for the attack, but the sophisticated nature in which it was carried out left no doubt as to who carried out the mission (Woods, 102–103). The killing of Nek Mohammad may have been tied to the failed attempt to assassinate President Musharraf. The CIA may have felt that by taking out Nek Mohammad, Musharraf would be in further debt to America and additional requests for assistance would be granted. The reaction from the tribal region was shock and anger. His death played a role in rallying more militants to the cause of jihad and subsequently it may have helped in the eventual galvanization of the Pakistani Taliban (TTP).

Over the next two years, Pakistan attempted to conceal the role of the United States. Early on, Pakistan was able to have a semblance of control over the operation as they requested pre-warnings of pending attacks and, furthermore, informed the Americans to keep the missions limited to particular areas of the tribal region. Wikileaks would uncover the details of this tacit agreement in subsequent years.

Once the decision was made to accelerate the drone campaign in Pakistan, the U.S. authorities, working with Pakistani intelligence, attempted to deny responsibility for many subsequent attacks. In late October 2006, a seminary for boys in the village of Chenegai in the Bajaur tribal agency headed by Maulvi Liaqat, a member of the outlawed TNSM, suffered a direct hit. The total destruction of the madrassa, including the dismembered bodies of the boys mostly aged 12 to 17 was horrific. The death toll of 81 was mostly young men including students as young as 7 (Cockburn, 220–221). The Pakistanis in the area were certain that this was an American operation, but it was concealed by the Pakistani military in accordance with a 2004 deal signed between the countries. Pakistan quickly asserted that the school was a main terrorist training center. The journalists investigating the incident were only able to confirm the killing of one known person tied to terrorism, Maulvi Liaqat. As the investigation continued, it was indeed clear that the attack had killed numerous young children and that the victims were innocent noncombatants. This drone attack had the lasting impact of destroying the very recently signed peace agreement between the Pakistani military and the tribal authorities in Bajaur.

The supposed role of the Pakistani military in the attack led to a vicious reprisal. This would become the pattern during the war on terror: A Pakistan attack by the authorities would lead to retaliation by the militants. In this case, a suicide attack a week later against troops in Dargai led to 42 deaths. This was the most significant loss of life for the Pakistani military since the start of the war on terror. Growing pressure on the Musharraf regime led to the decision to go public with the fact that the bombing of the school had indeed been carried out by the U.S. military. Publicly, the Pakistan government claimed that they requested that the United States halt future drone strikes, but privately this may not have been the case (Hussain, 73). What is clear from the tragic events was that the drone attack caused the level of violence to increase and created new militants who would be fighting the Americans and Pakistani military. In subsequent interviews, American officials including the new director of the CIA, Michael Hayden, did not confirm that this was a U.S. operation.

It became evident that the centerpiece of the U.S. drone operations would be the Waziristan region. Intelligence gathered following the fall of the Taliban regime in late 2001 clearly indicated that the majority of militants, including remnants of Al Qaeda, had made their way into the FATA region during 2002. The region was familiar to the Americans who had previously exploited the militants, encouraging them to wage jihad against the godless Soviet Union in the 1980s after they had occupied Afghanistan. The disillusioned peasants in the territories suffered economically in what is considered to be one of the poorest areas in all of South Asia. The assistance to the region did not help to develop the area economically but probably played a role in radicalizing it. Aid was funneled to the more militant anti-Soviet factions, and money was spent on printing Qurans rather than trying to modernize the infrastructure and educational system. The region became central to the war on terror in the aftermath of the Tora Bora fiasco as terrorists sought sanctuary in the tribal areas. Several Pakistani ISI operatives claim the drones were monitoring the tribal areas fairly early in 2002. The focus initially was on areas controlled and frequented by the notorious Haqqani network (Johnson, 7–8).

The administration was reluctant to take military action based on the desire to avoid the potential destabilization of the Pakistani state. The Bush foreign policy team realized that Musharraf was being heavily criticized, so the goal was to avoid emboldening the militant elements in the country that opposed him. Additionally, the objective was more focused on capturing terrorists rather than killing them. This was partially based on the desire to gain further intelligence on Al Qaeda and other militant groups in the area.

An indication of the success of this strategy was the capture of Abu Zubaydah in Faisalabad in 2002. It is estimated that nearly 700 Al Qaeda militants were apprehended by the Pakistani military in the early years of the war on terror. It is worth noting that cooperation between the United States and Pakistan was at its zenith, and the success of the joint operations is unquestionable (Rashid, 224–225). Apprehending militants further radicalized the tribal region and American efforts in Pakistan became more visible.

The Bush administration would not launch another drone attack until 2005 when the CIA targeted Al Qaeda operative Haitham al-Yemeni in North Waziristan. The secret assassination mission was quickly leaked to the press, which led to international protests for the clear violation of international law. It was noted by critics that no attempt to apprehend him was ever made making this case of extra-judicial execution. The Bush administration lashed out against the international community whenever any criticism of policies was aired. It was obvious that a total disregard of international law would be the norm under Bush (Woods, 104).

A disturbing trend with the increasing use of drones has been the targeting of reporters and journalists covering the story. One study claimed that 42 journalists have been killed (over half murdered) because of their work covering the war in Pakistan. As the drone attacks increased, attempt to conceal the covert actions of the U.S. military and intelligence community were undertaken. PBS journalist Hayatullah Khan traveled to North Waziristan to investigate the drone campaign. His photographs in the region included clear evidence of the U.S. direct role in the bombing campaign. Khan received dead threats and ultimatums, and eventually he was kidnapped and murdered with his body being discovered in the tribal region in the summer of 2006. Family and friends spoke out against the Pakistani government and specifically the ISI that they blamed for his death. The public notoriety of the pleas must have impacted the security apparatus. The following year, Khan's widow was blown up in a successful assassination carried out in her home. Another high-profile investigative journalist, Syed Saleem Shahzad, was kidnapped in Islamabad, and later his beaten corpse was found with all speculation pointing to the Pakistani intelligence service (Gall, 259). Pleas to the U.S. government had little impact as the administration continued to back the Musharraf regime, which blamed Al Qaeda for the murders of journalist.

The next major drone fiasco took place in January 2006 when the United States attacked the village of Damadola in the Bajaur Agency, causing close to 20 deaths. The question of who was killed in the attack was debated. Doubt was raised about the American claims of key mid-level Al Qaeda members being successfully targeted during the attack. Later statements by village locals asserted that most of the casualties were members of an extended family. This particular event sparked the most aggressive backlash from Pakistani authorities thus far. Part of the dilemma was the fact that Pakistan had started to delineate "good" Taliban from the "bad" Taliban. The "good" Taliban worked with the Pakistani authorities and did not directly target the Pakistani military. The "bad" Taliban were the militants who had the ultimate goal of using violence to remove Musharraf and establish a Taliban-style theocracy in Pakistan. Pakistani authorities had cut several deals with the "good" Taliban and found the continuation of drone strikes by the United States to be counterproductive to their long-term goals. For the first time, a clear rift and policy disagreement between the United States and Pakistan had emerged (Goldberg, 58–59). The lingering fear over the coming years was that the United States would again abandon Pakistan once the terrorist threat in Afghanistan had been eliminated. The perceived U.S. betrayal of the partnership was still painfully apparent.

From the perspective of the Musharraf administration, having the Taliban alternative in the region helped to counterbalance the growing influence and strength of India. The relationship with elements of the Taliban seemed to become closer as the U.S. interest in the war on terror shifted from Afghanistan to Iraq. It was also clear to American policy makers that the Pakistani military and intelligence community was directly assisting Taliban efforts in Afghanistan. Documents leaked by Wikileaks confirmed that the ISI assisted Taliban and Al Qaeda efforts in cross-border missions as early as 2004. These missions would have been directed against U.S. military personal. On several occasions, it was reported by U.S. commanders that militant fighters were resupplied and aided by ISI operatives. The Pakistani military leadership privately claims that in numerous instances the United States and Pakistani interest simply did not coincide.

By the final year of the Bush administration, changes were made. A more assertive U.S. policy was undertaken as CIA director Michael Hayden convinced the president to no longer abide by earlier agreements negotiated with Musharraf regarding the drone policy in the tribal region. The tone was no longer one of compromise or negotiation but frustration followed by demands (Cockburn, 223–224). Drone attacks in 2008 were increased and included successful attacks that eliminated several key Al Qaeda operatives most notably Abu Laith al-Libi.

In addition to ramping-up attacks, the Bush administration also increased the use of signature strikes that would be renamed personality strikes. The goal was to target specific individuals who followed a particular behavior pattern. This controversial tactic was criticized by human rights and international law advocates (Woods, 110–111). These attacks would devastate regions and communities where citizens lived, causing considerable collateral damage. Initially, the Pakistani administration did not care about the civilian damage (at least privately), as long as targets that were hostile to the state (most significantly "bad" Taliban) were taken out. The tone of the Pakistani government changed as the number of attacks increased dramatically. In the final months of the Bush presidency, ground forces launched incursions into the South Waziristan region. Code-named Operation Cottonmouth, the raid led to civilian casualties, and follow-up attempts by American special operation forces were met with resistance from Pakistan ground forces. In addition, the drone campaign accelerated as Bush's departure neared. This increase in the drone war was probably due to the fact that Bush was nearing the end of his tenure in office, but an additional factor was the growing distrust and resentment between the Pakistani and U.S. governments.

OBAMA AND THE DRONE CAMPAIGN

From the time Barack Obama was elected President in 2008, his policy regarding the war on terror was to shift the focus of the campaign back to the Afghanistan-Pakistan theater away from the preoccupation with Iraq that had consumed the second term of the Bush presidency. During a seminal appearance at West Point in December 2009, Obama stated, "I am convinced that our security is at stake in Afghanistan and Pakistan. This is the epicenter of the violent extremism practiced by Al Qaeda. It is from here that we were attacked on 9/11, and it is from here that new attacks are being plotted as I speak." Obama campaigned on the issue, as he was highly critical of Bush's decision to abandon the AfPak War for Iraq. The emphasis on Iraq was draining desperately needed resources from the campaign in Afghanistan. Candidate Obama had seen the intelligence reports stating that Pakistan was a key base for Taliban and Al Qaeda operations. Estimates from the intelligence community made it clear that terrorist militants in the region had regrouped and had sanctuary and support in the Pakistan tribal areas. Obama realized that the most significant threat from the militant bases would be to our interests in Afghanistan.

The air war in Afghanistan had inflicted significant civilian casualties in the final year of the Bush presidency. These inadvertent mishaps that led to civilian deaths were a public relations catastrophe for the United States and a propaganda victory for the insurgents. The vast majority of the operations leading to civilian deaths were actually not drone related. It is worth noting that drones conducted only 7 percent of the nearly 2,000 airstrikes carried out in 2008 (Coll, 4–5). The majority of drone operations were still in the Iraqi theater of operations.

Obama was adamant that drone warfare was the direction the U.S. military needed to take as the war on terror progressed. The precise nature of drones and the low risk factor regarding American casualties were ideal for the new administration. Obama and his foreign policy team believed that the increasing use of drones would reduce the cost of lethal force, especially in Pakistan. Since the United States was not at war in Pakistan, this policy seemed to be the logical direction to take because any overt action by the Americans would be politically problematic. The United States would not need to seek counsel with Pakistan prior to initiating an operation.

Many within the military hierarchy realized how counterproductive the air war was if civilian casualties were incurred. General Stanley

McChrystal, former commander of JSOC understood that any successful counterinsurgency strategy needed to keep civilian casualties at a minimum. As the architect of the famous COIN policy, McChrystal would voice both publicly and privately his adamant belief that the strategic defeats suffered due to civilian deaths could ultimately cost the United States the war. Major General Michael Flynn agreed with McChrystal stating that killing insurgents usually multiplies enemy combatants by drawing in new recruits. Modeling software was implemented during the Obama presidency that would supposedly help lessen civilian deaths. Analysts and drone crews could evaluate the impact of a strike on the civilian population in order to decide whether to recommend an attack on a particular target. Whether a drone attack was launched on the tribal region of Afghanistan or Pakistan, it is important to remember the impact the strike would have on the Pashtuns. The obsession that the Pashtun community had regarding revenge and justice meant that some sort of retaliation from the victim's families or tribal members would always be expected (Ahmed, 84–86).

President Obama made it clear to Pakistan that he intended to redirect U.S. efforts back to the AfPak theater of operations. Meetings between Pakistan military and intelligence leaders and Vice President Joe Biden clarified the American position. The Pakistani Taliban was increasing cross-border raids into Afghanistan from the Waziristan area. The two main leaders that concerned U.S. officials were Mullah Nazir, the leader of the Ahmadzai Wazir tribe in South Waziristan, and Baitullah Mehsud, the overall leader of the Pakistan Taliban. In addition, the Obama administration wanted the Pakistanis to take a more assertive stand against the Haqqani network that operated freely in both Afghanistan and Pakistan.

Nazir was a native of Wana and schooled in one of the regional madrassas founded during the anti-Soviet campaign of the 1980s. Nazir was also connected to the Afghan Taliban leader Mullah Omar, serving on the ruling council known as the Quetta Shura. His forces based in South Waziristan had been increasing attacks against American positions in eastern Afghanistan. He also provided sanctuary for Al Qaeda operatives still located in the tribal region. From the U.S. perspective, Nazir was a high-value target. The Pakistani intelligence and military establishment viewed the situation much differently (Woods, 151–152). Nazir had been instrumental in suppressing the Uzbek Islamists who had been fermenting anti-Pakistani tension in the Waziristan region. He was considered a "good" Taliban member and a loyal asset to the regime. The Pakistan intelligence leaders convinced the United States that they would go after Nazir.

Within the first few days of the Obama presidency, the extent of the administration's commitment to the drone strategy was confirmed. Strikes launched into Zeraki in North Waziristan and Wana in the South were carried out on the same day. Reports of nearly a dozen insurgents being killed, including high-valued targets, were leaked to media outlets. The Pakistan government accounts questioned the U.S. report. Independent sources later confirmed that several children were killed in the strikes with the final death toll estimated at 14, and the number of militants eliminated may have been less than reported. Eventually, survivors who were injured in the drone raid filed lawsuits. This legal action brought to light questions as to whether the United States was in violation of international principles of proportionality and proper precautions in launching this drone attack, which utilized the notorious Hellfire missile. Multiple sources confirmed that a group of tribal elders gathered in Zeraki in a hujra (a main hospitality/meeting area in a Waziri home where male visitors gather). Malik Gulistan Khan, who was a tribal elder who happened to be pro-government and a noted peace negotiator in the region, was conducting the meeting. The accounts of the drone attack were graphic as survivors were severely burned with serious shrapnel-induced wounds and significant damage to limbs, ears, and eyes (Living Under Drones, 70–71). The bodies of the dead were blown apart with parts scattered throughout the bombing location. The death and destruction was only part of the anguish, as survivors and residents from the location suffered the mental and emotional damage associated with such significant trauma. In addition, the tribal elders meeting were the breadwinners, and their loss caused economic distress throughout the community. Furthermore, additional side effects included property damage and the dislocation of numerous families.

Subsequent research confirmed that CIA director Michael Hayden had authorized this initial attack of the Obama presidency. Air Force operators in Las Vegas, Nevada, conducted the mission nearly 6,000 miles from the site of the attack. According to Chris Jones, this was the 46th and final authorized attack by the former Air Force general (Jones, 153). This was the first of nearly 300 drone strikes carried out in Pakistan by President Obama in his first term in office. The supposed new message of tolerance and respect to the Muslim world was being quickly squandered by the new administration. The U.S. government has continually refused to comment on any actions regarding abuse during drone attacks, leaving a dark cloud over the previous administration's commitment to human rights.

The Obama administration quickly turned to the goal of trying to eliminate the leader of the Pakistani Taliban, Baitullah Mehsud. Mehsud was the most wanted militant in South Waziristan. At his peak of power, Mehsud may have commanded close to 20,000 militants in the region. The area was known to be a main safe haven for Al Qaeda fighters, who at times were involved in cross-border attacks against U.S. forces. Mehsud became the central figure among the Pakistani insurgency following the assassination of Nek Mohammed in 2004. Mehsud was instrumental in bringing the alliance of militant groups together, and his successful organization and leadership abilities led to a $5 million bounty being placed on his head by the United States. The TTP organization had successfully assassinated Benazir Bhutto in December 2007 and was launching suicide attacks into urban areas on a regular basis. Over 220 attacks had been carried out during the first term of the Obama administration, killing over 3,200 civilians (Woods, 155–156). In addition to the Bhutto mission, the TTP had captured Pakistani forces, leading to concessions and peace accords being signed at numerous points.

The first substantiated attempt on Mehsud occurred in late June 2009. Rumors had circulated, and an NSA phone intercept picked up a conversation reporting that the militant leader was close to acquiring a nuclear device. This was of course never actually confirmed, and chatter like this was common in the intelligence community. A subordinate of Mehsud, Khwaz Wali Mehsud, was assassinated, and the CIA believed that he might attend his fallen comrade's funeral. A drone strike was launched at the funeral, killing over 80 people including several children, but Baitullah Mehsud was not among them. This particular attack and the fact that this was deliberate would lead to war crime allegations against the Obama administration. Joby Warrick stated, "I don't think there's a whole lot of thinking or calculating of the moral cost of going after these individuals" (Cockburn, 229). Six weeks later, the CIA campaign got their man as the TTP leader was blown in two by a drone strike, while receiving a rooftop massage by his wife. The attack killed approximately 10 people, including several civilians. President Obama was pleased and went out of his way to call the targeter with congratulations, as well as noting the assassination during his weekly radio address.

With U.S. encouragement and intelligence support, the Pakistani military took advantage of Mehsud's death to undertake the most ambitious offensive of the conflict. Operation Rah-e-Nijat, the Road to Salvation, was an attempt to break the backs of the Pakistani Taliban in South Waziristan. Over 350,000 civilians would be displaced in the fighting, as the military sent in over 30,000 troops in the offensive. The TTP forces eventually abandoned the region, as the insurgency seemed to be in disarray. On the surface, the first year of the Obama presidency ended with a feeling of confidence that the war effort in Pakistan was on the right track.

The initial euphoria by the end of 2009 cloaked serious problems regarding the war in terror in Pakistan. First, the militants were indeed routed by the Pakistani military, but most were not killed or captured, but simply fled to the region of North Waziristan. Second, the civilian displacement and extremely high level of IDPs turned much of the tribal region against the Pakistan government as well as the United States. Finally, the financial toll was significant to all parties involved. The strain on the Pakistani state was astronomical, and the level of desperation that now consumed the population radicalized people even further, playing into the hands of the extremists (Ahmed, 73–76).

During the same time span that American military was engaged in drone operations in the tribal regions pursuing the likes of Baitullah Mehsud, there was growing concern over the situation in the Swat region. Militants were gaining ground and the Pakistani government seemed on the ropes signing a permanent cease-fire with the insurgents in February 2009. With the TTP emboldened and only 120 miles north of the capital Islamabad, the new U.S. administration showed growing concern. With encouragement and support from the Obama administration, the Pakistani military launched an offensive into the region during the spring, retaking key strategic points in the area. The TNSM militants under the leadership of the future Pakistani Taliban leader Maulana Fazlullah were forced to resort to guerilla tactics and many fled across the border into Afghanistan (Hussain, 160–162). The end result of this operation was one of the largest civilian displacements of the entire war on terror.

Following the death of Baitullah Mehsud, his cousin Hakimullah Mehsud emerged as the new leader of the Pakistani Taliban. Considered by intelligence experts to be more capable and charismatic, he encouraged suicide attacks as a way to combat U.S. and Pakistani military efforts in the region. Hakimullah was able to devise a plan to use a Jordan physician as a double agent to conduct a lethal attack on CIA operatives in Khost, Afghanistan. The doctor, Humam Balawi, had convinced Jordanian intelligence agents that he was willing to work from the inside of Al Qaeda on behalf of the CIA. This would be a significant development for the agencies since the United States had never been able to place an operative in Al Qaeda or the Taliban. Balawi was instructed by Hakimullah to try and set up a meeting at the heavily guarded base at Khost. The U.S. intelligence officers erred and allowed Humam to enter the area without going through the normal checkpoints. This mistake was costly, and on December 30, 2009, Balawi detonated a suicide vest, killing seven CIA agents, including long-time agent Jennifer Matthews, who was involved in tireless efforts to track down Al Qaeda leaders, including Osama bin Laden. By all accounts, this high-valued operation secured a sense of revenge for the TTP and Al Qaeda operatives that had been killed in drone attacks (Bergen, 210–211). Hakimullah's posting of a video with the suicide attacker prior to the mission was payback for the killing of his cousin earlier that summer. The retaliation by the Americans included 11 Hellfire attacks over a period of 19 days. Several of the strikes targeted possible locations where Hakimullah was thought to be, but, ultimately, the militant leader escaped the attacks.

The intensity of the drone attacks continued in 2010 with an attack occurring once every three days (Cockburn, 230). Ironically, as the drone war accelerated, the Pakistani Taliban being targeted tended to be more of the "good" Taliban, who were on friendly terms with the Pakistani ISI. This would of course be counterproductive in the overall war on terror strategy.

DRONES: LEGAL/ETHICAL/MORAL PROBLEMS

The drone policy in Pakistan was beset with problems of a multifaceted nature. The damage went beyond the obvious immediate impacts of death, injury, and destruction. Findings from human rights organizations and independent journalistic organizations confirmed policies that were in blatant disregard of human life and callously indifferent to human suffering.

The first aspect of drone attacks that showed a reckless indifference was in the area of victim assistance. The United States had engaged in the process of double tap, which means hitting a target strike site multiple times in quick succession. The impact of such secondary strikes is to kill and maim first responders who are trying to rescue the injured or retrieve the dead bodies. Local residents and tribesmen carrying out rescue work were killed on multiple occasions in follow-up strikes, according to Chris Woods in his work for the Bureau of Investigative Journalists. The impact of this is that citizens will not give immediate assistance for fear of the double tap occurring. In many cases, the villagers wait up to half an hour before approaching the location. Villagers realized that any initial attempts at recovery could lead to death or serious injury.

A second significant impact of the drone attacks was on the economic well-being of the populations living in the immediate area. The economic impact includes damage to property, medical costs incurred by the victims, and the loss of primary breadwinners (Living with Drones, 77). Because housing compounds are structured in a style in which extended families live together, any strike on a particular residence can lead to significant property damage, creating a crisis situation within the immediate community. Since many of the areas targeted by drones in regions like North Waziristan are already extremely impoverished, such damage can prove to be catastrophic. When drone strikes kill the primary earners in a family, there is no alternative source of income within the village. This can typically lead to children dropping out of school to enter the workforce at an earlier age as well as creating families that are dependent on community charity in order to survive. This loss of the main breadwinner can also radicalize the youth that are left behind.

The devastation caused by drone attacks can also lead to astronomical medical bills for the injured person and family. Victims in the Waziristan area end had to seek medical treatment in private hospitals in Peshawar, where the cost can be financially devastating. No compensation from the United States has been offered for the damages sustained in the drone attacks in the tribal region of Pakistan (Woods, 160–161). Ironically, the military does have a payment policy for damages incurred in similar situations in Afghanistan.

One of the most significant areas of concern regarding the use of drones is the devastating impact it has on the mental well-being of the citizens living in the affected region. There is no way to know who or what the drones are targeting once the buzzing sound is apparent. Studies conducted in areas impacted by the drones report civilians living in a constant state of fear and extremely high stress levels. Citizens are constantly frightened and cannot escape the mental stress they live under on a daily basis. Mental health professionals predict the citizens impacted will have future trauma, sometimes referred to as anticipatory anxiety, which is common in war zones. When the civilians hear the drone sound, they run to seek shelter. People are concerned that they can be targeted at any time. Reports from the New York University and Stanford Law Schools refer to the issue of uncontrollability, which is common in civilians living in the tribal areas. No matter what the civilians were doing, they were always thinking the drones would strike. This sense of powerlessness to control their situation and environment creates long-term mental problems, which can also impact civilian's well-being. In addition, posttraumatic stress disorder has become a common occurrence, as well as emotional breakdowns. Sleep deprivation is also a problem, as is loss of appetite and anger, and irritability (Living Under Drones, 83). A sense of sadness and despair consumes the citizens, as so many innocent lives are lost. Interviews mention people being unhappy and afraid because of the terror of the drone attacks. The devastation on the children in the tribal areas is probably the most profound. Once children have been exposed to the horrors of such violence, the mental devastation is long term, and the images will stay with them into adulthood. The difficulty in obtaining anti-anxiety and anti-depressants makes treatment problematic. Children hear the drones all of the time, cannot function well in society, and are afraid to venture out.

Access to education has also been totally disrupted because of the drone policy. Shahbaz Kabir stated, "education was always a problem in Waziristan, but after the drone attacks, it got even worse. A lot of the children—most of the children—had to stop going to school" (Living Under Drones, 86). With already abysmal literacy rates in the Waziristan region, the area cannot afford to see further disruption to the education of children. Several issues relating to education have been impacted by the drone attacks. The physical and emotional devastation makes learning difficult. Student concentration levels and determination to study are adversely impacted by the threat of drone attacks. The financial stress incurred by families in villages devastated by the attacks eroded the educational infrastructure. Children might also be called on to tend to injured family members or possibly having to take over as breadwinners for the family.

It was also reported that many students stayed out of school for fear of being targeted on the way to or from the school buildings. In some cases, school employees have stopped working for fear of attacks. Human rights groups have confirmed that drones hit educational facilities on numerous occasions, making this fear legitimate.

A reprehensible part of the drone policy is the impact on funerals and burial traditions in the tribal areas. The cultural and religious practices in North Waziristan have been altered by the U.S. attacks. Citizens are afraid to attend funerals because of constant targeting by drones. In a culture and community in which religion is so significant, this is devastating. Burying the deceased soon after death is a religious duty, and the community involvement in funerals has always been important in the tribal regions. The "Living Under Drones" report states, "proper burial ceremonies and grieving rituals are essential to reducing or preventing psychological distress during times of large-scale disaster, and thus erosion of ceremonies attendant to death is likely to have a significant impact on the way communities grieve and deal with the loss of strike victims." A horrifying twist on this issue is the fact that missile strikes often incinerate the victims' bodies, leaving them in pieces and unidentifiable and making traditional burial practices impossible.

Furthermore, social and cultural gatherings that are so important to tribal communities have been totally disrupted. Day-to-day community activities can no longer be carried out for fear of attack. Gatherings where people would commonly meet and entertain guests can no longer take place. Thus, community dynamics have been altered in a serious way. People congregating together are believed to increase the likelihood of intelligence agents perceiving them to be possible terrorists gathering and thus meriting an attack. The economic fallout to communities is also significant. Attendance in bazaars has declined and trade has of course dwindled. Car or truck travel for the purpose of commerce from the tribal areas to Afghanistan has decreased because of the increased possibility of attacks. Since the risk factor is higher, businessmen making the journey have increased the cost considerably.

The centerpiece of tribal customs is the jirga system. The community-based jirga helps to resolve disputes and solidify agreements between tribal elders and leaders. The entire Pashtun community and social code is strongly based on having a functional jirga system. Since gathering in large numbers increases the risk factors, the use of jirgas has decreased significantly, which in turn has disrupted the fabric of the community and the communal order (Ahmed, 44–47).

A final area adversely impacted by the drone policy has been the community trust in Waziristan society. Many tribal leaders believe that particular individuals or factions becoming informants for U.S. intelligence agencies, such as the CIA, are settling scores. It is suspected that tracking devices or chips are dropped in areas where the CIA will launch a strike. In many cases, these devices are placed in a location where a tribal enemy might live in order to remove a political rival or settle a feud. The CIA has no way to confirm whether these tracking devices are actually placed in a terrorist home or location. This trend is extremely troubling as rivals are taken out or acts of revenge carried out by the United States in order to give particular groups advantages in tribal disputes. This leads to mistrust and paranoia within tribal culture. Everyone is constantly alert, and the community trust has been eradicated.

CIVIL SOCIETY IN DECLINE: TROUBLING TRENDS IN PAKISTAN

As the war on terrorism dragged on, religious minorities became the frequent targets of legal and social discrimination. During the tenure of General Zia, parliament approved dramatic changes to the penal code, which collectively became known as the blasphemy laws. These changes led to more intolerance and, ultimately, persecution of minority groups within the country. The critical question was centered on the role of religion in the life of Pakistanis.

The battle ground between a more tolerant Pakistan and those promoting rigid fundamentalist country was coming into play during 2010. The intensity of the struggle became clear when the governor of Punjab, Salman Taseer, was gunned down in Islamabad by a bodyguard who was angered over his statements advocating the relaxation of the blasphemy laws passed by the legislature in 2008. Taseer was a voice of moderation and tolerance in Pakistan. He openly criticized the blasphemy law for blatantly leading to the discrimination of religious minorities in the country. Many citizens openly praised Taseer's death, stating that he was interfering in the government's interpretation of Islam (Caryl, 2–3).

Taseer's assassin, Mumtaz Qadri, claimed the governor was an apostate for opposing the blasphemy law. He was given a hero's welcome upon his arrival at the courthouse. Young lawyers showered the assassin with rose petals as he walked outside heading toward arraignment. This scene was most disturbing because the common narrative of the religious fundamentalists being the uneducated poor from the remote tribal regions is simply not totally accurate. Extremism is spreading across the country and includes elements in both the rural as well as urban areas. Noted South Asian historian Mubarak Ali estimates that the religious right in Pakistan now constitutes approximately 30 percent of the country (McCarthy, 2). What was once considered extreme has now become mainstream. Many party leaders and officials remained silent following the assassination, showing that the fundamentalists have been effective in intimidating several of the leaders.

Unfortunately, the Taseer assassination was not an isolated incident. On March 2, 2011, four gunmen in Islamabad killed Pakistan's federal minister of minorities, Shahbaz Bhatti. He was also an outspoken critic of the blasphemy law and stated his belief that minority persecution would continue until the legislation was amended or repealed. Bhatti knew that his life was in danger after Taseer's death two months earlier. In a prerecorded statement that was to be released if he was assassinated, he stated, "The forces of violence, militants, banned organizations, Taliban and Al Qaeda, want to impose their radical philosophy in Pakistan and whoever stands against it, they threaten him" (Rashid, "An Army without a Country," 1). This growing trend toward intolerance and the embracing of elements of jihadism is troubling. Army chief General Ashfaq Kayani refused to condemn the attacks and went as far as to state that many of his soldiers supported the actions of the assassins. The military and intelligence community has trained and armed extremists dating back to the anti-Soviet campaign so controlling or moderating these elements now is problematic. They have also in many cases become the targets of terrorist attacks as over 2,000 soldiers were killed in a five-year span.

Part of the religious revival and turn toward extremism is due to the Pakistani government's friendly relations with the United States. As the drone policy and the war on terror kills thousands of Pakistani citizens, damages property, and destroys the livelihood of so many citizens, the result is a backlash against the West. The trust factor between the United States and Pakistan remained low, but over the next year, the situation would hit rock bottom.

THE SEARCH FOR OSAMA BIN LADEN

The whereabouts of Osama bin Laden had frustrated U.S. policy makers for nearly a decade following the September 11 attacks. The blunder at Tora Bora in January 2002 proved to be costly as the Al Qaeda leader disappeared and the trail had remained cold with few substantial leads emerging. Amazingly, over the next decade, bin Laden's followers and residents of the tribal region remained steadfast in their loyalty as no one divulged any clues that could have helped the U.S. intelligence community track the world's most wanted fugitive.

The miscalculations that caused the near destruction of Al Qaeda fell on the shoulders of bin Laden. He underestimated the American resolve as he erroneously believed that America was a "paper tiger" unable to commit to any sustained military operation that might incur casualties (Riedel, 80–81). The Al Qaeda leader did not think that America would launch an invasion of Afghanistan following the 9/11 attacks. Bin Laden speculated that America would respond with cruise missile attacks as they had after the bombings in Nairobi and Dar al Salam in 1998 (Bergen, "Manhunt,"

18–19). He noted that America was unwilling to sustain any sizeable troop deploy, as shown by their reactions to the attacks on the marine barracks in Lebanon in October 1983, Somalia in October 1993, and the infamous Black Hawk Down fiasco. The loss and humiliation of the Vietnam War had forever changed the American psyche. Bin Laden believed that the 9/11 attacks would lead to the American withdrawal from the region, and the eventual fall of Israel, and the eventual emergence of Taliban-style regimes throughout the region (Jones, 75–76). Bin Laden's miscalculation led to the degradation of the terrorist organization as they lost thousands of fighters and the vital sanctuary of Afghanistan.

Shortly after the 9/11 attacks, the U.S. intelligence community had worked on a plan to turn high-level Taliban leaders against bin Laden. The CIA station chief Robert Grenier initiated a meeting in Quetta, Pakistan, with Taliban number two Mullah Osmani in late September 2001 with the goal of getting the regime to turn on the Al Qaeda leader prior to commencing U.S. military operations. Even though nothing productive came out of this meeting, it showed a level of anxiety and frustration between the Taliban and Al Qaeda.

Within weeks of the commencement of U.S. military operations, the Al Qaeda contingent with bin Laden was trapped at Tora Bora. After sustaining heavy casualties, bin Laden abandoned the battlefield, circling back into Afghanistan and staying with a trusted friend, Awad Gul, in Jalalabad. After a short period of rest, bin Laden headed into Kunar Province. The inhospitable terrain and intense loyalty of the population made this the ideal location to seek sanctuary. Bin Laden released several videos encouraging his followers to continue the fight. The Al Qaeda leader had aged considerably and looked shaken, and it was obvious he had sustained some sort of injury because he did not move his left side. American officials were furious that the opportunity to kill the architect of the 9/11 attacks had been squandered (Burke, 66–68).

HIDDEN FROM SIGHT: OSAMA BIN LADEN 2002–2011

The organization that Osama bin Laden had formed in 1998 was in dire straits by early 2002. The leadership mostly dispersed into Pakistan, with some of the militants heading to the densely populated urban areas, while others sought sanctuary in the remote tribal regions. The organization would need to reevaluate both its structure and function. The group had an extensive bureaucracy that included business affairs, military planning, media outreach, and numerous other subagencies (Bergen, "Manhunt," 55). The organization had disabilities benefits, paid vacations, medical coverage, and salary schedules. This would all change, of course, because of the attacks of 9/11. Key operatives that ran the day-to-day operations were killed, captured, or in hiding. Muhammad Atef, the organizational expert of the group, died in a U.S. airstrike in November 2001. Other key managers were dispersed in remote areas. Numerous members of Al Qaeda were upset over the ill-fated decision to launch the 9/11 attacks. The damage to the group was monumental, and recovery seemed to be impossible. The most scathing critique of Al Qaeda came from Abu Musab al-Suri, who penned a 1,500-page manuscript on the movement. Suri, a Syrian intellectual, had argued for a less hierarchical Al Qaeda that would be more flexible and able to maintain long-term viability (Burke, 154–155). Suri stated that at least 4,000 Al Qaeda fighters had been killed or captured in the initial conflict, which devastated the military capacity of the group. Suri's statement about the destruction of the Taliban regime and other groups that had allied with Al Qaeda was blunt and critical. This public condemnation of Osama bin Laden and the actions taken were quite unusual for the organization. Al Qaeda did try to repair the damage and released reports and public statements celebrating the success of the operation. This at times seemed like damage control, and the group no longer had the ability to organize and plan in any significant way.

The United States planned covert actions in order to track down and apprehend key Al Qaeda operatives globally. Operation Greystone would be one of the most elaborate operations in U.S. history. This controversial program would include enhanced interrogation techniques, including waterboarding and the use of secret prisons, in order to facilitate the operation. Much of the focus was trying to find links that could help in locating the key Al Qaeda leaders, including bin Laden and Ayman Zawahiri. The Bush administration was concerned over reports that the Al Qaeda leadership had been in contact with Pakistani nuclear scientists during the summer of 2001. Throughout most of 2002, nothing was heard from bin Laden leading some to speculate that he was indeed dead. The situation changed when Al Jazeera received an audiotape on November 12 that gave proof that bin Laden was alive. The headline of "Bin Laden Alive" was demoralizing to the Bush administration that had been hopeful that bin Laden was deceased. The tape included Al Qaeda's leader referencing events from the past several months, including the notorious Bali nightclub bombing that killed several hundred civilians in October 2002 (Burke, 157).

The realization that bin Laden was still leading Al Qaeda led to intense speculation about his whereabouts. The consensus was the tribal region of Pakistan, but some intelligence experts believed he might have fled to the northern region of the country close to Chitral. Others speculated that he might have made it to Azad Kashmir. As the Pakistani military and security forces started to gather more intel on Al Qaeda operatives, a pattern developed of locating militants within Pakistan's massive urban areas. Al Qaeda leaders Khalid Sheikh Mohammed (KSM) and Ramzi bin al-Shibh granted an interview from their hideout in Karachi. Subsequently, Al-Shibh was captured in a raid, which provided Pakistani and American officials with an abundance of information about several of the key leaders' whereabouts following the fall of the Taliban regime. It became apparent that Karachi was a vital center of Al Qaeda activity as most of the group's banking transactions were funneled through the city. Several months later, the Pakistani authorities received a tip from an informant about the possible location of KSM. The informant was scheduled to meet with the terrorist leader, and the lure of the handsome reward money ($25 dollars) played a role in the decision to turn on one of Al Qaeda's most wanted leaders. The nighttime raid was conducted on February 28 and led to the capture of KSM in Rawalpindi. Ironically, the city is the home to the headquarters of the Pakistan military. The intelligence gathered from KSM's computer was beneficial and gave agents a unique perspective on the inner workings of Al Qaeda (Jones, 102–103). KSM had lived on the edge and did not abide by the conservative social norms of bin Laden and Zawahiri. He drank, womanized, and lived a rather decadent lifestyle. His capture was indeed gratifying as he planned and helped to fund the September 11 attacks, the Bali bombing, and played a direct role in the murder of Daniel Pearl.

The period from 2002 to 2005 saw multiple high-ranking Al Qaeda officials killed or captured, mostly in Pakistan's urban centers. In addition to KSM and al-Shibh, high-ranking operatives, including Abu Zubaydah, Walid bin Attash, Ahmed Khalfan Ghailani, and Abu Faraj al-Libi, were all apprehended in Pakistan. According to Peter Bergen, 369 militants associated with Al Qaeda were captured in the first five years of the war on terror (102–103). It was apparent that the use of technology by members needed to be limited, but this created an inability to organize and communicate with members effectively. The U.S. Counterterrorism Center expanded from 300 to 1,500 staff members following 9/11. The agency was also creating new areas of expertise in order to more effectively track terrorist activities. The success of counterterrorism measures by the U.S. and Pakistani authorities precipitated the decision by Al Qaeda to relocate in mass to the tribal regions of Pakistan in order to limit detection and apprehension. This would change the very nature of the war on terror.

THE BASE SHIFTS LOCATION: AL QAEDA IN THE TRIBAL REGIONS

Relocating and establishing stable bases within the tribal area of Pakistan were vital to the reformation of Al Qaeda. In addition, Western interests shifted from the Afghanistan-Pakistan theater of operations to Iraq. The first major large-scale successful operation carried out that was connected to Pakistan was the London bombing of July 2005. Four suicide bombers detonated bombs in the London Underground and on a bus, killing 52 people. This was the worst terrorist attack in British history. Al Qaeda claimed the attack was revenge for British support for the Iraq war effort. The operatives that carried out the mission were trained in Waziristan. One of the significant changes taking place was that many of the operatives trained in the tribal belt had Western backgrounds. This fact made carrying out operations much easier (Norell, 90–92).

Western intelligence agents attempted to strike against Al Qaeda in early 2006. On January 13, a bombing raid was carried out in Damadola, Pakistan, in the Bajaur district at a compound that was believed to house Ayman Zawahiri. The location was hit by Hellfire missiles, killing a number of militants and civilians, but Zawahiri was not among them. This shift in focus to the tribal regions with an emphasis on North Waziristan was based on intelligence data showing that training facilities for the Taliban and Al Qaeda were being established in the area. The focus in these facilities was mostly bomb making, small-scale arms training, and assassination techniques (Jones, 227).

Osama bin Laden also seemed to take on a more prominent public relations role in 2006. Early in the year, numerous tapes were released featuring bin Laden that seemed to assert a more active and strategic role for Al Qaeda's number one. The reappearance of bin Laden and the reestablishment of physical bases in Pakistan's tribal region alarmed the U.S. intelligence community. The trouble was that the U.S. military had committed to the war effort in Iraq. This decision by the Bush administration played a role in the rebirth of Al Qaeda in the remote regions of Pakistan. National Intelligence estimates state that the group had changed dramatically from the structural set up at the time of the 9/11 attacks. Al Qaeda was now highly decentralized with multiple networks and a much more global outlook. The organization had affiliates in dozens of countries, which created more difficulties in tracking the group's activities. It was impossible for the Al Qaeda franchises to actually contact the leadership. The militants knew the key targets, and, when possible, operatives would receive training in the remote tribal areas. This system was not without problems as some affiliate groups would go rogue and create havoc within the jihadist community. In addition, philosophical differences emerged over strategy and tactics as to whether to create sectarian divisions by attacking Shiites, or to targeting corrupt Muslim governments and Western interests (Yusuf, 1–3).

Intelligence gathering was also difficult due to the overemphasis on Iraq. Limited resources remained in the AfPak areas of operation. The surge in Iraq drained the best counterterrorism operatives as well desperately needed resources. Several advisors from the Bush administration, including Robert Grenier, Michael Hayden, and Steve Kappes, and Michael Leiter, pressed for a more aggressive program centered on the tribal areas. These advisors wanted more drones, agents on the ground in the country, and increased cross-border raids using Special Operations

Forces (Bergen, 72). As stated earlier, the drone's usage did indeed increase
in the last year of the Bush presidency. The success rate was significant as
half of the key Al Qaeda leaders residing in the tribal areas were killed
during the final six months of 2008. Furthermore, the administration gave
the green light for cross-border raids into South Waziristan, which proved
to be counterproductive and a public relations disaster as several women
and children were killed during operations conducted in the fall of 2008.
These cross-border incursions infuriated the Pakistani military and intelligence community as both General Parvez Kayani and ISI head Ahmed
Shuja Pasha logged official protests against the American actions. Overall,
the frustrating part of the attacks in the tribal region from the perspective
of President Bush was of course that neither of the top two Al Qaeda leaders was located by the time he left office in January 2009.

   After years of frustration and angst over the trail going dry, intelligence
officers at CIA headquarters came up with an idea that would eventually
pay huge dividends. Bin Laden was difficult to track because of his careful
planning and security measures dating back to the early 1990s. He moved
frequently and always had a heavily armed security entourage with him.
The key would be to map out the associates who knew him best, including
family and friends. The bin Laden unit at CIA headquarters was formed
in December 1995. On several occasions prior to 9/11, the team pointed to
opportunities where bin Laden could have been taken out. Some calculate
as few as three, while others, including Michael Scheuer, the leader of the
bin Laden unit, claimed it was approximately ten. Several officials believed
that bin Laden could have been taken out in February 1999 when they had
confirmed his location on a hunting expedition near Kandahar, but he was
with government officials from the United Arab Emirates. A strike could
have been a diplomatic catastrophe, so it was called off (Kux, 349).

   The first option for the CIA team was to look at possible protectors of bin
Laden. His allies from the Soviet war in the 1980s included the Haqqani
family, which controlled large swaths of territory in Afghanistan and Pakistan. The area of Waziristan would have been the most obvious place for
the sheik to seek sanctuary under the protection of the family patriarch
Jalaluddin Haqqani. The lack of any credible intelligence coming out of
the region led the CIA to nix the Waziristan area off the probable list where
bin Laden might be hiding. A second option where bin Laden could have
sought protection was from Gulbuddin Hekmatyar, the warlord from the
earlier conflicts. Even though the two had collaborated on earlier operations, they were not close enough where bin Laden would have trusted
him with his life. Other former allies that might have been possible links
to bin Laden were also crossed off the list, including Mullah Omar and
Mohammed Khalis.

   Over 30 tapes were released by Osama bin Laden following the 9/11
attacks. Years of analyzing these tapes never revealed a key clue about

the location of the world's most wanted fugitive. Thousands of leads were investigated at the CIA and Pentagon by intelligence officials without any success. The tapes revealed bin Laden to be in good health, and his attire was neat and clean, leading experts to believe he was not living in some remote primitive location. An additional problem was that no human intelligence was available to help in the tracking of bin Laden (Bergen, "Manhunt," 106–107). The agencies involved had become so overreliant on technology that the human element had been significantly downgraded.

The intelligence community attempted to follow-up on hundreds of leads, many of which were far-fetched. In addition, the CIA studied previous manhunt operations, including the Israel mission to capture Adolf Eichmann and the successful mission by the Columbian authorities working with the CIA to kill Colombian drug lord Pablo Escobar. In addition, analysts studied the Russian mission against Chechen leader Dzhokhar Dudayev and the FBI mission to locate Olympic bomber Eric Rudolph. Bin Laden's paranoia even prior to the 9/11 attacks made him difficult to track. He had never used a cell phone on a regular basis, so tracking him through his use of technology was virtually impossible.

Eventually, the CIA contacted Brad Garrett, whose claim to fame was the tracking of Aimal Kansi, who was responsible for the attack on the agency headquarters in January 1993. Garrett located him in 1997 after receiving a tip from a Pakistani informant in the central Pakistani city of Dera Ghazi Khan. Garrett's consultation with the authorities included a clear message that the United States should not trust the Pakistani authorities. Leaks were commonplace, so he encouraged the agencies to act alone in any operations to apprehend bin Laden or other top operatives. The issue again came back to the lack of reliable human intelligence for developing leads about the whereabouts of Osama bin Laden.

Four years after the 9/11 attacks, Al Qaeda was active in multiple countries with franchise operations in Lebanon, Iraq, Yemen, Somalia, and a number of other nations. The CIA reassigned members of the team that had been hunting bin Laden as the realization of a growing global jihadist problem was becoming apparent (Burke, 150–152). The hope that a detainee at Guantanamo would provide the critical piece of intelligence never materialized. Also, it proved impossible to ever infiltrate the Al Qaeda network with a spy. The counterterrorism community was demoralized by the lack of substantial leads.

A PLAN AND A BREAK IN THE CASE

Key operatives that had worked the bin Laden case came up with a plan that included locating the courier network and possible family members, which might lead to a break in the case. Operatives also felt that tracking his outreach to the media and the senior leadership might prove to be beneficial. Ultimately, the most promising avenue to explore would be the courier network. The analysis pointed to several conclusions by the end of 2006. Osama bin Laden was probably not moving around frequently and was not meeting face-to-face with any of his key leadership team. Bin Laden was not living in a harsh environment in the sophisticated cave complexes of the tribal regions. None of the Al Qaeda operatives captured in subsequent years had ever actually seen Osama. Furthermore, the security team that had protected him for so many years had been killed or captured in the post-9/11 fighting. Having a sizeable entourage would have also drawn attention to him so he was more than likely with a tiny group of followers. A close reading of bin Laden's life did point to the importance of family for the leader of Al Qaeda (Bergen, "Manhunt," 70–71). This led agents to speculate that he might be living with one or more of his wives and family members. If this was the case, it was also speculated that bin Laden was probably living in an urban area, like Karachi or Lahore.

The trail to bin Laden started with the 20th hijacker, a Saudi named Mohammed al-Qahtani. He was detained at the Orlando airport in August 2001 and refused entry into the United States by a suspicious customs agent, who realized he did not speak English and had purchased a one-way ticket into America. Qahtani was captured during the retreat to Tora Bora in December 2001. He was tortured by the interrogators for 48 days and at one point mentioned the name of an Al Qaeda operative that KSM had told him to contact by the name of Abu Ahmed al-Kuwaiti. This name surfaced later as the man who trained many of the 9/11 attackers and later helped bin Laden escape from Tora Bora. Another detainee, Hassan Ghul, told the CIA that Kuwaiti had traveled frequently with bin Laden and was one of his key couriers. He also had a very close relationship with Al Qaeda's number three, Abu Faraj al-Libi. Interestingly, Libi resided in Abbottabad, but intelligence agents did not carefully look at the city as a likely location for bin Laden for several years. The problem in finding Abu Ahmed al-Kuwaiti was that operatives used a number of aliases and because so many members of the organization had been killed in the years since 9/11, the likelihood of finding him was scant. The search for al-Kuwaiti would be slow, but his connection seemed to be the most promising courier lead thus far (Bowden, 63–64).

Once President Barak Obama assumed the presidency, the focal point of the war on terror shifted gradually back to the AfPak theater of operations. Obama had run stating that the Bush administration was fighting on the wrong battlefield in the war on terror. Obama's aggressive stance and liberal use of drone strikes surprised many who felt he would be more cautious and soft in matters of foreign policy. In addition, he quickly became obsessed with apprehending or killing Osama bin Laden. Obama ordered CIA director Leon Panetta to increase efforts to track down the Al Qaeda leader. Most of the top-tier intelligence officers did tell the president that it was the overwhelming consensus that he was in Pakistan (Bergen, 115). Within six months after assuming the presidency, Obama had another follow-up meeting with key intelligence leaders pressing them to come up with a clear and detailed plan of action for bringing bin Laden to justice.

The intelligence community finally seemed to catch a break when they placed a supposed Jordan spy inside the Al Qaeda network. Jordanian officials had arrested Humam al-Balawi, a Jordanian pediatrician, in 2009. Once in custody, he stated his willingness to go to the tribal regions to gather intel on the Taliban and Al Qaeda. The CIA station chief in Khost Jennifer Matthews set up a meeting with Balawi at the Forward Operating Base Chapman on December 30. The desire to have a coordinal first meeting with Balawi caused the security to be lax. This led to a grave tragedy as Balawi had a suicide vest strapped onto his body, which he detonated killing seven CIA agents including Matthews. This attack was the single worst day for the intelligence community since the Beirut embassy bombing of 1983 (Bergen, "Manhunt," 118–120).

A sense of urgency about the growing threat from Al Qaeda and specifically the training operations in the Pakistani tribal areas was becoming a stark reality. In the fall of 2009, Najibullah Zazi planned to launch a martyrdom operation in the Manhattan subway on the eighth anniversary of the 9/11 attacks. Zazi was an Afghan American who was trained by Al Qaeda in Pakistan. FBI agents who had been following him once he had returned from the region apprehended the operative.

Within three months, another attack was adverted when on Christmas Day Umar Farouk Abdulmutallab, a Nigerian from an affluent family, attempted to detonate explosives that were placed in his underwear while he was aboard flight 253 from Amsterdam heading to Detroit. The plastic explosives were not detected by airport security and had it not been for the quick action of the passengers, along with the possible faulty construction of the bomb, 300 lives would have probably been lost.

A third major plot in less than a year with a connection to the tribal region was an attempt in Times Square on a Saturday night in May 2010. Faisal Shahzad, an American of Pakistani origin tried unsuccessfully to blow up an SUV filled with explosives. The Taliban had trained Shahzad in Waziristan. U.S. officials were furious with Pakistani authorities, but this seemed illogical since the attacker was indeed a U.S. citizen. The government was now sending considerably more intelligence agents into Pakistan, as it was undoubtedly the epicenter of terrorism training and activity (Rashid, "Pakistan on the Brink," 154–155). Frustration was mounting within the intelligence community, as Pakistan cooperation seemed lackadaisical at times.

A phone call was intercepted confirming that the courier Kuwaiti was not only alive but also active within Al Qaeda circles. He took careful steps to ensure that his phone could not be traced to the Abbottabad region by making sure to take the battery out and not place it back in until he was several hours away around Peshawar. The CIA eventually tracked Kuwaiti to a large compound in Abbottabad that quickly received scrutiny from the intelligence officers following the courier. Agency operatives briefed Director Panetta that a large compound in the city seemed to be going to extraordinary measures to keep a high level of secrecy. For months, U.S. efforts to breach the compound were unsuccessful as the occupant's trash was buried, the children living in the compound were home schooled and never ventured out, and the structure was built in a way to protect the occupants from surveillance. Intelligence officers also tried to set up a vaccination program in order to infiltrate the compound, which proved unsuccessful.

Agents working the bin Laden case did not reach a consensus on the likelihood of the Al Qaeda leader being at the location. Several longtime bin Laden trackers gave a greater than 90 percent probability that he was at the Abbottabad location, while others put the percentage as low as 40 percent. The doubt about bin Laden being located at the compound was threefold according to Peter Bergen's analysis of CIA accounts. Abbottabad was the center of Pakistan military training and home to the largest military school in the country. Second, a large group of children were living in the compound, which would seem like a significant security risk. Third, the compound was much larger than the surrounding neighborhood structures, making it stand out to visitors. Finally, the probability that Osama bin Laden had been in the Abbottabad location for six years seemed unbelievable (Schmidle, "Getting Bin Laden," 4–6). Close surveillance of the compound over a period of several months led to the realization that three separate families resided in the structure. Satellite images could only confirm that a tall "pacer" would walk every day and that this particular individual never left the compound for any reason. Unfortunately, all the evidence presented was circumstantial.

The Kuwaiti brothers who ended up as the caretakers of bin Laden in his final six years at the Abbottabad compound were originally from northern Pakistan but had lived in the Gulf region most of their lives. They could easily travel between Pakistan and the Arab world without drawing much suspicion. The brothers were longtime members of Al Qaeda, and their role as couriers would prove invaluable in keeping Osama bin Laden connected to the outside world. Most information transported out of the compound ended up with bin Laden's chief of staff, Atiyah Abdul Rahman, a key member of Al Qaeda and of Libyan descent. The logistical challenge of trying to direct the Al Qaeda franchises globally was significant. Disagreements were commonplace, as affiliates like Al Qaeda in Iraq under Abu Musab Abu Zarqawi had philosophical differences with the main Al Qaeda leadership. Throughout bin Laden's time in Abbottabad, he became convinced of the importance of media and public relations in the conflict with the West. He thus felt the tactics of Zarqawi that emphasized egregious violence tarnished the group's image. The main focus needed to be attacking the "far enemy," the United States (Scott-Clark and Levy, 240–241). The hope was for a spectacular attack to coincide with the 10th anniversary of 9/11. Al Qaeda was beset with several problems, including financial issues, new technology innovations by the West, such as drones that were making Al Qaeda's day-to-day operations more difficult, and the relevance of the terrorism group in the wake of the Arab Spring uprisings. It seemed that Al Qaeda did not offer the Muslim world any solutions to the pressing social and economic problems confronting the average citizen (Bergen, 148).

The struggle within the U.S. government about staging an attack on the possible location of bin Laden in Abbottabad was intense. Sharp disagreements between key players in the Obama White House made the decision challenging. The intelligence was inconclusive, and unfortunately, it was doubtful it would get any better in the foreseeable future. The longer the United States waited, the higher the probability that a leak of some sort could occur.

Special Operations had become routine for the U.S. military. In the Afghan theater alone, the number had increased tenfold between 2008 and 2010. The overseer of the missions was the Joint Special Operations Command (JSOC), which was able to act without congressional oversight. They were not as accountable as the CIA with a clear goal of intelligence gathering and commencing covert actions to target enemies that threatened U.S. interests in the region.

President Obama was presented multiple courses of action in regard to the situation in Abbottabad. A B-2 bomber could flatten the compound, killing all the inhabitants. The same type of outcome could occur if a surgical drone strike was used. In both cases, clear evidence that bin Laden was dead might not be verifiable. A SEAL raid would be risky but would provide clear evidence of whether bin Laden was actually one of the inhabitants. The raid included the obvious possibility of casualties and even a potential firefight with the Pakistan military. The helicopters would also need a refueling stop, which further lengthened the time the SEALS would be in Pakistani airspace. A key incentive with the raid option was that it could provide the opportunity to secure intelligence that might be with bin Laden in the compound quarters. In all three options, the violation of Pakistan sovereignty would be blatant, and the possibility of irreparable damage to the relationship was clear (Schmidle, "Getting Bin Laden," 5–6).

Admiral Mike Mullen, Defense Department top policy analyst Michele Flournoy, CIA director Leon Panetta, and counterterrorism advisor John Brennan were the strongest advocates for the raid options (Bergen, "Manhunt," 174–175). To many of the advisors, this was the best evidence on bin Laden since his escape from Tora Bora. All parties involved realized that the intelligence was never going to provide certainty that it was bin Laden. Mullen was very close to General Kayani, but he had made it clear to him on several occasions that if the United States had the opportunity to get bin Laden or Zawahiri, he would not hesitate to take quick and decisive action. Two key Obama advisors voiced opposition against the raid option. Vice President Joe Biden worried about the possible implosion of relations with Pakistan. He wanted to wait until more clear-cut intelligence could be gathered, while Defense Secretary Robert Gates came out as the most vocal critic of the plan. Gates had been involved in Operation Eagle Claw, the 1979 failed mission to rescue the hostages from Iran. The failure of the mission was considered critical in Carter's failed bid to win reelection in 1980. Gates felt that President Obama should proceed with caution regarding the Abbottabad operation.

An additional glitch in the proposed operation was the case of Raymond Davis. In January 2011, Davis, who was a CIA contractor, killed two Pakistani citizens in Lahore. Davis claimed self-defense because he was threatened as the two men attempted to rob him. Many Pakistanis felt he was not justified and wanted him charged and executed for his crime. This episode heightened tensions, and the United States was eventually forced to pay $2 million in blood money to secure his release (Davidson, 2–3). The Pakistanis were becoming increasingly critical of the increased CIA presence in their country and warned of possible crackdowns in the near future.

The military was well prepared for this type of operation, having conducted hundreds of such raids since 9/11. The team that would carry out the raid trained in Colorado and Dam Neck, Virginia, before departing for Bagram Air Base in Afghanistan. General McRaven assured the president and his team that the operation could be completed in approximately 30 minutes. The problem that concerned the military leaders and the dozen or so White House officials aware of the operation was the significant amount of time the SEALS would spend in Pakistan territory. Approximately two-dozen meetings were held in the time leading up to the raid before President Obama made the final decision (Scott-Clark and Levy, 379–381).

The target date of May 1 was pushed back 24 hours because of heavy cloud cover. The mission named Operation Neptune Spear was undertaken Sunday evening. The surreal notion that bin Laden was living for six years a mile from Pakistan's elite military academy was astounding. The flight time for the state-of-the-art MH-60 Black Hawk helicopters was 90 minutes. The mission quickly suffered a severe setback as one of the two Black Hawks had to force land as the unexpectedly high temps coupled with a heavier-than-expected weight caused it to malfunction once it arrived on the grounds of the compound in Abbottabad. The tail of the chopper clipped the exterior wall, breaking off the tail rotor. The expert landing by the pilot was critical in ensuring that none of the SEALs were injured and the operation could proceed quickly.

Upon entering the compound, the SEALs quickly encountered bin Laden's courier Kuwaiti and killed him. The commandos proceeded on killing Abrat (Kuwaiti's brother) and his wife. The SEALs then dispatched bin Laden's unarmed son Khalid. Upon encountering bin Laden, the SEALs shot his wife, Amal, wounding her in the leg. Bin Laden was killed with a shot to the chest and eye. The message was sent to McRaven that Geronimo (the code name for bin Laden) was EKIA (enemy killed in action) (Schmidle, "Getting Bin Laden," 13). The president had been watching a live feed of the raid from the White House Situation Room with key advisors, including Secretary of State Hillary Clinton, Vice President Biden, CIA director Panetta, and several select officials.

The mission now shifted to destroying the downed helicopter and gathering the enormous stash of information from bin Laden's living quarters. Finally, photograph recognition needed to be taken as well as DNA samples to guarantee that they had the right man. The body of bin Laden would be taken from the compound in order to dispose it of at sea. As the SEALs gathered the intel, crowds of onlookers had to be dispersed. The SEALs compiled computers, cell phones, thumb drives, computer disks, and DVDs (Schmidle, 14). As the chopper was blown up, the team departed after a total operation time of slightly over three hours. The facial analysis and later DNA test confirmed the identity.

President Obama was pressured to make an announcement fairly quickly after the raid ended. Because of the helicopter mishap, the operation could not be concealed for very long. Furthermore, it was decided that the possibility of a leak was high, so the decision was made to go public with a live announcement on Sunday evening. Admiral Mullen notified General Kayani by phone, and Obama called Pakistani president Asif Ali Zardari, who was grateful that the group indirectly responsible for his wife's murder had been brought to justice. Obama also notified former presidents George Bush and Bill Clinton. Approximately 55 million Americans listened to Obama's announcement that the architect of the 9/11 attacks against American had been eliminated (Bergen, "Manhunt," 239).

It was decided that bin Laden would be disposed of at sea after proper Muslim burial procedures were followed. In accordance with Islamic customs, the burial occurred within 24 hours after his death. The body was dropped into the Arabian Sea at approximately 2:00 am Washington time on May 2 with the event witnessed by a handful of soldiers on the flight deck of the USS *Carl Vinson*.

Back in Washington, intelligence experts started to comb through the materials taken from the Abbottabad compound. Over one hundred operatives worked 24/7 to translate and interpret the information. One important fact that did emerge quickly was that bin Laden still had control over

Al Qaeda and was still planning operations. He had not been in total isolation, semi-retired, and unable to reach the organization.

The Pakistani police arrived at the scene of the raid shortly after the departure of the SEALS. The officials found 14 children handcuffed, several screaming women, and four dead bodies. The helicopter was burning, and the scene was becoming chaotic. When General Pasha, head of the ISI, was notified, his subordinates incorrectly informed him that a Pakistani helicopter had crashed, but since they did not have the ability to fly at night, he knew something was seriously wrong. Since the Abbottabad region is in close proximity to some of the nuclear weapons, the security situation was serious. Quickly after the details were released, the military and security apparatus started to go into damage control regarding the onslaught of negative public relations since the world's most wanted man had been living in such close proximity to key security installations for over six years (Soherwordi and Khattak, 353–354).

The Pakistani leadership quickly expressed disproval for how the relationship with the United States was evolving. The partnership seemed to be very one-sided as the United States acted unilaterally making decisions that cost Pakistani lives and made the ability to govern challenging. From increased drone strikes to the Raymond Davis case to the proliferation of U.S. intelligence agents secretly operating in Pakistan, the perception was one of a lack of trust. The bin Laden raid was the culminating event, however. Both the army and intelligence agencies were embarrassed, and the public confidence in these institutions was at an all-time low. It seemed that the relationship was harmed beyond repair.

Within the United States, the strain was also very apparent and accusations that the Pakistani government had been protecting bin Laden quickly surfaced in the Congress. Within the media, rumors also circulated that bin Laden's whereabouts were known by a select group within the highest level of the ISI. Since Pakistan had received billions of dollars in aid from the United States since 9/11, the frustration level was high. Several members of Congress including Mike Rogers, a Michigan Republican, publicly condemned the regime and especially the intelligence community in Pakistan (Goldberg and Ambinder, 54). Senator John Kerry was sent to Pakistan to try and mend the relationship. He met with Kayani and Pasha to attempt to heal the rift. Kerry also wanted the CIA to question bin Laden's wives who were being detained.

CONTROVERSY SURROUNDING THE WHEREABOUTS OF OSAMA BIN LADEN

The public and scholarly debate about bin Laden's relationship with Pakistani officials remains unresolved. Al Qaeda experts and prominent writers Seth Jones and Peter Bergen state that no clear evidence has proven that the Pakistani hierarchy knew that bin Laden had been living in Pakistan for six years. In the ensuing period, several conflicting accounts with differing degrees of creditability have surfaced. The most notable critic of the standard view comes from *The New York Times* reporter and author of *The Wrong Enemy: America in Afghanistan 2001–2014*, Carlotta Gall. During her more than a decade of reporting from the frontlines of the war on terror, Gall became one of the leading voices telling the public the story of the post-9/11 policies of the United States. In her view, the Abbottabad compound was designated as a safe house, which meant it was under the watch and protection of the Pakistani military or intelligence agencies. The compound was known as the Waziristan haveli or mansion that was known to provide sanctuary for tribal militants traveling or recuperating. These safe houses were typically located in secure neighborhoods. They usually had high walls, and the focus was on seclusion and security, and, in many cases, there would be armed guards. At times, key militant leaders have been held in such locations, and the local security apparatus is keenly aware of these locations and know to avoid disrupting these facilities. Gall's informants stated that the ISI plays a game in which they help to track down some militants to help the United States in the war on terror, while others are provided protection from the same forces. In the case of the Abbottabad compound, no guards were involved, but bin Laden's movements would have been strictly monitored. With the compound being literally in the backyard of the Kakul Military Academy, no one really believed that his whereabouts were unknown or that the 40-minute SEAL raid could have been carried out without forewarned knowledge. Gall stated that police and intelligence agencies have informants throughout the city.

Gall said that it took months of investigation and interviews before she came up with the key to breaking open the case. According to a source inside the ISI, she discovered that a special desk assigned to handle Osama bin Laden existed. His main handler did not report to a superior in order to provide a clear sense of plausible deniability. The upper level of the ISI was aware of the inner workings of the bin Laden desk. The fact that bin Laden was placed in this safe house by Pakistani officials explains why the compound did not have any escape routes or, backdoors, or places to hide in. Bin Laden realized that he was solely dependent on the Pakistani authorities, and if they turned on him, he would have no way out. Gall also believes that bin Laden had told his colleagues in Al Qaeda about the chance of betrayal by his Pakistani handlers. General Helmly stated the probability that the ISI knew in an e-mail exchange with Gall in 2013. Pakistani retired general Ziauddin Butt also told Gall that General Musharraf and Ejaz Shah (head of Internal Security in Pakistan) had approved moving bin Laden into the safe house several years earlier. Shah stated, "Nobody can believe he was there without people knowing . . . In a Pakistani village, they notice even a stray dog" (Gall, 250). Her research shows that Lieutenant General Nadeem Taj, Chief of Staff Ashfaq Parvez Kayani, and ISI head General Ahmad Shuja Pasha all would have known of bin Laden's whereabouts. The final damming detail was Gall's claim that the United States had evidence that Pasha knew of bin Laden's location because of an intercepted phone call after the raid. American officials were not interested in releasing this information because it served no purpose and would further complicate the already difficult relationship in the post-raid period. The Obama administration claimed that no clear evidence pointed to Pakistani knowledge of bin Laden being in Abbottabad. Several critics claim the administration was covering up the details to maintain the Pakistani assistance in the war on terror.

The information gathered from the raid revealed that bin Laden had been maintaining correspondence with Taliban leader Mullah Omar, LeT leader Hafiz Saeed, and a number of other militant leaders. Many of these individuals maintained close ties with the ISI, providing further circumstantial evidence pointing to a wider conspiracy surrounding the Pakistani knowledge of bin Laden's whereabouts. According to Gall and other investigative journalists, bin Laden did travel from the Abbottabad compound in order to meet with Al Qaeda leaders and other militants and to help facilitate terrorist activities. In 2009, bin Laden had met with Qari Saifullah Akhtar in Kohat, Pakistan. Akhtar is one of the most important connections between the militants and the ISI. He was the man personally responsible for helping Mullah Omar escape from Kandahar in 2001 and was credited with the successful plot to assassinate Benazir Bhutto in 2007. Akhtar wanted bin Laden's help in launching an attack against Pakistan's Army Headquarters in Rawalpindi. Bin Laden felt this was a counterproductive move and refused to help with the mission because the main goal of global jihad should be attacking the United States. An attack on Pakistan would destroy the needed sanctuary that Al Qaeda and other militant groups needed in order to survive. This meeting was known by Pakistani officials, which Gall puts forth as evidence that elements of the government knew about bin Laden's location in Pakistan. In any case, what was clear throughout this time period was that Pakistani insurgents and Al Qaeda remained in contact. Virtually all of the militants captured in the post-9/11 period were found in the residences of Islamist supporters in the country (Jones, 88–89).

The aftermath of the raid opened up the Pakistani military and intelligence community to intense criticism. The supposed ineptitude of the armed forces made many citizens and critics in the media believe that the nation could be vulnerable to an attack from its main rival, India. The decade of support for the United States had been counterproductive according to many pundits, and Pakistan was weaker than ever from backing the West. In addition, Pakistan was being constantly berated by American officials and the Western media for a failure to do more in regards to the war on terror.

The situation in Pakistan heated up in late May as militants targeted the Naval Station outside of Karachi, killing 10 and causing millions of dollars in damage to equipment purchased from the United States at the location, including surveillance planes. In this time period after the bin Laden raid, America wanted to see an amped-up effort on the part of the Pakistanis. The reaction ended up just the opposite as a more nationalistic, combative Pakistan was emerging. The violation of sovereignty, along with the Raymond Davis fiasco and the U.S. growing network of CIA agents working inside Pakistan, made the government more hostile to American efforts (Markey, 208–209).

Pakistani policy turned in disturbing directions as the CIA station chief in Islamabad was exposed and one of the country's leading journalists, Saleem Shahzad, was kidnapped and brutally murdered on the orders of the ISI. The Pakistan government was also allowing militant activity to flourish as operatives from the Haqqani network launched an attack on the Inter-Continental Hotel in Kabul. Furthermore, U.S. requests to help in the apprehension of Mullah Omar and Sirajuddin Haqqani were disregarded. Matters only worsened through the summer and fall of 2011. A spike in cross-border militancy activity occurred as a truck bomb attack planned and coordinated from Pakistani safe havens was carried out at the U.S. military base in Wardak Province. Days later, the U.S. embassy in Kabul was attacked by militants from the Haqqani network. Finally, the former president of Afghanistan, Burhanuddin Rabbani, was killed by a suicide bomber while en route to peace talks in Kabul. Authorities believed the ISI had a hand in the assassination. U.S. officials went public, condemning Pakistani officials during congressional testimony and in the media (Rashid, 181).

Relations between the countries were in a free fall and hit a new low following a November U.S. airstrike that accidently killed 24 soldiers from the Pakistani Army stationed on the Afghan-Pakistan border. The Pakistan government retaliated by closing the border to NATO supply trucks heading into Afghanistan. The standstill would last for seven months, proving costly to the Western powers fighting the insurgency in Afghanistan. Experts believed that the government and military were in conflict and a coup possibility might be in the works. When evidence surfaced that the United States might intervene to stop a coup, anger in Pakistan intensified even further.

A STRIKE AGAINST GENDER EMPOWERMENT: THE CASE OF MALALA YOUSAFZAI

Once the Pakistani Taliban had solidified its position in the tribal region, they worked toward the stated goal of implementing sharia and establishing a conservative social order. Within the Swat region, their presence was ominous. The insurgents wore long straggly hair and beards and black turbans proclaiming slogans such as "sharia law or martyrdom." One of the key targets of the movement was girls' schools (Khattak, 292–293). The regional commander (and future leader of the TTP) was Maulana Fazlullah, known commonly as "Radio Mullah." His propaganda war against the Pakistani government and the evils of Western influence were aired through his nightly radio broadcasts. His charismatic style made him popular with the locals, who were fed up with the high levels of corruption and the lack of a functioning judicial system. His attacks on Western media and technology led to television, CD, and DVD burnings, as well as the outlawing of virtually all forms of music. However, the most hostile attacks were reserved for women. Warnings were issued about women appearing outside of their homes, and extremely modest dress was required. Female education was discouraged, and schools like the Khushal Academy (ran by Malala Yousafzai's father) received threats. The leader of the TNSM, Sufi Mohammad, went as far as to proclaim from prison that there should not be education for women. Girls who dropped out were praised on the nightly radio broadcast. As the insurgents' grip over the region tightened, local sharia courts began operating, ordering floggings and the halt to international programs trying to eradicate polio. The vaccination program was supposedly a Western plot to sterilize the women so that the population would die out (Yousafzai, 120).

By the fall of 2006, regional violence was intensifying as suicide attacks were becoming more commonplace in response to American drone operations. An attack at the army barracks at Dargai killed 42 members of the Pakistani armed forces. This was the beginning of a deadly chapter in the terror campaign in Pakistan. The militants also started attacking and murdering local political agents and mullahs who did not preach the extremist philosophy of the Taliban. Threats and attacks against girls' schools were becoming common, as Ziauddin Yousafzai found a note pinned to the front door of the school warning that the institution was Western inspired and preaching infidel ideas.

Malala's account of this early period paints a picture of growing boldness on the part of the militants. Slowly, but surely, the fundamental parts of normal, everyday life in the Swat region were being altered. From the restrictions on music to the eradication of symbols of religious diversity and works of art to the limitations on travel to the glorious tourist attractions, Swat was being altered in adverse ways. The threats from the Taliban were becoming more serious with the goal of instilling fear within the population. Furthermore, the country in general was in peril by 2007, as political disruptions in Islamabad and elsewhere preoccupied the Pakistani authorities.

Even when President Musharraf moved aggressively into Swat, the militants held firm. It seemed like a true civil war was emerging. This was also the time period when the militants gathered to officially form a united front known as the Tehrik-i-Taliban-Pakistan (TTP). The militants spread fear in the region as they targeted the police and military. Through these dark times, Malala's father kept his school operating, as it became a safe haven and sanctuary for the youth in the adjacent area. By the end of 2008, over 400 schools in the region were damaged or destroyed, and the dropout rate for females was very high. In Malala's class, the number of students had decreased from 27 down to 10 (Yousafzai, 157).

Eventually, Malala was given the opportunity to appear in the media to discuss the importance of education for girls. This was a bold and dangerous move, but it was needed in order to give the people a voice and to counter the negative stereotypes concerning Pakistan. This powerful platform for Malala was important in combating the messages coming from extremists like Maulana Fazlullah. Eventually, Malala was contacted to secretly write a diary that would be published by the BBC. The entries would appear in a blog. The international media was looking for a voice for the Pakistani citizenry and Malala was the perfect representative. *The New York Times* aired a documentary, "Class Dismissed in Swat Valley," and supporters, such as Stanford student Shiza Shahid, became ardent supporters of her cause. The Taliban eventually forced all girls' schools to close with threats of death for those who did not follow the edict. In one striking excerpt, Malala stated, "The Taliban could take our pens and books, but they couldn't stop our minds from thinking" (Yousafzai, 146).

Many community leaders in Swat had decided that the TTP was here to stay and started working with them. The security apparatus seemed unwilling or unable to combat the Taliban. Many residents felt that some Pakistani officials supported the efforts of Talibanization in the region. The citizens of the region seemed to be caught in a no-win situation between increased militancy and corrupt officials that had zero trust within the community (Abbas, 146). Over a third of the population of Mingora had fled the region, and the Pakistani military had moved in over 12,000 troops to the area.

A peace deal was negotiated between the TTP and the government, but, as was always the case, it did not last for very long. The Taliban was overconfident, and when Sufi Mohammad proclaimed that the militants would soon move on to Islamabad, danger seemed eminent. The Obama administration pressed the Pakistanis to take action in order to secure the region. The military launched Operation True Path in order to retake Swat (Khattak, 307). This massive operation required all residents to leave the area. Malala and her family were to be Internally Displaced Persons (IDPs). Nearly two million residents were forced from their homes in the spring of 2009.

Malala's family ended up residing with relatives in the village of Karshat in Shangla Province. During the exile, they had the opportunity to travel to Islamabad, where Malala was able to meet with the U.S. envoy for Afghanistan and Pakistan, Richard Holbrooke. After three months, the family was able to return to their home in Mingora. The intense fighting devastated the area, and a large percentage of buildings were damaged during the operation. When Malala's father reached the Khushal School, they realized that the facility had become a battle zone. As for the Pakistani Taliban, the leadership had fled into Kunar Province in Afghanistan, including the inspirational leader Fazlullah. The military had arrested thousands, including many youngsters who had been trained as suicide bombers.

By late summer, schools were able to once again reopen. Malala had now become a very public figure, giving interviews and appearing on national television. She was also able to study journalism through her connections with the British organization Open Minds Pakistan. As things seemed to be returning to a sense of normalcy, another tragedy struck, as devastating floods swept across the northwest portion of the country. Over 1,600 people were dead, and 3 million left homeless. An estimated 20 million people were severely affected. The infrastructure including roads, bridges, irrigation canals, health-care facilities, schools, farms, and homes were destroyed, which led to massive food shortages. Diseases such as cholera were rampant, and a humanitarian catastrophe was underway. The tragedy allowed room for the TTP to initiate relief efforts. Numerous organizations that had been banned by the Pakistani government were at the forefront of relief efforts and won the hearts and minds of the citizenry. It seemed that the region was cursed as misfortune followed misfortune (Yousafzai, 215–216).

Throughout 2011 and 2012, Malala's notoriety increased as she was nominated for several distinguished honors. Schools and awards were even named in her honor. Her parents started to become worried that she could become a target of the extremists. Malala felt that the cause of championing education was far too important, and she did not back down from her obligation. Eventually, the police received tips from intelligence sources that Malala might be targeted for an attack from Taliban operatives. In addition, her school was also receiving threats and criticism. The use of suicide missions was the common tactic by this time period.

Malala did take precautions in her daily activities. On October 9, 2012, several months after she turned 14 years old, Malala was taking exams at school. As she rode the school van home, the vehicle was pulled over by two young armed gunmen. They asked, "Who is Malala?," and before she could even respond, they fired, lodging three bullets into her head. She survived after an ordeal that included Pakistani national helicopters; a Saudi Arabian jet; a hospital in Birmingham, England; and multiple surgeries.

The attack on Malala placed the TTP on the front page of global news coverage. The average citizen did not even know that a separate Taliban organization existed in Pakistan. This event gave the group maximum notoriety but also quickly brought to the forefront the disagreements within the movement. Regional TTP leader Adnan Rasheed wrote an open letter to Malala in the summer of 2013 following her speech at the United Nations. In his critique, he mentioned the double standard of how the drone attacks kill hundreds of children who are never recognized. The media never makes a fuss about the indiscriminate killings of so many innocent Pakistanis in the bombing missions. Rasheed said the Taliban's frustration with the West's lack of consistency in placing a value on human life is what causes the grievances and leads to the decision to take the necessary measures to protect the citizens (Sheikh, 6–7). Other criticism eventually trickled out. Author and niece of Benazir Bhutto, Fatima Bhutto, stated "why not Noor Aziz, eight years old when killed by a drone strike in Pakistan or others killed by drones in Yemen or Iraq?" Many critics saw Malala as a potential propaganda tool for advocating a more aggressive military campaign in Pakistan. Others even spoke of the "White Savior Complex" with the story of the native girl being saved by the white man. For many observers, it fit the historical racist narrative that has been institutionalized (Ryder, 178).

CHAPTER 7

Sharif and Beyond: Pakistan's Contemporary Struggle with Extremism

There have been continual twists and turns over the past several years as Pakistan has tried to reestablish firm control over territories once controlled by terrorist elements. The tactics used by terrorist organizations such as the Pakistani Taliban have changed, becoming more desperate and violent as suicide operations became the norm. Civilian casualties have increased, and sectarian violence is at an all-time high within the country. In the past few years, the military has taken a more assertive role in trying to combat the terrorist problem. As the Tehrik-e-Taliban Pakistan (TTP) has gone through yet another leadership transition, the movement seems to be fracturing with rival groups unable to form a common leadership structure. On the surface, this seems like a positive development for the government, but in many ways the ability to track and combat the militants could become more problematic. As the regime of Nawaz Sharif took office in June 2013, Pakistan entered a new era because the democratic transition took place in a relatively successful manner.

SHARIF AND BEYOND: PAKISTAN'S CONTEMPORARY STRUGGLE WITH EXTREMISM

Overthrown in a coup d'état in 1999, later jailed, and eventually exiled, no one expected a political comeback by Nawaz Sharif. The overwhelming victory of Sharif as prime minister was a monumental day in Pakistani history. It was a record third electoral triumph for the 63-year-old formally disgraced leader of the Muslim League. Sharif captured 244 of 294 ballots cast in the lower house of Parliament. The day was a watershed moment for Pakistani democracy as the country saw the first free and fair transfer of power from one civilian leader to the next. The election turnout surpassed 60 percent, another sign of a robust democracy. Sharif did not need a coalition government to be formed, which allows for a cleaner and less complicated transition. Furthermore, many opposition party members encouraged Sharif form a strong, stable government (Fair and Watson, "Pakistan's Enduring Challenge," 131–132).

The obstacles facing the new leader were ominous both domestically and internationally. Chronic fuel shortages, rampant unemployment, and a lack of basic services and essentials like clean drinking water were some of the many challenges facing the new administration. On the foreign policy front, Sharif quickly called for an end to the devastating drone strikes that were being carried out by the Obama administration. A new direction in dealing with terrorism was also high on Sharif's agenda. As always, the fragile relationship with neighboring India was another pressing challenge facing Sharif. The delicate situation with Afghanistan also needed to be handled in a more effective manner. Encouraging foreign investment would also be of vital importance to the new administration. In addition, Sharif would seek a multibillion dollar bailout from the International Monetary Fund. Several regional experts believed that Sharif was more trusted by the military hierarchy than his predecessor, Asif Ali Zardari. The days of the military being able to run rough shot over, the government seemed to be over and tighter scrutiny was applied in the wake of embarrassing discoveries released from Wikileaks. This factored into Sharif having more power over the military than in earlier experiences. Above all, the issue of trust both internally and externally needed to be restored.

THE PAKISTANI TALIBAN SUFFERS A LOSS: THE DEATH OF HAKIMULLAH MEHSUD

For the third time in under a decade, the leader of the Pakistani Taliban was killed by a U.S.-orchestrated drone strike when on November 6, 2013, Hakimullah Mehsud was assassinated in North Waziristan. The timing was interesting as the Taliban leadership was contacted by the government of Nawaz Sharif with the intent of undertaking peace talks. Mehsud was schooled at a small madrassa in the Hangu district. His initial claim to fame was the ambush of NATO convoys in Khyber and Peshawar. He was also the architect of the 2007 mission that captured over 300 Pakistani soldiers. Mehsud had gathered with key Taliban leaders to discuss the Pakistani initiative. Mehsud was outspoken and not shy about granting interviews and going public with his message of jihad. Just weeks before his death, he had given an interview to the BBC in the tribal regions. This reckless behavior played into his demise. The assassination could be seen as a key step in destabilizing the movement, but at the same time any remote chance at peace with the militants in the foreseeable future died with Mehsud. For the United States, Hakimullah Mehsud was an extremely high-valued target as he was known to have set in place the tragic suicide mission in December 2009 that led to the deaths of seven CIA operatives in eastern Afghanistan. This single event catapulted Mehsud to the top of the most wanted list as far as the United States was concerned (Craig, *Washington Post*, 1). The drone strike against Mehsud blindsided Pakistani officials, who were furious, accusing the United States of sabotaging the peace talks. The authorities went as far as to lodge a formal protest against the United States with all five permanent members of the UN Security Council. The government once again felt that the United States was taking advantage of Pakistan and totally disregarding the wishes of the authorities. The rhetoric from the TTP was fierce, as a spokesman for the group stated, "every drop of Hakimullah's blood will turn into a suicide bomber." Authorities placed the nation on high alert following the assassination.

The most serious implication stemming from the assassination was the further factionalization of the TTP. Even before Hakimullah's death, apparent rifts were widening. Disagreements over whether to pursue peace talks with the government were apparent. Hakimullah's second-in-command, Waliur Rehman, had been killed in a drone strike in May 2013, so a clear replacement was uncertain. A significant void emerged, and rival elements began jockeying to take over the helm.

A definite change of direction occurred with the surprising announcement of Mullah Fazlullah as the new emir of the TTP. The leadership factions of the TTP made the announcement after six days of deliberations. Interestingly, Fazlullah's appointment was a surprise because the base of his support was not in the heartland of the tribal regions of Pakistan but in the northwestern region of Swat (Sheikh, 34–35). However, the once powerful Mehsud tribe had been decimated by the U.S. drone campaign, and the two previous leaders of the TTP had been killed by drone strikes. Fazlullah was the notorious leader of the radicalization of the Swat region from 2007 to 2009. His followers were also responsible for the attempted assassination of Malala Yousafzai in 2012. He was known to have strong connections to both Al Qaeda and the Haqqani network. Furthermore, the Afghan Taliban also believed Fazlullah was the best choice to lead the organization. He was respected as a religious scholar (though his actual credentials are somewhat suspect), and it was believed he would act in accordance to the will of the Afghan Taliban. Fazlullah sought sanctuary in the Kunar region of Afghanistan after the massive Pakistan military incursion into the Swat region in 2009. The BBC reported that Fazlullah was in the Tirah valley in the Pakistan-Afghan border area following the military sweep of the region. During an interview conducted by BBC reporter Haroon Rashid, it was apparent that Fazlullah was a strict ideologue, strongly committed to the implementation of sharia through-out the region. His devotion to the cause was absolute and unwavering. During the brief interview, Fazlullah warned of impending attacks against Pakistan officials to send a lesson to the authorities. He noted that "the region was God's land and the Taliban could go anywhere and no one can stop us" (Guerin, BBC News, July 11, 2013). By appointing Fazlullah to the position of emir, the Pakistani Taliban was sending a strong message that future talks with the government would not occur. Still, the fact that the vast majority of the TTP fighters were centered in North and South Waziristan made the change in leadership somewhat unexpected and risky. Ultimately, the directional change in using more aggressive and fre-quent suicide attacks can be attributed to the decision to place Mullah Fazlullah in the key leadership post of the TTP.

THE ARMY TAKES THE OFFENSIVE: ZARB-E-AZB

A leadership shift in the Pakistan military occurred as longtime army chief Ashfaq Kayani handed over the reins to General Raheel Sharif in November 2013. Sharif made it clear that a more aggressive anti-terrorist policy would be implemented in both South and North Waziristan. His disproportionate retaliation against the TTP was apparent in operations conducted in Khajori and Mir Ali. Following a terrorist ambush against a military convoy and a suicide attack at a check point, General Sharif ordered a massive counterattack. The military operation included the use of helicopter gunships, mortars, and tanks against suspected militant strongholds. The media was forbidden from entering the site of the attack. The authorities claimed to have killed mostly foreign fighters (many from Uzbekistan). Civilians claimed enormous collateral damage, and Maulana Fazlur Rehman stated that the 60 or so killed in the attack were all civil-ians. In addition, houses and mosques were destroyed. This retaliation ushered in a new chapter in the campaign in North Waziristan (Sareen, 3–4). The military was now taking on a more aggressive tone in combat-ing the militants. The Sharif doctrine, as it would be coined, in many ways disregarded earlier agreements with the militants. Tribal leaders like Gul Bahadur had been left alone by the Pakistani military, but this changed with the promotion of General Sharif. The policy that shielded the "good" Taliban was a long-term strategy to prepare for the time when America was no longer engaged in the region. General Kayani had worried that once the U.S. war on terror ended, Pakistan needed to maintain a posi-tion in which loyal proxies were available to help secure Pakistani inter-est regionally. Kayani also felt that if a full-scale offensive were launched against the militants in the tribal areas, it would overextend the military. Finally, the political uncertainty in Pakistan and inability to build a firm consensus led to the policy considerations previously followed. Kayani's paranoia about the United States was well known, as he believed that the ultimate goal of the Americans was to destroy Pakistan's nuclear arsenal (Goldberg and Ambinder, 52). The new policy shift under Sharif, however, harmed more civilians and made winning the hearts and minds of the population more problematic.

In the months leading up to Zarb-e-Azb, extremists launched numerous suicide attacks that specifically targeted the military. The attacks included the massacre of over 20 Frontier Corps troops, who had been taken into Taliban custody, and a bus bombing that killed over a dozen. These attacks were followed by massive retaliation that in many cases led to the creation of more internally displaced people. To the surprise of many observers, Prime Minister Nawaz Sharif proposed peace talks with the TTP prior to making the final decision to launch Zarb-e-Azb. Explaining the peace proposal negotiations is complex, but three possible factors could have played into the decision. First, the lack of political consensus domestically may have been a key factor. Second, the danger of giving the military too much power might have also been a reason. Finally, if the mission failed, the potential blowback could destabilize the entire country (Sareen, 24–26). The government may have also been trying to exploit the increasing factionalization within the movement. Some elements of the TTP feared that Maulana Fazlullah had become too violent and irrational. In March, the Taliban announced a month-long ceasefire that could potentially lead to negotiations with the authorities. Three conditions were laid out by the TTP: suspension of military operations, release of noncombatants being held by the authorities, and the creation of a demilitarized zone. Unfortunately, attacks continued by some elements of the TTP. It is uncertain whether these were actually breakaway groups or this was just a claim by the TTP hierarchy to avoid the resumption of military operations. A TTP market attack in Islamabad and a government strike in the Tirah valley caused significant death and destruction. As measures and countermeasures were undertaken, it was apparent by the end of April that any chance of serious negotiations had ended. The peace attempts by the Pakistani authorities failed to make any inroads.

The TTP decision to facilitate a deadly attack on Karachi's International Airport on June 8 was an attempt to destabilize the economy of Pakistan, while potentially factionalizing the government on how to pursue the anti-terror campaign. The evening assault by 10 militants on the Jinnah International Airport lasted 6 hours leaving 36 dead. The attackers' goal of seizing planes and destroying state installations had, for the most part, failed. Commentators speculated that the militants hoped to bring down the aviation industry. Many of the dead were airport security personnel and airport employees.

The attackers had secured airport employee uniforms, and most were in their teens or early twenties. Dozens of grenades and rocket launchers and numerous assault weapons were seized during the operation. The terrorists were from Uzbekistan and probably connected to the notorious Islamic Movement of Uzbekistan (IMU), which had taken sanctuary in the South Waziristan region. The Pakistani authorities have been dealing with an increased presence of militants in urban areas, particularly in Karachi. The attack was precipitated by the aggressive drone campaign of the past several years.

The timing of the attack was interesting in that the TTP organization had split into two factions only a few weeks earlier. Shahidullah Shahid, a spokesperson for the militants, released a statement claiming responsibility and commenting that the attack was in response to the assassination of Hakimullah Mehsud in November 2013. The TTP also noted that the main goal of the attack was to cut off the supply line to NATO troops in Afghanistan (Javaid, 53–54). The group was adamant the peace overtures from Prime Minister Sharif had failed.

The Pakistan military announced on June 15, 2014, the commencement of Zarb-e-Azb, or "Strike of the Sword of the Prophet Mohammed," against Taliban positions throughout the tribal regions of Pakistan. The hype surrounding the proclamation of the operation was intense. Government spokesmen called the ensuing offensive "the mother of all military operations against the Pakistani Taliban" and a "war of survival for Pakistan." The attacks were centered against both foreign and local terrorists. One of the first targets hit was a IMU hideout in which the mastermind of the airport attack, Abu Abdur Rehman Almani, along with over a hundred mostly Uzbek militants were killed in a bombing raid. The mission was to be different than earlier anti-terrorist operations because the military and intelligence community no longer differentiated between "good" and "bad" Taliban. The announcement was looked upon with suspicion as the government had made similar statements on numerous occasions preceding anti-Taliban operations, only to follow through with a marginal effort. In addition, it was common knowledge that the ISI still maintained a close relationship with the Haqqani network, as well as prominent warlord Hafiz Gul Bahadur (both of whom were perceived as "good" Taliban) (Sareen, 7).

The explanation given for the decision was that the tribal region was a hub of terrorist activities and the main stronghold of the TTP. This was not a new revelation, as counterinsurgency experts had been stating this fact for over a decade. Starting in 2002, the Pakistani army had launched over a dozen major operations against insurgents in the tribal areas and FATA. The normal operational pattern included grandiose proclamations by the military followed by tight censorship and control of media access to the areas being attacked. The most devastating aspect of previous operations was the uprooting of the populations, which caused significant increases in the IDPs. The scorched earth tactics used by the military made the return of the population problematic and also damaged an already fragile economic system (Hameed, 101–103). Because of the earlier failed attempts, especially regarding gaining any sort of governmental or administrative control over the areas, and the inability to support any economic rebuilding efforts, there were doubts about the potential success of Zarb-e-Azb.

The main advantage the military had going into the operation was that the public and numerous interest groups in the country seemed to be rallying around stronger anti-terrorist policies. The growing use of suicide operations by the TTP may have played into the pro-military mind-set. Others cast doubt on the rally around the flag hype leading up to the operation. Critics believed this sort of fervor had occurred leading into earlier major operations only to subside once the operations became down and civilian casualties became commonplace. Another point of criticism was that if particular parties and organizations did not publicly support the military, harassment and intimidation would occur. Ultimately, the fact that the military had on so many occasions claimed that a fight for the survival of the nation was ensuing made the population cautious about their sincerity (Javaid, 50–52).

The military stated that the TTP was trapped in North Waziristan and would not be able to escape from the military onslaught. Unfortunately, as had been the case in nearly every major military operation, most militants and virtually all key leaders escaped to safer areas. Intelligence sources confirmed that foreign fighters had moved into Afghanistan prior to the commencement of the operation. Some of these fighters may have even made their way to Syria, which was becoming jihadist central. It is estimated that the TTP exodus was completed three weeks prior to the start of the operation (Sareen, 9). Another interesting twist to the story was that infighting within the Pakistani militants had broken out. Maulana Fazlullah was at odds with members of the Mehsud tribe. How much of this infighting was due to disagreements over how to deal with the Pakistani authorities is still uncertain. A final factor in the period leading up to the launch of Operation Zarb-e-Azb was the role of China. In early March, Uighur terrorists had hacked over 30 people to death in Kunming, China. Abdullah Mansour, the Uighur terrorist leader living in North Waziristan, made a bold proclamation, promising more attacks against the Chinese. Furthermore, operations were indeed carried out in China, which may have led to the Chinese government applying pressure on Pakistan to take action (Javaid, 51–52). The economic relationship between China and Pakistan had grown dramatically over the past decade or so; thus the Pakistani authorities needed to avoid jeopardizing this vital partnership. Finally, the United States had become impatient with the Pakistani refusal to take on the militants in North Waziristan. This was partially due to the fact that the Haqqanis had such close connections to the region and were directly responsible for coordinating attacks against American military personnel. Pakistani toleration for extremist elements operating in the region had to end.

The military entered the operation with a sense of overconfidence. The army strategy consisted of three stages: to separate the insurgents from the population; gain control over the territory held by the extremist; and denying the insurgents access to the population (Sareen, 30). Initial victories were secured, but, as had been the case with earlier operations, the military advances stalled. Strategic areas, like Miranshah and Mir Ali, were cleared of militants only to be reoccupied and cleared again in subsequent months. The ultimate evaluation of whether a mission was successful or not comes from whether the state can maintain the military gains made. Across the board this has not occurred. Once troops were withdrawn, the militants quickly reoccupied the area. Furthermore, the TTP launched targeted attacks and assassinations of key government supporters. Most important, the population dislocated by the military operations could not return to the areas in a reasonable amount of time and the number of IDPs reached close to a million (*Dawn*, "TTP Claims Attack on Karachi Airport," June 8, 2014). Concerns of safety coupled with the destruction of the infrastructure played into the disillusionment of the population.

The media hype by the government following the operation led to growing skepticism. Significant casualties and the destruction of weapon storage cases were reported but not confirmed. Authorities also claimed (without independent media verification) that suicide bomber and terrorist-training facilities were located and eliminated. Another disturbing aspect of the operation was that the identity of those killed could not be confirmed. This played into the militants' claims that the vast majority of those killed were actually civilians (Sareen, 39).

The aggressive push by the military was part of a trend toward more military influence in governmental decision making. Ambitious operations like Zarb-e-Azb allowed the military to control the public relations aspects of the government and shift the balance of power in a dangerous direction. Nawaz Sharif realized this as he walked a tightrope between wanting to be perceived as tough on terrorism, while at the same time attempting to nurture democracy and civil society in Pakistan (Rashid, *New York Review of Books*, 3).

North Waziristan was the central location for jihadists by the time that Operation Zarb-e-Azb was launched. Authorities believed that numerous groups had sought sanctuary in the area, as the perception of it being the final frontier for terrorists was commonplace. Pakistani authorities and U.S. intelligence sources had pinpointed nearly every recent extremist attack to the North Waziristan region. The area was noted for being a true international center of terrorism. Chechens, Uighurs, Uzbeks, Tajiks, Arabs, Afghans, Pashtuns, and Punjabis were all known to operate out of the area. For two weeks, the military used heavy aerial bombardments to soften the region prior to advancing with ground troops. Operation Zarb-e-Azb aimed to be much more broadly based, while earlier operations were precise and localized; this was going to be a sweep against both "good" and "bad" Taliban and would include areas that could provide sanctuaries or safe houses to extremist elements. The rhetoric did not seem to match the reality as groups and individual earlier designated as "good" Taliban were once again allowed to either move to new locations prior to the commencement of the operation or not be attacked by the Pakistani military. Neither the Haqqani network nor the notorious warlord Gul Bahadur was targeted in any significant way in the early stages of the operation.

One distinct advantage that Operation Zarb-e-Azb had in comparison to previous Pakistani military incursions was the increased factionalization of the TTP. Growing discord had mounted with the appointment of Maulana Fazlullah as the head of the TTP. Since he was the first TTP leader from outside the tribal regions, many militants did not trust him. The launching of Operation Zarb-e-Azb could be looked upon as a way to exploit the growing rift in the TTP or it could have potentially backfired and brought the disparate factions together. Early military advances faced very little opposition; that could mean the militants were dispersed in a chaotic fashion or that they retreated to wage more guerilla-style countermeasures. Ground assaults faced little resistance as the vast majority of areas entered by government forces were deserted and depopulated (Sareen, 24–25). The military was positioned in a way to avoid any militant movements from North to South Waziristan, but it seemed as if the breach had taken place prior to the commencement of the operation. The military leadership had told the government that the operation could be concluded in three weeks. By all rational accounts, this was an unrealistic timetable. In reality, the military seemed reluctant to pursue the militants into Shawal in the south or north of the Tochi River valley. The follow-up phase seemed nonexistent. Furthermore, it seemed as if the attention paid to the operation by political leaders and the media was not sustained. By November, the number of terrorists killed numbered close to 1,200, but no independent confirmation was possible. The TTP said the number of casualties was much lower, and most scholars believe that the overall cost of the operation was much more damaging to the Pakistani military (Sareen, 33). The financial impact was enormous, and the significant increase in the IDPs in the region was astronomical. The overall devastation to the economy and infrastructure is still not known. Another damaging aspect from the operation was speculation that the U.S. military provided intelligence and coordinates to assist Pakistan in the targeting of areas. Overall, it seemed as if the Pakistani government and military did not fully look at the implications of the operation before undertaking such an extensive mission. The backlash was felt most severely in the tragedy that unfolded in Peshawar.

PAKISTAN'S 9/11: THE SCHOOL MASSACRE IN PESHAWAR

December 16, 2014, marked the 43rd anniversary of the dreaded surrender of West Pakistani forces and the dismemberment of the country following the 1971 Bengali War. It would be on this noted anniversary that the TTP launched what was the deadliest and most notorious attack in Pakistan history with the slaughter of over 140 school children at the Army Public School in Peshawar, the capital city of Khyber Pakhtunkhwa. The attack represented one of the most horrific incidents in the brutal insurgency against the Pakistani state. At approximately 10:00 am, seven armed men disguised as soldiers stormed multiple classrooms and indiscriminately fired on children. By noon, a siege developed as military units surrounded the school. Fighting between the terrorists and the security personnel continued for eight hours before the army took control. Once security forces entered the compound and closed in on the combatants, they blew themselves up to avoid being captured (Craig and Constable, 4). The Pakistani government announced a three-day mourning period to honor the victims. The incident sent shockwaves across the nation and the world.

Statements condemning the attacks came from a wide variety of individuals and leaders. Barack Obama denounced the act of depravity and reiterated the U.S. support for counterterrorism measures. Malala Yousafzai released a statement from England that she was heartbroken by the atrocious and cowardly acts. Leader of Lashkar-e-Taiba, Hafiz Mohammad Saeed, stated that the attack was carried out by the enemies of Islam—barbarians operating under the name of Jihad. The Afghan Taliban quickly issued a press release stating that the intentional killing of innocent people, women, and children are against the basics of Islam.

The investigation into the massacre uncovered that the attackers arrived at the school by car and subsequently set the vehicle on fire as a diversion in order to make their entry into the campus less noticeable. In order to conceal their identity, the terrorists wore paramilitary uniforms and used a ladder to scale the rear wall on Warsak Road. After cutting the barbed wire and entering the main compound, the militants fired indiscriminately and tossed hand grenades in random directions. The killers entered the main auditorium, where students were congregated together for a first-aid in-service. The fact that so many students were in that central location was probably a factor in the tremendous death toll. The Pakistani Special Services Group launched a rescue operation approximately 15 minutes after the attack ensued, but most of the children had already been murdered. During the attack, the following message was intercepted by authorities: "We have killed all the children in the auditorium. What do we do now?," which was followed by "What for the army people, kill them before blowing yourself up." Authorities confirmed that the terrorist attackers were in contact with Senior TTP commander Umar Adizai. Intelligence experts believe that the individuals coordinating the operation were located in Nangarhar Province in eastern Afghanistan. According to reports, many family members of key TTP operatives were killed during the campaign in North Waziristan. Several days after the attack, video footage was released that showed Umar Mansoor claiming responsibility and justifying the massacre (Biberman and Zahid, 4–6).

As the rescue operation commenced by the Special Services Group, the number of militants was unknown. The SSG moved from block to block, placing a high priority on securing the junior section of the compound, where the younger students were located. The terrorists were eventually centered in the administration area, and, as forces closed in, four of the militants blew themselves up in the lobby of the building. Another fighter killed himself inside of the headmistress's office. The final two terrorists detonated themselves on adjacent sides of the block leading toward the administrative building. In all, over 2,500 students were in the school at the time of the attack. SSG forces rescued approximately 960 students and staff during the siege (Shay, 2–3).

Within days after the massacre, the Pakistani authorities decided to impose the death penalty on numerous terrorists with the sentences being carried out very quickly. Furthermore, the military conducted massive retaliatory strikes by air as well as with ground assaults. Sustaining the momentum to destroy the terrorist bases in the tribal region was challenging. Some commentators believed the Peshawar massacre was a game changer regarding the stance that Pakistan took concerning the war on terror. The attack showed how vulnerable the Pakistani state was to terrorism (Raza, 22–23). Security forces could not possibly combat these sorts of attacks, while many within the state apparatus indirectly supported the TTP operations in Pakistan or in close approximation to the border.

The citizen reaction to the tragedy was one of shock and disbelief. The typical response of fear seemed to be replaced with anger at the TTP. The demand for action was overwhelming, and any sympathy for the movement was gone. Some citizens were skeptical that the military would follow through with decisive action. Others claimed that the military solution would not accomplish the long-term goal of eradicating terrorism without a robust education system (Fishwick, *Guardian*, 4). Other citizens complained about the ISI connection to militancy in Pakistan. The population realized that change could not occur unless the intelligence community was committed to finally cutting ties with the Taliban.

In a statement released by the Pakistani Taliban spokesman Mohammad Khorasani, the organization claimed that the attack was in response to the carnage inflicted by the Pakistani military during Operation Zarb-e-Azb in North Waziristan. The civilian death toll during the nearly six months of the offensive was significant. In addition, the million plus IDPs left the region in a state of disarray.

One of the essential questions of the situation in the post-Peshawar period was whether the attack was a sign of a rejuvenated TTP or an act of desperation from a failing movement and ideology. The decision to strike a "soft" target rather than a military base or security location could be construed as a sign of diminished capacity (Biberman and Zahid, 4). Several indicators have led regional experts to point to a TTP in disarray. The damage wrought by the military through its most ambitious and aggressive campaign during Operation Zarb-e-Azb cannot be overstated. The severe factionalization of the leadership with Maulana Fazlullah as the head has played into the increased infighting within the organization. The Fazlullah faction's response, driven by a younger, more ruthless generation of commanders, led to the bloodiest attack in Pakistani history. Second, the conflict has become more diffused with an increasing sectarian focus. Increasing strikes against Shias and Sufis was the new norm. This could also be connected to the fact that some commanders have become tied to the Islamic State of Iraq and Syria (ISIS) chapter that was emerging in Pakistan. This strike was meant to maximize media coverage; most terrorist operations received scant coverage, as attacks had unfortunately become the norm in Pakistan. The shocking nature of this operation was bound to gain sensational coverage that could help the recruitment and possibly survival of the Fazlullah faction. Ironically, the massacre and subsequent response by the military did indeed lead to the resolution of the factionalization issue in the TTP, as Fazlullah emerged as the winner in the internal struggle by March 2015 (Biberman and Zahid, 7–8).

In the aftermath of the carnage, the Pakistan government passed the National Action Plan that included 20 key points to help eradicate the scourge of terrorism. The plan was created on December 25 and was undoubtedly the most detailed effort by the Pakistani state to destroy terrorism within the country. The most high-profile point of the plan was the lifting of the moratorium on the death penalty, which would mean the state would quickly begin executing convicts on death row (Raza, 23–25). The plan included the development of special military courts under the supervision of the army. The government also called for a revamping and overhaul of the criminal justice system. An aggressive campaign to eradicate armed gangs would be pursued as well as the strengthening of anti-terrorist institutions. Additionally, the goal of choking off the finances of terrorist groups would be pursued and funding for counterterrorism measures would be increased.

Public relations and legal efforts to end religious persecution were also stressed. Religious seminaries would go through strict regulations. One of the more controversial parts of the National Action Plan was the goal of censoring or closing newspapers, magazines, or literature that promoted extremism, sectarianism, or intolerance. Along this line, communication networks and social media sites suspected of aiding militants would be completely dismantled. The Action Plan also called for a more coherent strategy in dealing with Afghan refugees.

Other points in the Action Plan dealt more specifically with regional problems. Within the FATA region, a call for reforms including more focus on the repatriation of IDPs was advocated. A zero tolerance for militancy in Punjab was a stated goal in the document. The plan also called for the military to eradicate the terrorist cells in and around the Karachi area. The Balochistan area was to receive assistance in regard to any anti-terrorist activities. Finally, any sectarian violence was to be combatted with all necessary force.

The National Action Plan was very ambitious and in many ways unrealistic. Many experts dealing with terrorism in Pakistan consider progress made in regard to the plan temporary and artificial. The most glaring problem is that the plan does not address the fundamental root causes of terrorism. Others, including foreign policy writer Moeed Yusuf, criticize the plan for being just a list of bullet points without a true goal or agenda (Yusuf, "Not Really a Plan," 1–2). Furthermore, Pakistan still has an over-reliance on the military regarding the terrorism issue. Strengthening the legal system and civil society has to become a higher priority. Even though a reduction in attacks has occurred, the problem was far from eradicated.

KARACHI: A CASE STUDY IN INSTABILITY AND A BREEDING GROUND FOR EXTREMISM

The progress toward combatting the terrorist problem has been complicated by terrorism transitioning in part from the tribal regions to the more densely populated urban centers. Nowhere has this been more apparent than in the volatile megacity of Karachi. The government has neglected the city, and endemic mismanagement has created immense problems. In addition, according to the International Rescue Committee, "Ethno-political and sectarian interests and competition, intensified by internal migration, jihadist influx and unchecked movement of weapons, drugs, and black money, have created an explosive mix" (International Rescue Committee Report, 1). The political and economic systems are very exclusive regarding access to jobs, basic services, and justice. This makes it easy for jihadist and criminal gangs to recruit among the growing youth population in the city.

The fundamental problem in Karachi lies in the current demographic makeup of the city. Karachi is the largest city in Pakistan and is divided into six districts. Significant influxes increased the port town from a population of 435,000 in the 1940s to a megacity of 20 to 25 million today (Inskeep, 239). That number constitutes 10 to 12 percent of the Pakistani population and nearly a quarter of the urban numbers in the country. After partition, the percentage of Muslim residents increased from 42 percent to 96 percent by 1951. For the first 20 years of Pakistan's existence, Karachi would be the federal capital. It was moved to Islamabad in 1967. Numerous groups have entered the area because of natural disasters or increasing political and ethnic conflict in the tribal regions and FATA. The already overburdened infrastructure cannot provide for the growing numbers of citizens entering the city. Basic health care, transportation services, and housing are grossly inadequate. Approximately 70 percent of the city's population would be classified as poor, and there has been a significant increase in squatter settlements appearing. Because of this, organized crime and exploitative members of a growing informal economy took advantage of the situation. These areas became sanctuaries for extremist propaganda.

Tensions increased with the relocation of members of the Pakistani Taliban to Karachi following the government crackdown in Swat in 2009. The dynamic of the city changed after this influx with estimates of over 8,000 TTP members operating in the city by 2013 (International Crisis Group, 11). The militants became involved in criminal enterprises, including extortion and kidnapping. This was in addition to the already tense sectarian situation in Karachi, where anti-Shia groups like Lashkar-e-Jhangvi (LeJ) have been active for years. Karachi has been divided into pockets along ethnic, sectarian, and political lines because of the growing militant threat. Ultimately, Karachi was thrown into a wave of violence and lawlessness that created chaos in significant parts of the city. Sectarian hatred poisoned neighborhoods and aggressive hateful propaganda permeated social media websites. Children as young as 10 years old were raising sectarian slogans at rallies with a simple message that people belonging to the opposite sect were simply to be loathed (Abdullah, "Karachi: Where walls tell tales of sectarian conflict," *Herald Magazine*). The insecurity in Karachi played into the hands of extremists. As the fear level increased, the militants' influence grew.

The response from the government was dramatic. In September 2013, the interior ministry requested that the military send in the paramilitary Rangers in order to regain a semblance of control in Karachi. The request was put forth because of the deteriorating security situation. The federal cabinet approved of the Ranger operation on September 4. The four target areas the Rangers focused on were terrorism, kidnappings, extortion, and targeted killings (International Crisis Group, 12). The Rangers were given special police powers including shoot-to-kill and detaining suspects for 90 days without charges. The Ranger incursion almost immediately turned dark, as they were involved in significant human rights violations, including extrajudicial killings, disappearances, and torture (Human Rights Report). Troublingly, the duration of the operation was open ended. The operation quickly led to increased ethnic and political tensions that helped recruitment efforts for the gangs and terrorist organizations. The confusion over whether much of the action taken was political or sectarian in nature was disturbing. Several commentators believed the Ranger actions had simply put the criminal and jihadist groups underground without really solving the problem in any significant way. Even though overall crime numbers decreased, Karachi remained the most violent city in the country through 2016. Ethnic and religious tensions remain very high, and the societal ills facing Karachi are very much apparent.

The Karachi operation has led to significant problems regarding human rights. Estimates of the number of citizens arrested range from 6,000 to 10,000 with many never being formally charged. Accounts from detention facilities include ill-treatment, torture, and extreme trauma. Many times, bribes had to be paid in order to free prisoners. Civil society activities were routinely harassed as approximately 70 activists have been killed with another 125 missing. Often times, the Rangers' choices were politically motivated with members of the MQM party being a main target. Women were also the victims of sexual violence and attacks at the hands of the Rangers with little recourse available to them (International Crisis Group, 16–17).

When the Ranger operation was announced, numerous prominent jihadists temporarily fled the area but many have returned recently. Pro-jihadist madrassas have continued to operate freely and remain a powerful tool for the recruitment of militants opposing the government. Most important, numerous leaders and organizations promoting sectarian attacks against Shia and Sufi elements in the region have been left untouched. Banned groups have operated with ease indicating a green light for the continuation of religiously inspired violence (International Crisis Group, 13–14).

BEYOND THE PESHAWAR MASSACRE: ADVANCES AND SETBACKS IN THE WAR ON TERROR

Many analysts touted the progress made by Pakistan officials and the military in the aftermath of the school attack of December 2014. Intelligence data provided evidence that the sheer numbers of attacks declined. Whether this was due to the nationwide actions of the military and government authorities or the infighting and factionalization of the militants was unclear. This sense of increased security was anything but certain, as evidenced by the shocking Easter bombing in late March 2016.

A crowded park in Lahore, the capital of Punjab province, became the scene of unbelievable carnage as 74 civilians were killed and nearly

300 wounded. The attackers were members of Jamaat-ul-Ahrar, a splinter group of the Pakistani Taliban. The group claimed that the targets were Christians, but the reality was that the majority of the victims were Muslim with 30 being children (Bhojani, 1–2). Lahore is a frequent location during spring weekends with parks being especially crowded. The Gulshan-e-Iqbal Park was congested with numerous families congregating in the vicinity as sunset set in. The powerful blast ripped through a massively crowded area of the park adjacent to swings, trains, and several children attractions. The blast was so massive and fatal that there were pools of blood and scattered body parts in the park (*Dawn*, "At least 72 killed in suicide blast as terror revisits Lahore," 4). In a released statement, the group issued a warning to Prime Minister Nawaz Sharif stating, "We have entered Lahore." This was in reference to the fact that Sharif and his Pakistan Muslim League Party were based out of Lahore, which was considered the prime minister's stronghold. The prime minister's brother, Shahbaz Sharif, also governs the province. In addition, the terrorists wanted the government to halt military operations against their safe havens in the remote tribal areas bordering Afghanistan.

Unfortunately, attacks by extremists against religious and ethnic minorities in Punjab and nationwide have been all too common. Pakistan has recently witnessed some of the worst persecution and discrimination of religious minorities in its history (Ispahani, 2). The timing of the March 2016 attack might have been connected to the decision by the National Assembly to adopt a resolution to recognize Easter and the Hindu festivals of Holi and Diwali as public holidays. This was a move by the state to show tolerance and acceptance of other faiths within Pakistan.

This attack may have been a symptom of a more serious problem regarding the terrorism threat in Pakistan. The success of the intense campaigns and efforts over the past several years in the tribal areas and Pashtun-dominated regions such as Waziristan may have pushed the militants further to the east into the more densely populous urban centers. Many Punjabi politicians disregarded the tribal regions as almost a foreign land and not part of the essential construct of Pakistani identity. Punjab was considered safe from terrorist threat, but that is no longer the reality of the situation.

One of the controversial options discussed was to allow a more aggressive military presence in Punjab in order to root out and destroy terrorist operations. The army was demanding legal coverage for paramilitary rangers to launch aggressive actions against militant elements in the province. Both Nawaz and Shahbaz Sharif believed this could be an initial step toward a military play for power and possible coup d'état, opposed this proposal. The worry is that a mission creep would occur as the military deployment would go from initially being an anti-terrorist campaign to eliminating criminal syndicates, which might have hit close to home for the

Sharif family. Even if the army were able to take a more aggressive stance in Punjab, a serious complication would remain. Many of the militants have long been associated with the military in undertaking efforts to help the effort in Kashmir, such as Lashkar-e-Taiba and Jaish-e-Mohammad. This delicate balance could be jeopardized by any paramilitary incursion into the area.

In addition, the success of the Easter bombing showed gaps in the military's and government's ability to eliminate the terrorist threat. Furthermore, many commentators believe the fact that the targeted community was Christian was connected to the toxic blasphemy law that was being enforced more frequently and most notably in the Lahore area. The Taliban spokesman stated that the attack had two objectives: to kill Christians and to give a message to the government that it cannot deter the terrorists in their stronghold of Lahore (*New York Times*, "Another Bombing, This Time in Pakistan," March 28, 2016). Sadly, terrorist organizations acting in the name of faith have been destroying religious diversity across the region. This setback shows that the extremist problem continues to keep Pakistan in a state of fear and panic.

A NEW TWIST TO THE TERRORISM PROBLEM: THE ISLAMIC STATE ENTERS PAKISTAN

Most coverage of ISIS has centered on the expansion of the organization from its bases in Syria and Iraq into other regions of the Middle East and potentially North Africa. What was not addressed was the potential for the organization to expand eastward toward the trouble region of Afghanistan and Pakistan. ISIS was somewhat different in its global ambition versus most militant jihadist groups that focused on local or regional concerns.

Pakistan had long-standing ties to the founder of ISIS, Abu Musab Al-Zarqawi. He had set up training facilities in Afghanistan and was on good terms with the Taliban regime. Zarqawi's anti-Shia rhetoric resonated with numerous Pakistani militant factions but also alienated him from Al Qaeda leader Osama bin Laden. One of the main objectives of Zarqawi upon his return to Iraq was to wage intense sectarian violence against the Shia.

A key factor that helped the Islamic State gain a foothold in Pakistan was the sectarian nature of the ideology, a theme popular with numerous militant factions. Thus, the ISIS agenda fit nicely into the Sunni extremist narrative that became commonplace in Pakistan during the spread of Wahhabist ideology in the 1980s to 1990s. ISIS support networks have been identified in Karachi and Punjab.

The first indication of the Pakistani Taliban supporting ISIS came with a statement released by TTP spokesman Shahidullah Shahid, "Oh brothers of ISIS we are proud of you in your victories . . . we are with you, we will provide you with Mujahedeen and with every possible support" (Rashid, "Pakistan: The Allure of ISIS," 3). The TTP were in disarray as rifts developed over whether to launch indiscriminate attacks on civilian targets and whether to move forward in an attempt to negotiate with Pakistani authorities. This uncertainty along with the proclamation of the caliphate in the summer of 2014 opened the door for ISIS in the region. A select number of TTP commanders and militants pledged allegiance to ISIS. Many factions were undecided, supporting the efforts of the movement without giving full-fledged allegiance.

The key opening for ISIS was facilitated by the terrorist shift toward urban areas. The more settled regions of Pakistan were open to accepting the ISIS agenda. Urban areas, such as Karachi and Lahore, saw an influx of ISIS activities. Educated and middle-class citizens in the urban areas were susceptible to the ISIS message and propaganda, which was more widely available in cities. In addition, online recruiting efforts seem to be having an impact. Twenty-year-old medical student Noreen Leghari joined ISIS after being recruited through Facebook. She joined with ISIS in Lahore and was captured by authorities while planning a suicide mission. University graduates were recruited in Karachi to carry out the killing of Shiites in a bus attack. A final sign of an increasing ISIS presence was when protesters at the Jamia Hafsa in Islamabad proclaimed loyalty to Abu Bakr al-Baghdadi, stating that they were waiting for the caliphate to be established in Pakistan. Estimates of ISIS operatives in Pakistan range from 2,000 to 3,000. The remote tribal region where the TTP is centered has always been more difficult for ISIS to spread propaganda, but authorities have confiscated pamphlets and materials in Peshawar and in Balochistan Province during 2016 to 2017.

The ISIS threat in Pakistan troubled the Al Qaeda leadership, which worked closely with the TTP over the previous decade. In response to the ISIS decision to proclaim the caliphate, Al Qaeda announced a branch in South Asia known as AQIS. The announcement by Ayman al-Zawahiri, just three months after the caliphate was proclaimed, was an effort for the group to remain relevant in South Asia by expanding further into Pakistan and India. It is important to note that geographic considerations impacted the ability of both groups to spread in a significant fashion.

ISIS and Al Qaeda did share common ideological ties with both emerging out of militant Salafi school of thought. Many Pakistani families who spent time as guest workers in the Gulf States ended up adopting Salafi views. The San Bernardino attacker, Tashfeen Malik, became radicalized by the Salafi ideology when her family lived in Saudi Arabia. These experiences help to recruit new members to the ISIS cause. The Pakistani state was weary of ISIS efforts because of the inability to control and manipulate this faction of terrorists. ISIS would be willing and able to attack

Pakistani military and security targets (something that several factions of the TTP along with LeT avoid).

Potentially the most troubling element of the ISIS infiltration into Pakistan was the impact it would have on sectarian violence. A clear aim and objective of ISIS was to destroy and kill Shia Muslims. This of course was something that Al Qaeda had avoided in order to evade further infighting. Because of the anti-Shia objectives, ISIS has found a clear ally in the Pakistani group LeJ. A LeJ propaganda statement said: "All Shias are worthy of killing. We will rid Pakistan of unclean people . . . the Shias have no right to be here . . . We will make Pakistan their graveyard—their house will be destroyed by bombs and suicide bombers" (Zahid and Khan, 12). Sectarian violence had the potential to tear the country apart. Over the past 20 years, over 3,000 incidents of sectarian violence occurred in Pakistan. With the ongoing Iran-Saudi Arabia proxy battles occurring, the prospects of sectarian violence increasing are likely.

One point that undoubtedly limited the ability of ISIS to have sustained success in Pakistan was the fact that the ISIS success occurred only in the urban centers of the country. The prospects for gains in the tribal regions of the country were weak. Any attempts to infiltrate into FATA or other remote regions risked the resumption of American drone operations. It is also unlikely that the Pakistani authorities will tolerate any significant incursion of ISIS into the country. There is no strategic reason for Pakistani officials to turn a blind eye to ISIS activities as they did with LeT and at times Al Qaeda. Additionally, no coherent spokesperson emerged to lead ISIS outside of Iraq and Syria.

By the second half of 2016, ISIS appeared to be making its presence known in Pakistan. On August 8, a suicide bomber struck a hospital in Quetta, killing 74 people. Jamaat-ul-Ahrar, a splinter faction of the TTP that pledged alliance to ISIS, took responsibility for the attack. The province of Balochistan had become one of the most violent areas in Pakistan during recent years, which was partly because of the sectarian divisions in the region. Sunni extremist groups, such as LeJ, consistently targeted the Shia Hazara population. Members of Sharif's government and key military leaders, such as General Bajwa claim the attacks were an attempt to disrupt the economic advances made in the China-Pakistan Economic Corridor (CPEC), which was a multibillion-dollar infrastructural development project. The province had been the longtime home of the Afghan Taliban, who sought sanctuary in the region following the fall of the regime in 2001.

On October 24, 2016, the most significant attack against a police installation in Pakistani history occurred in Quetta. Heavily armed militants wearing suicide vests stormed the police academy, killing 61 and wounding 117. Most of the troops in the training facility were between the ages of 15 and 25. The attack occurred shortly after 11:00 pm, while the recruits were sleeping. The training location was situated in a highly secured area of Quetta. As the terror campaign continued, militants seemed to be targeting sensitive security and military locations whenever possible (A.S. Shah, 2).

The Islamic State group claimed responsibility for the attack, but some confusion existed because a faction of LeJ also released a statement taking credit. As with the majority of suicide attacks, two of the three bombers blew themselves up to maximize the casualty level. This attack showed growing evidence of a potential battle brewing between militants loyal to the TTP and other terrorist elements that pledged allegiance to the Islamic State. This factionalization was problematic for Pakistani authorities, as the groups may have been engaged in more attacks in order to outdo each other to maximize exposure and thus gain recruits.

Additional evidence of the TTP and ISIS continuing in a battle of trying to claim the leadership helm of terrorism in Pakistan continued throughout 2017. The TTP's deadly market bombing that killed 25 and wounded 50 took place in the city of Parachinar, the capital of the Kurram tribal region. This border town had been a center of resistance against the Pakistani Taliban and also opposed the notorious Haqqani network.

February 2017 witnessed an acceleration of violence in Pakistan with five suicide attacks occurring in the span of a week. From Lahore to Peshawar to Quetta, violent suicide incidents created chaos within the country. The deadliest attack took place at the gold-domed Sufi shire of Lal Shahbaz Qalandar in the town of Sehwan in Sindh Province. A total of 88 Sufi pilgrims were killed and over 250 wounded in the explosion. ISIS claimed responsibility for this attack in what was considered a further effort to destabilize Pakistan. The ISIS attacks focused mostly on either Sufi or Shia target groups that the Islamic State considered to be apostates.

The ISIS attacks were not just sectarian in nature. In mid-May 2017, a terrorist attack in Mastung, close to the Balochistan provincial capital of Quetta, targeted Senate deputy chairman, Abdul Ghafoor Haideri. The senator was wounded in the blast that killed 25 people and wounded close to 40. The attacker was wearing a suicide explosive vest. Haideri was a member of the right-wing religious party Jamaat Ulema Islam. At this point, no one was safe from the growing terror threat engulfing Pakistan.

REGIME CHANGE AND CRISIS: THE THIRD FALL OF SHARIF

For the third time in his long and turbulent political career, Nawaz Sharif was forced out of office without completing his full term. In late July 2017, Sharif stepped down after the Pakistani Supreme Court disqualified him on corruption charges. This change can be viewed as both positive and negative for the stability of democracy in Pakistan. The fact that the prime minister was held accountable by the judicial system shows a strengthening of rule of law and confirms the aspect of checks and balances so vital to a functioning democracy. On the negative side, Sharif's removal once again demonstrates that the proper electoral process in which ineffective leaders are removed via the ballot box does not play out in Pakistani politics.

The downfall of Sharif was the release of the Panama Papers, which had evidence that Sharif along with numerous other world leaders, secretly stashed assets in offshore bank accounts that were not declared to authorities in Pakistan. Sharif seemed to get off lightly as he was not formally charged with corruption (although investigations are still ongoing), will not have to serve any jail time, and was also able to keep the wealth he had accumulated. His only penalty was having to resign as prime minister of Pakistan. The reason for this was that he had violated the "morality clause" in the constitution, which states that leaders must be truthful and trustworthy. This was the first time the obscure constitutional clause had been used against a public official since its passage during the Zia administration in the 1980s. Even though Sharif is removed from office, he will still be the head of his powerful political party, the Pakistan Muslim League. His future remains uncertain as the political tension increases in Pakistan.

U.S. POLICY TOWARD PAKISTAN: TRUMP TAKES A HARD-LINE STANCE

President Donald Trump's August 21, 2017, speech was a stark departure regarding U.S. policy in South Asia because it called out Pakistan for turning a blind eye to terrorist groups operating out of the country. The administration with NATO backing has publicly condemned the military and intelligence communities for its duplicity regarding terrorist support. Trump stated, "We have been paying Pakistan billions and billions of dollars at the same time they are housing the very terrorists that we are fighting. It is time for Pakistan to demonstrate its commitment to civilization, order, and to peace" (Joshi, "Viewpoint," 1). The rhetoric from Trump may not equate with any tangible action. The relationship between the United States and Pakistan is symbiotic with both sides benefitting from the arrangement. It may be unlikely that the Trump administration is willing to sever this alliance in any substantial way. The use of Pakistani territory to supply American troops in Afghanistan and to conduct drone attacks in Pakistan are just two examples of how America benefits from the relationship. Finally, the intelligence data provided to the United States has been helpful in tracking down Al Qaeda and ISIS militants in South Asia.

If the Trump administration does take significant action against Pakistan, the fallout will be problematic. The closing of the supply routes will mean that the United States will have to find an alternative to supplying American military personnel at the same time that Trump is increasing troop levels in Afghanistan. This could be a logistical challenge for policy makers who are already stretched thin. Most policy experts do not believe that a decision by President Trump to cut aid to Pakistan will convince the government to change course. According to Abbas, "If you think strong statements or mere pressure from the United States, or taking away $300 million that is given to the military will be sufficient to really convince Pakistan to change its calculus, that is like really living in a fool's paradise" (Calamur, 2). Pakistani officials believe that they are once again the scapegoat for the failed American efforts in Afghanistan.

It will be difficult or nearly impossible for Pakistan to abandon a policy that has been in place for nearly four decades. The proxy wars in Afghanistan and support for extremist elements regionally allow Pakistan to keep a strong ally on its border in neighboring Afghanistan which in turn strengthens its hand in dealing with India. As Trump pivoted to building a stronger alliance with India, this in turn may feed into the paranoia of the Pakistan military and intelligence services. The Trump move could ultimately push Pakistan into a closer alliance with China. The $56 billion investment in building the One Belt One Road project in northern Pakistan is the centerpiece of the CPEC, which is designed to help China become the dominant regional power. Whether the Trump administration can pressure China regarding Pakistani support for terrorism remains to be seen.

PROTESTS AND INSTABILITY: DOMESTIC TURMOIL PLAGUES PAKISTAN

Events toward the end of 2017 showed increasing uncertainty and chaos regarding the future of Pakistan. The bizarre alliance of the army, ISI, judiciary, bureaucracy, and select politicians known as the "miltablishment" was engulfed in significant infighting about the future of the country. The closing of main roads into Islamabad for three weeks in November by a fringe group known as the Tehreek-e-Labaik (TEL), or the Movement in Service to the Finality of the Prophet, created chaos and led to several deaths and 200 injuries. Select members of the "miltablishment" that supplied food, blankets, and water to the protesters indirectly supported the 3,000 or so protesters.

The events centered on Law Minister Zahid Hamid, who was accused of blasphemy for a proposal that would have slightly changed the oath taken by incoming lawmakers, altering the language that declared the Prophet Muhammad as God's final prophet. Even though the government quickly dropped the change, this became the rallying cry for the TEL alliance. The most disturbing aspect of this turn of events was that the protesters were from the Sufi-inspired Barelvis sect, which happens to be the largest Sunni faction in Pakistan and has traditionally been the most peaceful and tolerant group within the country. This shift toward more militant action by the Barelvis could lead to chaos in Punjab and even interfaith conflict between rival Sunni groups.

Another troubling trend in 2017 was the reemergence of Lashkar-e-Taiba (LeT) as a significant force on the scene. The release of the controversial leader of LeT, Hafiz Saeed, who had been held under house arrest on terrorism charges, could impact the political dynamic in Pakistan. A court in Lahore dropped charges against Saeed who also has a $10 million bounty on his head from the United States for his role in the Mumbai attack of 2008. LeT has rebranded itself as a charitable organization and is forming a new political party, the Milli Muslim League, which plans to participate in future elections. This has further angered the Trump administration, which publicly called out the Pakistani government and promised to cut military aid. In addition, Trump resumed drone strikes and targeted militants in a late November attack.

Through all of this instability the army is the critical actor. They refused to reel in terrorist operatives even in the face of continued attacks in late 2017. A student hostel was bombed in November and a high-level police chief in Peshawar was assassinated. The future political scene could include a possible return of Sharif or a resurrected PPP under the guidance of Bilawal Bhutto, the son of the slain former leader, and a role for extremist parties. The role of the military in future democratic developments in Pakistan might lead to the solidification of gains that were made in recent election cycles or could derail the processes entirely. The future peace and security of South Asia hinges on this point.

POLICY RECOMMENDATIONS AND CHALLENGES FACING PAKISTAN

Regional chaos helped to fan the flames of extremist rhetoric across the South Asian subcontinent. Pakistan maneuvered into policy decisions that undermined the secular, inclusive country envisioned by Mohammad Ali Jinnah in 1947. Whether the government is democratically elected or a military dictatorship, the country continues to struggle with what seems to be insurmountable challenges. Pakistani society and leadership need a clear vision of the key priorities to address in order for tangible progress to be made.

The turmoil of the past decade has engulfed Pakistan and profoundly impacted the political, economic, and social dynamics of the country. The wounds inflicted on Pakistan had both internal and external causes. Separating the two can be difficult, if not impossible, since the internal situation in Pakistan is tied so closely to what occurs both regionally and internationally.

The first challenge that Pakistan must confront is the growing Islamic militancy that is tearing apart the state politically, socially, and economically. This will be enormously complicated to deal with because of the extreme factionalization of religious militants. What started off as religiously inspired opposition to the U.S. war on terror and American ground forces fighting in Afghanistan has turned into a convoluted mix of Taliban militant factions sometimes fighting against Western interests and sometimes fighting amongst themselves, increased sectarian violence, and pro-Al Qaeda and ISIS elements struggling to gain a foothold regionally. In order for Pakistan to begin to undertake reforms, it must take action to change this toxic climate that is consuming the country.

In order for Pakistan to combat the extremist threat engulfing the region, the relationship between Pakistan and the United States must be healed. The trust factor within both nations is low, and mutual animosity is apparent. Pakistanis feel that the United States does not respect their country and refuses to treat them with dignity. The examples of the Raymond Davis fiasco and the raid of Osama bin Laden's compound at Abbottabad are evidence supporting this perspective. The U.S. frustration stems from the double-dealing of nearly every Pakistani leader, and the military and intelligence communities allowing terrorist sanctuaries within Pakistan, who then enter Afghanistan and attack U.S. military personnel. In order to move forward effectively, change must occur.

A key to combatting the terrorist problem in Pakistan is the disruption of the financial networks that allow extremism to flourish across the region. Terrorist cells sustain their activities through illicit means, such as kidnappings, extortion rackets, and, most notably, illicit drug trafficking that benefits the militant networks across Pakistan and Afghanistan. The international community must work with Pakistani authorities to aggressively thwart these activities that fund extremism. Until this occurs, very few incentives are in place for terrorists to halt these actions.

Assistance to Pakistan should be geared toward infrastructure and economic development projects with less emphasis on aid that only benefits the military. These types of projects are highly visible and could help to change the negative public perceptions of the West. A strategic dialogue initiated in 2006 listed the key areas of concern, including education, energy, agriculture, and science and technology. The devastating earthquake centered in Kashmir during 2005 and the deadly region-wide flooding of 2010 opened a dire need for such assistance opportunities. Combatting terrorism cannot be the single focus and obsession of U.S.-Pakistani relations. Once the threat of extremism subsides, development has the potential to flourish in Pakistan.

Pakistan must work with regional partners to develop a South Asian economic organization. This could help mitigate the security concerns between India and Pakistan, but this can only occur when the relationship becomes mutually beneficial. The international community can help to promote economic development measures to facilitate this process. Forces within Pakistan that attempt to derail partnerships between the two regional powers need to be dealt with in a more effective manner.

It is clear that the overarching concern in Pakistan continues to be the security situation. The terrorism threat remains the dominant perception of Pakistan internationally. The tribal regions are still problematic partially because of the lack of opportunities for the citizens of FATA and Khyber Pakhtunkhwa Province. With low educations levels, lack of economic opportunities, and an active recruitment network from numerous extremist groups, the region will remain a troubled spot. The government must use a combination of military actions with coherent educational and economic opportunities to lessen the attraction of extremism. The withdrawal of Western forces from neighboring Afghanistan and the elimination of the use of drones can only help in these endeavors.

The security problems in other areas of Pakistan may be more problematic to deal with. Militants will be more difficult to track because of their increasing presence in urban areas. The densely populated neighborhoods in Lahore and Karachi provide ample areas for terrorists to plan and organize. In addition, the growing sectarian divide is creating a climate of fear and hostility and making particular areas ungovernable. Finally, the use of tactics, such as suicide missions, has dealt a serious blow to attempts at reconciliation within Pakistan and created an atmosphere in which foreign investment is difficult to promote.

The never-ending obsession with Kashmir must be dealt with in a comprehensive manner. Bringing closure to the Kashmir problem through a diplomatic settlement with India would benefit Pakistan economically and help promote the development of civil society. With 68 percent of the Pakistan population believing that Kashmir is still a very big problem, it is obvious that public perception and education must be addressed (Kapur, 132). Pro-government media, misguided educational curriculum, and constant rhetoric from the military establishment ferment this endemic fear in the society. Ending this dispute will open up more international assistance and long-term benefits to the country and the region. Resolving this long-standing issue with India will create enormous opportunities for Pakistan.

As long as the Afghan conflict remains unresolved, Pakistan cannot make progress toward stability. The hostile relations between Afghanistan and Pakistan facilitate the actions of multiple terrorist organizations. Without this festering regional conflict, the problem of terrorism in Pakistan would be much easier to contain and possibly eliminate. With a border stretching over 1,600 miles and ethnic and tribal associations that strongly connect the two states, the peace of one nation cannot be separated from the other. The insecurity of the border regions must be contained, and this becomes less complicated once American military personal are removed from the equation. In order to facilitate a move toward regional peace, Pakistan must cut ties to the notorious Haqqani network. Without marginalizing this organization, security cannot be achieved. Accomplishing this will also eliminate much of the illicit activities that destabilize the region, such as the drug trade and extortion rackets. Getting buy in from the Pakistan government and intelligence community for a negotiated settlement with numerous factions, including elements of the Taliban, will be necessary in order to achieve regional stability. Once an accord is negotiated, efforts to strengthen civil society and institutions in both states can be seriously undertaken.

The issue of nuclear security regarding the terrorism threat is of paramount importance. The fact that Pakistan is known as the main provider of nuclear technology to rogue states like Iran and North Korea is troubling. Counterterrorism efforts are centered mostly on keeping nuclear weapons out of the hands of terrorists. This is the main security objective of the United States as well as the international community. Jihadist sympathizers infiltrate the intelligence community and segments of the Pakistani military. Estimates list approximately 15 sites across the country where terrorists could acquire nuclear materials. The nuclear issue is the prime example of disconnects between Pakistan and the United States. From the perspective of Pakistan, the greatest concern and risk is the U.S. design on dismantling the nuclear program. Steps being taken by Pakistan authorities are not centered on a possible jihadist attack but on threats of a U.S. raid against the nuclear facilities. This shows the adversarial role between the two countries in recent years. Until the aspect of trust is rebuilt, the nuclear issue will continue to hamper progress between Pakistan and the Western powers.

Unfortunately, the reality of dealing with the overarching security concerns in Pakistan is still beset by the problems of accountability and corruption within the Pakistan military and intelligence communities. According to author Lawrence Wright, "despite all the suffering the war on terror had brought to Pakistan, the military was addicted to the money it generated" (Wright, 6). In addition, the military has made millions in investments, such as real estate, hotels, and shopping malls, which have been mostly funded by U.S. financial assistance. When the military funding is funneled into the actual security realm, it usually goes to the Pakistani military stationed on the Indian border and does not target the terrorist issue in the tribal regions or any elements associated with the TTP or Al Qaeda. The continuation of the war on terror benefits these corrupt elements within the country. This exemplifies a failure of leadership from the top-down. The ruling elite, the bureaucracy, and the elected representatives refuse to take on the military and intelligence establishments. The dark side of the Pakistan intelligence power is evident in that the secret faction of the ISI known as the S Wing (composed of retired officers) operates in the realm of helping radical elements ferment terrorism and regional instability. These secretive subgroups help to promote Pakistani security interests in Kashmir as well as ensuring Afghanistan does not begin to align too closely to India in regional politics. The most troubling statement on the magnitude of the Pakistani security situation came from chairman of the Joint Chiefs of Staff, Admiral Michael Mullen, during his congressional testimony in September 2011, 10 years after the 9/11 attacks. Mullen claimed that the Haqqani network was operating as a "veritable arm" of the Pakistani state in Afghanistan and was orchestrating direct attacks against U.S. military personnel (including an attack on the U.S. embassy in Kabul). Pakistan was undermining U.S. interests and potentially warranting sanctions (Gall, 261). His scathing testimony (backed by the Secretary of Defense Leon Panetta) basically accused Pakistan of being a state sponsor of terrorism. This example of calling out the Pakistani leadership showed a level of accountability and transparency that has been woefully lacking during the troubling partnership between the United States and Pakistan.

Change must start with serious education reforms and the nurturing of civil society within the country because the education sector is in dire need of help. The Brookings Institute released a study stating that the illiteracy in Pakistan is actually increasing, and the educational infrastructure resembles that of a poor sub-Saharan nation (Riedel, 135). Spending on education has been insufficient for decades with the bulk of funding going to the security sectors. Unfortunately, this does not impact the still flourishing and mostly unregulated madrassa system. Without more accountability in this area, any significant progress will be difficult to attain. According to Saqib Khan and Umbreen Javaid, "The lack of education and employment opportunities creates a pool of discontented and marginalized youth who can be recruited by religious or militant groups" (Khan and Javaid, 11). This battle for the hearts and minds of the growing underclass within Pakistan is an enormous challenge. As ISIS attempts to attract the youth within Pakistan, they promote the myth of the caliphate. Their propaganda touts a romantic illusion of life under a caliphate since the fall of the Ottoman Empire. According to Iman Malik, this utopian fantasy bolsters recruitment and support for the Islamic State (Strasser, 1–2). The literacy rate is at an abysmal level with Pakistan ranking near the bottom of the global index. These uneducated masses (especially within the youth bulge) make the society prone to sectarian rhetoric. It is troubling to note that even the public school curriculum includes units on the history of jihad and describes Hindus as the enemies of Pakistan (Kapur, 132–133). From the onset, Saudi financial assistance funded the Wahhabist brand of Islam that has been entrenched in the country for over 30 years. Unless the government is able to promote economic change and reinvest in an overhaul of the educational system, progress will be difficult. Extremist leadership within the madrassas wants the Taliban in Afghanistan to serve as a model for Pakistan's future. An objective look at the failure of this type of antiquated system is clear evidence of what Pakistan would fall into if a Talibanization movement were successful. Organizations like the Bacha Khan Educational Foundation, which promotes the teaching of a more modern curriculum in rural areas such as FATA and Khyber Pakhtunkhwa, are desperately needed.

Pakistan's civil society institutions have been historically weak. What is needed in Pakistan is a civil society that allows for honest debate and that checks the excesses of the government. In addition, the support of free speech must become a higher priority within the country. Support for these initiatives will disrupt the perverted narrative of extremism. Incidents like the brutal murder of prominent Pakistani journalist Saleem Shahzad show the extent to which the intelligence community in Pakistan will go in order to silence critics. Some semblance of progress has occurred regarding this, most notably the lawyer's movement for judicial independence of 2007 that emerged in support of Chief Justice Iftikhar Muhammad Chaudhry. Local groups throughout the country are trying to make a difference in diminishing the violence. Strengthening solidarity, communal identity, and social cohesion are key elements according to international studies professor Anita Weiss. NGOs have had mixed results in Pakistan; some have worked as a cover for Islam radical elements, while others with a more progressive pro-Western agenda have been subject to rigid government oversight. Several grassroots organizations have emerged in recent years that have attempted to turn the tide away from radical intolerance. In urban areas, organizations such as "I Am Karachi" were formed to combat religiously hateful rhetoric and graffiti targeting the Shia and Ahmadiya minority communities. Other organizations have emerged in Karachi and other cities to assist slum children and education for women about their legal rights. A counter-extremism educational movement called Khudi has been working to develop a democratic culture in Pakistan and help promote religious tolerance. Through workshops that generate debates and discussions with the youth, Khudi hopes to promote civil society nationwide. The key to success in developing civil society may be the ability to mobilize the media in a productive manner. Recent episodes have seen the media playing a positive role in exposing the abuses of the regime and the military. Unfortunately, the media has also continued to be used by the state to promote causes and issues that are counter to the promotion of civil society in Pakistan.

However, this momentum and the gains toward tolerance and respect for diversity and free speech have not been fully sustained. In some ways, the religious conservatives' support for the murders of Taseer and Bhatti is evidence of an alarming trend. Militants can use the madrassa system and propaganda to ferment intolerance and hatred. The massive turnouts in support of the blasphemy laws and conservative policies show the polarization within Pakistani society.

The situation looks bleak regarding the issue of sectarian violence within Pakistan. The resurgence of Sunni-Shia violence in the past decade is the most disturbing trend in contemporary Pakistan and is potentially the most threatening to the future of the country. As radical Salafis elements entered Pakistan during the war on terror, the tribal dynamic was disrupted, and the religious establishment that had dominated the area imploded. This has directly led to significant increases in religious-inspired acts of violence. Support for sectarian organizations remains high as funding from abroad helps to promote intolerance. In addition, the criminal justice system continues to fail the people of Pakistan as individuals committing acts of religious terrorism are not prosecuted or are eventually acquitted. If the madrassa system does not undergo reform, the problem of sectarian-inspired violence cannot be eliminated. Finally, many of the leaders promulgating sectarian violence remain closely connected to political leaders and members of the military and intelligence communities. In order to control sectarian violence, the relationship between state agents and extremists must be ended.

Pakistan must also do more regarding the issue of gender relations within the country. Violence against women is still endemic in Pakistan, and a climate of impunity and state inaction remains in place (ICG Report, April 8, 2015). Both the criminal justice system and the legislative branch have failed to make significant progress regarding gender-related violence. The problem is more significant in the tribal regions, including Khyber Pakhtunkhwa and FATA.

The Pakistani state has turned a blind eye to violence and discrimination against women in part to appease the militants within the country. Legislation has been passed, but until societal attitudes change and educational reform is implemented, legal change is meaningless. Crimes against women are disregarded by law enforcement, and justice is too often denied to women throughout Pakistan. Human rights monitors, such as the International Crisis Group, document these disturbing trends. Criminal offenses against women go unpunished, especially in the tribal areas. Sexual violence and state-sanctioned discrimination is pervasive, and leaders and activists are key targets for radical elements.

Several options appear as Pakistan looks for models to help guide the transition to a post-conflict society where terrorism has been marginalized. Until recently, Turkey was a model for their ability to manage religious diversity within a framework that stressed openness and inclusivity. However, dark trends and recent government action under Erdoğan have thrown the Turkish case into a somewhat chaotic situation. The other example of a Muslim society that embraces tolerance within a relatively diverse society is Indonesia. The educational policies of the country help steer the society in the right direction. The culture of the country, as well as the legal framework, offers avenues where success can be achieved. If Pakistan can embrace diversity and gear the education system and grass-roots civil society in positive directions, the terrorism problem can become manageable, at the very least. Until change occurs, the country will remain a troubled land.

Bibliography

Abbas, Hassan. *Pakistan's Troubled Frontier*. Washington, DC: The Jamestown Foundation, 2009.

Abbas, Hassan. *The Taliban Revival: Violence and Extremism on the Pakistan-Afghanistan Frontier*. New Haven, CT: Yale University Press, 2014.

Abdullah, Hasan. "Karachi: Where Walls Tell Tales of Sectarian Conflict." *Herald Magazine*. November 8, 2016. https://herald.dawn.com/news/1153580.

Ahmed, Akbar. *The Thistle and the Drone: How America's War on Terror Became a Global War on Tribal Islam*. Washington, DC: Brookings Institution Press, 2013.

"Another Bombing, This Time in Pakistan." *New York Times*. March 28, 2016.

Baig, Assed. "Malala Yousafzai and the White Saviour Complex." *Media Diversified*. October 8, 2013.

Bass, Gary. *The Blood Telegram: Nixon, Kissinger, and a Forgotten Genocide*. New York: Alfred A. Knopf, 2013.

"The Battle for Punjab." *The Economist*. April 2, 2016.

Beehner, Lionel, and Joseph Young. "Special Operations or Drones?" *The National Interest*. November 4, 2013.

Bergen, Peter L. *The Longest War: The Enduring Conflict between America and Al-Qaeda*. New York: Free Press, 2011.

Bergen, Peter L. *Man Hunt: The Ten-Year Search for Bin Laden from 9/11 to Abbottabad*. New York: Crown Publishers, 2012.

Bergen, Peter L. *Talibanistan: Negotiating the Borders between Terror, Politics, and Religion*. Oxford: Oxford University Press, 2013.

Bergen, Peter, and Jennifer Rowland. "Drone Wars." *Washington Quarterly* 36, no. 3 (2013): 7–26.

Bergen, Peter, Mike Mazarr, Steve Coll, Touqir Hussain, Mohsin S. Khan, Thomas Lynch III, William Milam, Shuja Nawaz, Joel Rayburn, Joshua T. White,

Andrew Wilder, Huma Yusuf, and Moeed W. Yusuf. "Pakistan and the United States: At a Strategic Crossroads." Washington, DC: New America Foundation. September 2011.

Bhojani, Fatima. "ISIS Is on the Decline in the Middle East but Its Influence in Pakistan Is Rising." *Washington Post*. May 5, 2017.

Biberman, Yelena, and Farhan Zahid. "Why Terrorists Target Children: Outbidding, Desperation, and Extremism in the Peshawar and Beslan School Massacres." *Terrorism and Political Violence*. February 9, 2016. doi:10.1080/09546 553.2015.1135425.

Blood, Peter R. *Pakistan: A Country Study*. Washington, DC: U.S. Library of Congress, 1994.

"Blood for Money for Blood." *The Economist*. May 3, 2012.

Bose, Sumantra. *Kashmir: Roots of Conflict, Paths to Peace*. Cambridge, MA: Harvard University Press, 2003.

Bowden, Mark. *The Finish: Killing of Osama Bin Laden*. New York: Atlantic Monthly Press, 2012.

Boyle, Michael J. "The Costs and Consequences of Drone Warfare." *International Affairs* 89, no. 1 (2013): 1–29.

Brenner, Marie. "Anatomy of a Siege." *Vanity Fair*. November 2009.

Brown, Vahid, and Don Rassler. *Fountainhead of Jihad: The Haqqani Nexus, 1973–2012*. New York: Columbia University Press, 2013.

Burke, Jason. *The 9/11 Wars*. London: Allen Lane, 2011.

Burki, Khan Zeb. "Rise of Taliban in Waziristan." *The Dialogue* 5, no. 3 (2010): 188–211.

Calamur, Krishnadev. "Trump and the Pakistan Problem." *Atlantic*. August 22, 2017. https://www.theatlantic.com/international/archive/2017/08/trump-pakistan-afghanistan/537564/.

Caryl, Christian. "Pakistan: When the State Loses Control." *New York Review of Books*. January 6, 2011. http://www.nybooks.com/daily/2011/01/06/pakistan-when-state-loses-control/.

Chicago Project on Security & Threats. "Suicide Attack Database." *Scholarship with Impact: University of Chicago*. October 12, 2016.

Clarke, Ryan. "Lakshar-I-Taiba: The Fallacy of Subservient Proxies and the Future of Islamist Terrorism in India." Carlisle, PA: United States Army Way College Publications. March 1, 2010.

Cockburn, Andrew. *Kill Chain: The Rise of the High-Tech Assassins*. New York: Henry Holt and Company, 2015.

Coll, Steve. *Ghost Wars the Secret History of the CIA, Afghanistan, and Bin Laden, from the Soviet Invasion to September 10, 2001*. New York: Penguin, 2004.

Constable, Pamela. *Playing with Fire: Pakistan at War with Itself*. New York: The Random House, 2011.

Craig, Tim. "Drone Kills Taliban Chief Hakimullah Mehsud; Pakistan Accuses U.S. of Derailing Peace Talks." *Washington Post*. November 2, 2013.

Craig, Tim. "Karachi Airport Attack Shows Growing Threat Posed by Pakistani Taliban." *Washington Post*. June 9, 2014.

Craig, Tim. "Nawaz Sharif Is Formally Elected Prime Minister of Pakistan." *Washington Post*. June 5, 2013.

Craig, Tim, and Pamela Constable. "In Pakistan, Taliban Massacre of Schoolchildren Fuels Broad Outrage." *Washington Post*. December 16, 2014.

Daveed, Gartenstein-Ross, and Nathaniel Ross. "How al-Qaeda Survived the Islamic State Challenge." Washington, DC: Hudson Institute. January 13, 2017.

Davidson, Amy. "Raymond Davis: Guns, Cars, and Bagels." *New Yorker*. October 5, 2011.

"The Easter Bombing Is the Latest Reminder That Pakistan Must Stop Tolerating Terrorism." *Washington Post*. March 30, 2016.

Fair, C. Christine. *The Evolution of the Global Terrorist Threat: 9/11 to Osama bin Laden's Death*. New York: Columbia University Press, 2014.

Fair, C. Christine. *Fighting to the End: The Pakistan Army's Way of War*. New York: Oxford University Press, 2014.

Fair, C. Christine. "Lakshar-e-Tayiba and the Pakistani State." *Survival* 53, no. 4 (2011): 29–52.

Fair, C. Christine. "Why the Pakistani Army Is Here to Stay: Prospects for Civilian Governance." *International Affairs* 87, no. 3 (2011): 571–588.

Fair, C. Christine, and Sarah Watson. *Pakistan's Enduring Challenges*. Philadelphia, PA: University of Pennsylvania Press, 2015.

Fair, C. Christine, and Seth G. Jones. "Pakistan's War Within." *Survival* 51, no. 6 (2009): 161–188.

Fair, C. Christine, and Sumit Ganguly. "An Unworthy Ally: Time for Washington to Cut Pakistan Loose." *Foreign Affairs*. August 18, 2015.

Farwell, James P. *The Pakistani Cauldron: Conspiracy, Assassination & Instability*. Washington, DC: Potomac Books, 2011.

Fazli, Shehryar. "Sectarianism and Conflict: The View from Pakistan." *DIIS*. June 2012.

Filkins, Dexter. *The Forever War*. New York: Alfred A. Knopf, 2008.

Fishwick, Carmen. "Peshawar School Massacre: This Is Pakistan's 9/11—Now Is the Time to Act," *Guardian*. December 19, 2014.

Foust, Joshua. "U.S. Drones Make Peace with Pakistan Less Likely." *Atlantic*. July 12, 2012.

Gabol, Imran. "At Least 72 Killed in Suicide Blast as Terror Revisits Lahore." *Dawn*. March 27, 2016.

Gall, Carlotta. *The Wrong Enemy: America in Afghanistan, 2001–2014*. Boston: Houghton Mifflin Harcourt, 2014.

Ghufran, Nasreen. "Pushtun Ethnonationalism and the Taliban Insurgency in the North West Frontier Province of Pakistan." *Asian Survey* 49, no. 6 (2009): 1092–1114.

Goldberg, Jeffrey, and Marc Ambinder. "The Ally from Hell." *Atlantic*. December 2011.

Goodson, Larry P. "Pakistan—The Most Dangerous Place in the World." Carlisle, PA: Strategic Studies Institute. July 2009.

Gopal, Anand, Mansur Khan Mahsud, and Brian Fishman. "The Battle for Pakistan: Militancy and Conflict in North Waziristan." *New America Journal.* (April 19, 2010): 1–3.

Grare, Frederic. "Pakistan's Foreign and Security Policies after the 2013 General Election: The Judge, the Politician and the Military." *International Affairs* 89, no. 4 (2013): 987–1001.

Greg, Myre. "Pakistan Weakens Militants, but Can It Defeat Them?" *NPR.* March 28, 2016.

Guerin, Orla. "Malala Yousafzai: Battling for an Education in Pakistan." BBC News. July 11, 2013. http://www.bbc.com/news/world-asia-23268708.

Gul, Imtiaz. *The Most Dangerous Place: Pakistan's Lawless Frontier.* New York: Penguin Books, 2009.

Gunaratna, Rohan. "Al Qaeda in the Tribal Areas of Pakistan and Beyond." *Studies in Conflict & Terrorism* 31, no. 9 (2008): 775–807.

Gunaratna, Rohan, and Khuram Iqbal. *Pakistan: Terrorism Ground Zero.* London: Reaktion Books, 2011.

Hameed, Nida. "Struggling IDPS of North Waziristan in the Wake of Operation Zarb-e-Azb." *NDU Journal* (2015): 95–112.

Haqqani, Husain. *Magnificent Delusions: Pakistan, the United States, and an Epic History of Misunderstanding.* New York: PublicAffairs, 2013.

Hashim, Asad. "Bomb Attack Kills at Least 25 in Pakistan's Balochistan." *Al Jazeera.* May 12, 2017.

Hilton, Isabel. "The Pashtun Code: How a Long-Ungovernable Tribe May Determine the Future of Afghanistan." *New Yorker.* December 3, 2001.

Hiro, Dilip. *Apocalyptic Realm: Jihadists in South Asia.* New Haven, CT: Yale University Press, 2012.

Hussain, Zahid. *Frontline Pakistan: The Struggle with Militant Islam.* New York: Columbia University Press, 2007.

Hussain, Zahid. *The Scorpion's Tail: The Relentless Rise of Islamic Militants in Pakistan—and How It Threatens America.* New York: Free Press, 2010.

Inskeep, Steve. *Instant City: Life and Death in Karachi.* New York: Penguin Books, 2011.

International Crisis Group. "Pakistan: Countering Militancy in PATA." *Asia Report N°242.* January 15, 2013.

International Crisis Group. "Pakistan: Madrasas, Extremism and the Military." July 29, 2002. https://www.crisisgroup.org/asia/south-asia/pakistan/pakistan-madrasas-extremism-and-military.

International Crisis Group. "Pakistan: Stoking the Fire in Karachi." *Asia Report N°242.* February 15, 2017.

International Human Rights and Conflict Resolution Clinic (Stanford Law School) and Global Justice Clinic (NYU School of Law). "Death, Injury, and Trauma to Civilians from US Drone Practices in Pakistan." *Living Under Drones.* (September 25, 2012): 1–182.

Iqbal, Khuram. *The Making of Pakistani Human Bombs.* Lanham, MD: Lexington Books, 2015.

Islam, Heba. "20 Questions We Should Be Asking after the Peshawar Massacre." *Dawn.* December 20, 2014.

Ispahani, Farahnaz. *Purifying the Land of the Pure: A History of Pakistan's Religious Minorities.* New York: Oxford University Press, 2017.

Jaffrelot, Christophine. *The Pakistan Paradox: Instability and Resilience.* New York: Oxford University Press, 2015.

Jalal, Ayesha. *The Struggle for Pakistan: A Muslim Homeland and Global Politics*. Cambridge, MA: The Belknap Press of Harvard University Press, 2014.

Javaid, Umbreen. "Operation Zarb-e-Azb: A Successful Initiative to Curtail Terrorism." *South Asian Studies* 30, no. 2 (2015): 43–58.

Johnson, Thomas H., and M. Chris Mason. "No Sign until the Burst of Fire: Understanding the Pakistan-Afghanistan Frontier." *International Security* 32, no. 4 (Spring 2008): 41–77. doi:10.1162/isec.2008.32.4.41.

Jones, Seth. *Hunting in the Shadows: The Pursuit of Al Qa'ida since 9/11*. New York: W.W. Norton & Company, 2012.

Joshi, Shashank. "The Broken US-Pakistan Relationship." *Current History* 111, no. 744 (2012): 141–147.

Joshi, Shashank. "Viewpoint: Why Trump's Threats to Pakistan Raise Serious Questions." BBC News. August 25, 2017. http://www.bbc.com/news/world-asia-41042316.

Kapur, S. Paul. *Jihad as Grand Strategy: Islamist Militancy, National Security, and the Pakistani State*. New York: Oxford University Press, 2017.

Kfir, Isaac. "Understanding the Roots of Sectarian Violence in Pakistan." *Institute for National Security and Counterterrorism*. February 22, 2013.

Khalid, Iram, and Naveed Arooj. "Conflict in Waziristan." *South Asian Studies* 29, no. 2 (2014): 559–582.

Khan, Akbar Nasir. "Analyzing Suicide Attacks in Pakistan." *Conflict and Peace Studies* 3, no. 4 (2010): 1–5.

Khan, Ismail. "Attack at Bacha Khan University in Pakistan Leaves at Least 22 Dead." *New York Times*. January 20, 2016.

Khan, Riaz. *Afghanistan and Pakistan: Conflict, Extremism, and Resistance to Modernity*. Washington, DC: Woodrow Wilson Center Press, 2011.

Khan, Saqib, and Umbreen Javaid. "Extremism in Contemporary Pakistan: Threats, Causes and Future Policy." *South Asian Studies* 31, no. 2 (2016): 7–16.

Kronstadt, Alan K. "Pakistan-U.S. Relations: Issues for the 114th Congress." *Congressional Research Service*. May 14, 2015.

Kronstadt, Alan K., and Kenneth Katzman. "Islamist Militancy in the Pakistan-Afghanistan Border Region and U.S. Policy." *Congressional Research Service*. November 21, 2008.

Kux, Dennis. *The United States and Pakistan, 1947–2000: Disenchanted Allies*. Washington, DC: Woodrow Wilson Center Press, 2001.

Lanche, Jeremie. "Suicide Terrorism in Pakistan: An Assessment." New Delhi, India: Institute of Peace and Conflict Studies. September 2009.

Lieven, Anatol. *Pakistan: A Hard Country*. New York: PublicAffairs, 2011.

Malik, Iffat. *Kashmir: Ethnic Conflict International Dispute*. Karachi: Oxford University Press, 2002.

Malik, Iftikhar. *Pakistan: Democracy, Terrorism, and the Building of a Nation*. Northampton, MA: Olive Branch Press, 2010.

Markey, Daniel S. *No Exit from Pakistan: America's Tortured Relationship with Islamabad*. New York: Cambridge University Press, 2013.

Masood, Salman. "A Wave of Grief and Anger after a Pakistani Shrine Is Bombed." *New York Times*. February 17, 2017.

McCarthy, Julie. "Extremist Intimidation Chills Pakistan Secular Society." *NPR*. January 24, 2011.

McKelvey, Tara. "Covering Obama's Secret War." *Columbia Journalism Review.* (May/June 2011): 1–12.

Mirza, Waqas. "Pakistan's Brutal Military Operation in North Waziristan Is Funded by US Tax Dollars." *Muftah.* December 10, 2014.

Musharraf, Pervez. *In the Line of Fire: A Memoir.* New York: Free Press, 2006.

Mustafa, Ali. "Why the Pakistani Taliban Massacred 134 Children at a School in Peshawar." *Vice News.* December 17, 2014.

Naseemullah, Adnan. "Why the Pakistani Taliban's Massacre of Children Reveals Its Weakness." *Washington Post.* December 18, 2014.

Nawaz, Shuja. "FATA—A Most Dangerous Place: Meeting the Challenge of Militancy and Terror in the Federally Administered Tribal Areas of Pakistan." Washington, DC: Center for Strategic and International Studies. January 2009.

Nilsson, Kirk H. "Dealing with Terrorist Sanctuary in Pakistan's Federally Administered Tribal Areas." Carlisle, PA: United States Army War College. March 27, 2009.

Norell, Magnus. *Militancy in the Pakistani Federally Administered Tribal Areas (FATA) and Afghanistan.* Report no. FOI-R--2727--SE. FOI, Swedish Defence Research Agency. Stockholm: FOI, 2010.

"Pakistan: 2008 Country Reports on Human Rights Practices." News release. February 25, 2009. Bureau of Democracy, Human Rights, and Labor, U.S. Department of State, Diplomacy in Action.

Parvez, Tariq, and Mehwish Rani. "An Appraisal of Pakistan's Anti-Terrorism Act." Washington, DC: United States Institute of Peace. August 3, 2015.

Peterson, Matt. "Is Obama's Drone War Moral?" *Atlantic.* August 18, 2016.

Qazi, Shehzad H. *An Extended Profile of the Pakistani Taliban.* Washington, DC: Institute for Social Policy and Understanding. August 2011.

Rabasa, Angel, Robert D. Blackwill, Peter Chalk, Kim Cragin, C. Christine Fair, Brian A. Jackson, Brian Michael Jenkins, Seth G. Jones, Nathaniel Shestak, and Ashley J. Tellis. "The Lessons of Mumbai." RAND Corporation, 2009.

Rafiq, Arif. "Pakistan's Resurgent Sectarian War." *United States Institute of Peace.* November 5, 2014.

Rana, Muhammad Amir. "Pakistan Security Report: Internal Security Matrix 2014." Islamabad, Pakistan: Pak Institute for Peace Studies. January 4, 2015.

Rashid, Ahmed. *Descent into Chaos: The U.S. and the Disaster in Pakistan, Afghanistan, and Central Asia.* New York: Penguin Books, 2008.

Rashid, Ahmed. "Pakistan: The Allure of ISIS." *NYR Daily.* October 6, 2014.

Rashid, Ahmed. "Pakistan: The Army Steps In." *NYR Daily.* April 12, 2016.

Rashid, Ahmed. *Pakistan on the Brink: The Future of America, Pakistan, and Afghanistan.* New York: Viking, 2012.

Rassler, Don, C. Christine Fair, Anirban Ghosh, Arif Jamal, and Nadia Shoeb. "The Fighters of Lakshar-e-Taiba: Recruitment, Training, Deployment and Death." West Point, NY: Combating Terrorism Center at West Point. April 2013.

Raza, Syed Sami. "After the Peshawar School Attack: Law and Politics of the Death Sentence in Pakistan." *Counter Terrorist Trends and Analyses* 7, no. 5 (June 2015): 22–27.

Riedel, Bruce. *Deadly Embrace: Pakistan, America, and the Future of the Global Jihad.* Washington, DC: Brookings Institution Press, 2011.

Riedel, Bruce. "The Mumbai Massacre and Its Implications for America and South Asia." *Journal of International Affairs* 63, no. 1 (2009): 111–126.

Ryder, Phyllis Mentzell. "Beyond Critique: Global Activism and the Case of Malala Yousafzai." *Literacy in Composition Studies* 3, no. 1 (2015): 175–187.

Sareen, Sushant. "ZARB-e-AZB: An Evaluation of Pakistan Army's Anti-Taliban Operations in North Waziristan." Chanakyapuri, India: Vivekananda International Foundation. December 2014.

Schmidle, Nicholas. "Getting Bin Laden: What Happened That Night in Abbottabad." *New Yorker.* August 8, 2011.

Schmidle, Nicholas. *To Live or to Perish Forever: Two Tumultuous Years in Pakistan.* New York: Henry Holt and Company, 2009.

Schmidt, John R. *The Unraveling: Pakistan in the Age of Jihad.* New York: Farrar, Straus and Giroux, 2011.

Schofield, Victoria. *Kashmir in Conflict: India, Pakistan, and the Unfinished War.* London: I.B. Tauris and Co, 2000.

Scott-Clark, Cathy, and Adrian Levy. *The Exile: The Stunning Inside Story of Osama Bin Laden and Al Qaeda in Flight.* New York: Bloomsbury, 2017.

Semple, Michael. "The Pakistan's Taliban Movement: An Appraisal." Belfast, Northern Ireland, UK: Institute for the Study of Conflict Transformation and Social Justice. November 2014.

Sethi, Mira. "The Child Martyrs of Pakistan." *New York Times.* December 16, 2015.

Shah, Aqil. *The Army and Democracy: Military Politics in Pakistan.* Cambridge, MA: Harvard University, 2014.

Shah, Syed Ali. "61 Killed in Twin Suicide Attacks as Terrorists Storm Police Training College in Quetta." *Dawn.* October 24, 2016.

Shahzad, Syed Saleem. *Inside Al-Qaeda and the Taliban beyond Bin Laden and 9/11.* London: Pluto Press, 2011.

Shaw, Ian, and Majed Akhter. "The Unbearable Humanness of Drone Warfare in FATA, Pakistan." *Antipode* 44, no. 4 (2012): 1490–1509.

Shay, Shaul. "The School Massacre in Peshawar (Pakistan)." International Institute for Counter-Terrorism (ICT). December 22, 2014. http://www.ict.org.il/Article/1269/The-School-Massacre-in-Peshawar-Pakistan#gsc.tab=0.

Sheikh, Mona. *Guardians of God: Inside the Religious Mind of the Pakistani Taliban.* New Delhi: Oxford University Press, 2016.

Sheikh, Mona. "Sacred Pillars of Violence: Findings from a Study of the Pakistani Taliban." *Politics, Religion, & Ideology* 13, no. 4 (2012): 439–454.

Siddique, Qandeel. "The Red Mosque Operation and Its Impact on the Growth of the Pakistani Taliban." Kjeller, Norway: Norwegian Defence Research Establishment. October 8, 2008.

Siddique, Qandeel. "Tehrik-E-Taliban Pakistan: An Attempt to Deconstruct the Umbrella Organization and the Reasons for Its Growth in Pakistan's North-West." *DIIS Report.* November 30, 2010.

Snow, Matthew. "When Idols Turn to Sand: How the West Nearly Killed Malala Yousafzai." *Foreign Policy Journal.* March 27, 2013.

Soherwordi, Syed Hussain Shaheed, and Shaid Ali Khattak. "Operation Geronimo: Assassination of Osama Bin Ladin and Its Implications on the US-Pakistan Relations, War on Terror, Pakistan and Al-Qaeda." *South Asian Studies* 26, no. 2 (2011): 349–365.

Stoessinger, John George. *Why Nations Go to War*. 8th ed. Boston, MA: Wadsworth, 2001.

Strasser, Fred. "South Asia: Rising Extremism Opens War for ISIS." *USIP*. May 9, 2017.

Tankel, Stephen. "Lashkar-e-Taiba in Perspective: An Evolving Threat." Washington, DC: New America Foundation. February 2010.

"'Targeted Killing' Policies Violate the Right to Life," *Amnesty International USA*. June 15, 2012.

Tellis, Ashley J. "The Menace That Is Lashkar-e-Taiba." Washington, DC: Carnegie Endowment for International Peace. March 2012.

Templin, James D. "Religious Education of Pakistan's Deobandi Madaris and Radicalisation." *Counter Terrorist Trends and Analysis* 7, no. 5 (June 2015): 15–21.

"TTP Claims Attack on Karachi Airport." *Dawn*. June 8, 2014.

Walsh, Decan. "Assault on Pakistan Airport Signals Taliban's Reach and Resilience." *New York Times*. June 9, 2014.

Weaver, Mary Anne. *Pakistan: In the Shadow of Jihad and Afghanistan*. New York: Farrar, Straus and Giroux, 2002.

Weaver, Mary Anne. *Pakistan: Deep Inside the World's Most Frightening State*. New York: Farrar, Straus and Giroux, 2010.

Weiss, Anita. "Can Civil Society Tame Violence Extremism in Pakistan?" *Current History*. April 2016.

Woods, Chris. *Sudden Justice: America's Secret Drone Wars*. New York: Oxford University Press, 2015.

Wright, Lawrence. "The Double Game: The Unintended Consequences of American Funding in Pakistan." *New Yorker*. May 16, 2011.

Yasmeen, Samina. "Pakistan, Militancy and Identity: Parallel Struggles." *Australian Journal of International Affairs* 67, no. 2 (2013): 157–175.

Yousafzai, Malala. *I Am Malala*: *The Girl Who Stood Up for Education and Was Shot by the Taliban*. New York: Little, Brown and Company, 2013.

Yusuf, Moeed. "Not Really a Plan." *Dawn*. September 13, 2016.

Zahid, Farhan. "The Successes and Failures of Pakistan's Operation Zarb-e-Azb." *Terrorism Monitor* 13, no. 14 (2015): 5–6.

Zahid, Farhan, and Muhammad Ismail Khan. "Prospects of the Islamic State in Pakistan." *Hudson Institute*. January 29, 2017.

Zeb, Fatima. "Zarb-e-Azb: One Year On." *ACLED*. September 17, 2015.

Ziring, Lawrence. *Pakistan: At the Crosscurrent of History*. Oxford: Oneworld Publications, 2003.

Index

Abdullah, Hamna, 99
Abdullah, Maulana, 95–96
Abdulmutallab, Umar Farouk, 157
Action Plan. *See* National Action Plan
Adizai, Umar, 181
Afghanistan: Obama and drone campaign in, 140–45; Soviet invasion of, 26–30; Taliban movement in, 40
Afghan National Front, 29
Ahl-e-Hadith, 128, 130
Ahmad, Mehmood, 50–51
Ahmad, Qazi Hussain, 63
Ahmad Gailani, Pir Sayed, 30
Ahmadis, 23–24
Ahmed, Akbar, 77
Aidid, Mohammed, 45
Akhtar, Qari Saifullah, 95, 164
Al-Baghdadi, Abu Bakr, 188
Ali, Chaudhary Rahmat, 2
Ali, Mubarak, 148
Al Jazeera, 89
Al-Libi, Abu Faraj, 152
Al-Libi, Abu Laith, 139
All Parties Hurriyat Conference (APHC), 70
Almani, Abu Abdur Rehman, 176
Al Qaeda, 86; anti-Americanism of, events leading to, 44; Azzam

and, 43; bin Laden and, 42–44; declaration of global jihad, 46–47; Holy Tuesday operation of, 49–50; ISIS threat in Pakistan and, 188–89; in Pakistan, search for, 67–69; Pakistan ties with, 45, 47; Qutb and, 42–43; Rahman and, 44, 46; Taliban leaders and, influence on, 42; terrorist attacks, 47–48; in tribal regions of Pakistan, 152–55; Zawahiri and, 43–44
Al-Shibh, Ramzi bin, 69, 151–52
Al Walid, Abu, 46
Amir Hamza mosque, 99
Anatomy of a Siege (Brenner), 134
Annan, Kofi, 59–60
Anticipatory anxiety, 146
ArmorGroup, 115
Army Public School massacre, Peshawar, 180–83
Ataturk, Kemal, 42
Atef, Mohammed, 49, 150–51
Atoms for Peace program, 11
Attash, Walid bin, 152
Attlee, Clement, 6
Awakening, 42
Awami League, 13, 15, 16–17
Awami National Party (ANP), 106, 108

About the Author

WILLIAM J. TOPICH is chair of the Department of Social Science at Pulaski Academy, a college preparatory school in Little Rock, Arkansas. His is also an adjunct professor in the Department of Political Science at the University of Arkansas at Little Rock. His courses include global terrorism and politics of the developing world. Topich is the coauthor of *The History of Myanmar* and is a contributor to *The Vietnam War: Handbook of the Literature and Research*. Topich conducted research in Cambodia in the late 1990s and in Pakistan in the summer of 2010.